D1283102

LIGHTS IN NASSAU HALL

A BOOK OF
THE BICENTENNIAL

PRINCETON
1746-1946

BY CHARLES G. OSGOOD

PRINCETON, NEW JERSEY
PRINCETON UNIVERSITY PRESS
1951

London: Geoffrey Cumberlege, Oxford University Press

Printed in the United States of America by
Princeton University Press at Princeton, New Jersey

Foreword

THE Executive Committee appointed by the Board of Trustees of Princeton University to plan and carry out the Bicentennial Program of 1946-1947 gave serious thought to the production of a book which would serve not only as an historical record but would attempt also to capture the spirit which animated the program. The late Walter E. Hope, who served as Chairman of this Committee, felt particularly that publication of such a book was an important part of the duty of the Committee. Now that the book has been completed, it is fitting that it has been dedicated by the author to his memory.

The Committee considered itself fortunate in persuading Professor Charles G. Osgood to undertake the preparation of the manuscript. He was not a member of the official organization of the Bicentennial and thus could view the program with a degree of objectivity and detachment impossible for those concerned with the planning and management of the long series of events.

With complete confidence in Professor Osgood, the Committee made it clear that he was to have an entirely free hand. This volume is in a very real sense his own view of the Princeton Bicentennial in the perspective which the delay of a few years in publication has permitted.

In only two respects did the Committee attempt to provide suggestions. One was the proposal that the manuscript should include an adequate presentation of the two centuries of Princeton's history which the Bicentennial Program was designed to commemorate. This seemed particularly essential because the Program itself was so forward-looking that throughout its course Princeton's history was perhaps inadequately stressed.

The other suggestion was that Professor Osgood should feel no obligation to follow any pattern set by other books which have been written about similar academic celebrations. Many of the facts pertaining to the Bicentennial are recorded in the later sections of this book, but no attempt has been made to set down a detailed account of methods and procedures adopted. A file of such procedures and methods, complete to the most minute detail, has been preserved in the archives of the Firestone Library. It is available to those in other institutions who, in the course of organizing similar programs, may wish to take advantage of our experience at Princeton.

For the Committee:
ARTHUR E. FOX
Secretary

Preface

THIS book has been compiled less for men now living than for readers yet unborn. In deciding what to omit and what to set down, the writer has submitted the choice to the imagined curiosity of the few who may pick it up in the year of grace 2046 or thereabouts. How much they will be edified by what is here recorded no one can say. They may be amused, they may be bored; they may wish we had left untold things that we have told, or told things that we have left untold. Whatever they may think, a record of this sort concerns those who took part in the events less than their descendants, and with the writing has gone the hope that it might gratify some antiquarian taste in generations to come.

But we hope that the book will also find some contemporary use, especially in helping to clarify at large the conception of what Princeton has been, is, and intends to be, and to disabuse the minds of any who still think of her as smug, or idle, or creed-bound, or luxurious, or aloof, or inbred. Such revision of estimate was indeed confessed by some who saw Princeton for the first time during the Bicentennial. We hope hereby to extend it.

Mere grateful acknowledgment is no adequate recognition of the part of Colonel Arthur E. Fox in the making of this book. With criticism, correction, advice, suggestion, materials, and cheerful patience his help has been indispensable to an extent that entitles him to be considered its co-author.

One there was whom of all others we should have wished to please with this record of the Bicentennial Year—Walter Ewing Hope—whose service to his beloved Princeton, not only in her year of jubilee, but at all times, was selfless and entire. To his memory, therefore, we would devote these labors.

The late Walter E. Hope (with former President Herbert Hoover)

Contents

Lights
in Nassau Hall

CHAPTER I

Two Centuries Abuilding

"SIR," said Imlac, "my history will not be long: the life that is devoted to knowledge passes silently away, and is very little diversified by events." With this observation of Dr. Samuel Johnson's one can only agree. Indeed, we may readily extend it from the scholar's life to the life of an institution "devoted to knowledge." For the soul of a college or university is just that devotion. The long quest and slow discovery, the quiet expanding influence of personality upon personality, of mind upon mind, the silent interdependent growth of knowledge and power and spirit, the slow, unconscious advance towards maturity, from day to day, in both teacher and taught—these constitute the essential life of a college, and of these its real history is made. But it is a history that does not submit to chronicle; it is too subtle, too hidden, proceeding by regular and often monotonous routine of reading and conference and inquiry, with rare and exciting moments of realization, which, if recordable at all, belong to biography rather than to history.

But the soul and essence of a college seem through the years to entertain a strange overgrowth, like the ivy on its walls, of sentiment and romance. Its friendships, its great personalities, its architecture, its sports and pranks, its traditions and atmosphere and quaint customs, its "old characters," even its enterprises of finance and discovery, its combination of learned age with exuberant youth, blend into a kind of picturesque charm to which the outside world is readily susceptible and responsive. In fact these more external aspects of a college are pretty faithful exponents of its essential history, of its "life devoted to knowledge"; and, of course, the older it is the richer they grow.

The history of Princeton, as of many institutions, has moved under the momentum of great personalities; and their practical, intellectual, and spiritual energies, having passed into the college, have persisted long after their times. But to transmit themselves in this way they had to find there receptive spirits, and the numerous list of those who caught their fire and carried on can never be compiled.

Princeton's history has also been peculiarly involved with great issues and movements. Indeed Princeton was born of a profound religious movement known as the Great Awakening. This was but a provincial overflow of the Enthusiastic Movement which swept England in the Eighteenth Century under the leadership of Wesley and Whitefield. The fiery spirit of the early Puritan settlers had in three generations cooled into a complacent Calvinism, serene and secure in its learned theological formulas.

But there were spiritual counselors who felt that this was not enough for salvation, that an emotional experience possessing the whole soul of a man, a "conversion" in the old sense, was indispensable. And they went preaching through the land, swaying vast crowds with a sense of sin, a fear of Hell, and a high ecstasy of assurance that they were "saved." These flaming evangelists and their followers were known as the New Lights. They were naturally regarded with aversion and contempt by the Old Side, the clergy intellectually and theologically at ease in Zion. Though zealots they might be, the New Lights were not sciolists. They included men of such stature as Jonathan Edwards, Gilbert Tennent and his brother John, the devout David Brainerd, who was expelled from Yale for his "enthusiasm," and Princeton founders Jonathan Dickinson and Aaron Burr.

Dr. Francis L. Patton used to say, with his accustomed wit, "Beware lest your religion, though it may stand trial in the court of the emotions, be non-suited in the court of the intellect." And the New Lights, well aware of this truth, and smarting under Old Side contempt, felt the need among their young clergy, not only of "emotional experience," but of education. Yale and Harvard were too far away, and too Old Side in any case. So the venerable William Tennent gathered his four sons and other young men around him near Hartsville, Pennsylvania, in what came to be known as the "Log College," and taught them theology and such liberal arts as he could command. This was not the equivalent of a New England or British education, to be sure, and the Old Side, entrenched in the synod of Philadelphia, made active objection to the callow but zealous and successful young preachers coming forth from the Log College and other like schools.

Wherefore, in this crying New Light need of education, four clergymen, with the support of three strong laymen, devised the plans for a new college to be located in New Jersey. The clergymen, whose names should be well remembered by all generations of Princeton men, were Jonathan Dickinson, pastor at Elizabeth, Aaron Burr, pastor at Newark, John Pierson, pastor at Woodbridge, and Ebenezer Pemberton, pastor of the First Presbyterian Church in New York. All were graduates of Yale. Supporting them were William Smith, Peter Livingston, and William Peartree Smith, all of New York. The standards of the new college were to be equal to those of New England or British institutions, and though it was definitely a New Light college, it followed the tolerant tradition of the colony in its charter, which provided that it would not exclude "any Person of any religious Denomination whatsoever from free and Equal Liberty and Advantage of Education, or from any of the Liberties, Priviledges or immunities of the Said College on account of his or their being of a Religious profession Different from the said Trustees of the College. . . ."

High were the hopes and resolute the purpose which finally overcame the Anglican and Old Side obstruction; and on October 22, 1746, the official birthday of Princeton, the first charter was signed by Governor John Hamilton. Two years later a new charter was signed by the new Governor, Jonathan Belcher, a staunch and much-needed defender of the infant college. The new charter was essentially identical with the first, except that the Board of Trustees was enlarged to 23, including the Governor. Of these, nine were graduates of Yale, four of Harvard, and three of the Log College.

Beginning with the little group of ten or a dozen students gathered in or around President Dickinson's parsonage in Elizabeth, Princeton's first twenty years were high in the glories of her history. During that time she overrode what seemed insuperable obstacles—death, poverty, and heckling of her enemies. Her five presidents were all devoted and enlightened men. Only two of them, however, served for more than two years. The revered Jonathan Dickinson lived but four and a half months in office, and the great Jonathan Edwards only a few weeks. But between them, from 1748 to 1757, fell the nine-year administration of Aaron Burr. The few lads who had gathered under the lamented Dickinson moved to Burr's parsonage in Newark, and here the college continued for eight strenuous years.

Burr was young, popular, eloquent, learned, and energetic, and he literally poured out his life for Princeton. Finance was his first worry. Subscriptions were insufficient. A lottery met with only qualified success. Then Samuel Davies and Gilbert Tennent braved Atlantic dangers to spend a year, 1754, in Great Britain and Ireland in a rather fruitless quest of funds. The matter of a local habitation for the new college had already been settled, and the little village of Princeton bore away the honor in competition with Newark, Elizabeth, and New Brunswick. Gradually, through the next two years, Nassau Hall assumed its plain and solemn form; and late in 1756 the college, now increased to three tutors and some seventy students, took possession. Nassau Hall, derived from English originals by architect Robert Smith, made a sensation in its day. It was the largest building in the colonies. It housed all of the college but the President, and contained refectory and offices, class-rooms, prayer hall or chapel, and dormitory. Close by they built the President's house, now the Dean's House, whose spacious and mellow dignity against the sombre shadows of Nassau Hall brings Princeton near to the stout and generous spirit of her hard beginnings. In gratitude to Governor Belcher for his loyal support from the outset, the Trustees would have named the new college building Belcher Hall. But the Governor becomingly declined the honor in favor of his deep admiration for William III and suggested "Nassau Hall." The Trustees readily agreed; and hence the multitudinous uses of the name "Nassau" to this very day.

Burr's satisfaction as he looked upon Nassau Hall and considered all that he had done for the college should have been great. But it was to be short-lived. He had, all at one time, done his full pastoral duty by the church in Newark, borne his full part in teaching, supervised the college's affairs, and travelled up and down the land in quest of funds and students when travel was a slow ordeal. He had burned himself out. But he had established the college in its course, past all its tremulous beginnings, and should be remembered as one of Princeton's great Presidents.

His successor, the great Jonathan Edwards, came to Princeton but to die, yet even by his brief association and death he enriched the Princeton tradition. For the next eight years the college carried on under the gentle Samuel

Davies and the redoubtable Samuel Finley, whose death in 1766 ended the first climacteric of Princeton.

The second began with the advent from Scotland of John Witherspoon. He had been elected in the hope that an eminent and uncommitted leader from abroad might heal the breach between Old Side and New Light. At first Witherspoon declined the call in deference to his wife's fear of the New World; but when at last she yielded to the suasion of Richard Stockton and the charming young Benjamin Rush, Princeton 1760, he accepted re-election and set out for America.

He was now 46. He had been bred of stout country clerical stock and trained at Edinburgh in much the same course of study that prevailed at Princeton in his day. He was a solid scholar and wielded a style that projected the man himself—logical, tough, vigorous, and unembellished. In the Scottish Church for twenty years he had with clear and deep convictions fought valiantly for a liberal party against the over-ripe "Moderates," serene, secure, and "intellectual." The issues were in many respects not unlike those between New Light and Old Side, and, more significantly, between the colonists and the mother country in the War for Independence. In Scotland republican ideas were in lively circulation. Witherspoon was not averse to contest at any time, especially if moral convictions were involved. Thus, when he stepped with his family from the *Peggy* on to the Philadelphia wharf on August 7, 1768, he was entering, perhaps unawares, upon a scene almost ideally set for the last 26 years of his career. In talents, experience, character, and conviction he was ready for the part.

Colleges prosper under two kinds of administration. Usually they carry forward under the direction of a prudent, energetic, faithful man and his carefully chosen assistants. More rarely they are blessed with the gift of a great and dominant personality who permeates the uttermost fibre and fabric of the institution with his fiery spirit and his clairvoyant mind. Such was Witherspoon.

His portraits show a massive, high, rough-hewn head, a big nose, a mouth firm but delicately chiseled, with the heavy modeling of chin and jaw that betokens strong physical instincts. About the eyes lurks a trace of inscrutable Scotch humor. He evidently had a deal of Scotch charm, like that of Burns, less of manners and more of manliness.

He found the college finances in a hopeless muddle of arrears and neglect. By appeals to the public, by lottery, by Spartan economy he in two years restored them to the black. Meanwhile he travelled through the South and New England, preaching, making friends and reputation, gathering funds, enlisting students, studying America, and rapidly becoming a patriot. He even planned a tour of the West Indies. He effected reforms in the curriculum and in the grammar school which at that time was preparing boys for college. He reinforced the library with books from overseas, and purchased scientific apparatus, including the famous Rittenhouse orrery, which he snatched from under the indignant nose of the University of Pennsylvania. Witherspoon with all else was canny. He rapidly became a power in the Presbyterian Church, and by his generous and transcendent influence subdued the old differences. He repeatedly advanced money out of his own pocket for college or church, some of which was never repaid.

Meanwhile was kindling the baptism of fire. In 1770 the students had intercepted and burned with ceremony an "unpatriotic" letter on its way from New York merchants to the merchants of Philadelphia. In 1774 they burned the college steward's winter supply of tea by way of underscoring the Boston Tea Party. The campus reverberated with patriotic oratory and resolutions. Witherspoon himself was much preoccupied with the overthrow of the royal government in New Jersey, and in 1776 he signed the Declaration of Independence.

Then the war broke over Princeton. In November college was disbanded. In December the British occupied Princeton and Nassau Hall, plundering and devastating. On January 3, 1777, Washington made his famous early-morning surprise attack and drove the British out in disorder. In the bombardment of Nassau Hall this now venerable shrine was consecrated by wounds from several cannon-shots, one of which is still visible as a stigma of honor. One shot even demolished the portrait of George II, the "Founder."*

For five months after the battle American troops in Nassau Hall did more damage than the British; they wrecked the organ and orrery, stole the books, and smashed things generally. For an ensuing year the dismantled place was used for a military hospital. Late in 1778 a few students crept back, and slow repairs began. From ten students in 1779, the number rose to ninety in 1786.

But the pressing condition of recovery was financial. Witherspoon got damages from Congress, but with post-war inflation and general poverty, neither appeals to friends, nor a lottery, nor petitions to legislature or Congress availed anything. Witherspoon himself, though disapproving, was sent abroad for eight months, only to meet, as he expected, with polite refusals. But somehow or other,

* Six and a half years later the Trustees voted to replace it with a portrait of Washington by Charles Willson Peale. That year Congress had received Washington in Nassau Hall and, at the commencement exercises the following month, Washington had given fifty guineas "as a testimony of his respect for the college." It is not unlikely that much of the gift was used to pay for the portrait. From its ancient frame in Nassau Hall, it continues to shed its patriotic blessing on all generations of Princeton men.

in his canny way, he managed to keep house and carry the college into better days.

For the six years from 1776 to 1782 Witherspoon was absent much of the time as a member of Congress; but even through the darkest days, while the college was in session, his indomitable spirit enlivened it. During the last eight years of his life his son-in-law, Samuel Stanhope Smith, appointed Vice-President in 1786, relieved him of many administrative burdens, but deferred to his counsel and opinion.

In 1782 Witherspoon left the President's House for his farm and newly-built house, which he named Tusculum, and there he lived out his last twelve years. Thence he rode into town to preach or lecture; and thither members of the lower classes repaired for informal instruction in the classics. And there, blind, but famous and well-beloved, he died quietly in his chair at the age of 71.

Princeton, through the successive tradition of Harvard and Yale, is, as it were, the granddaughter of the English Cambridge. But other strains have entered into her making. After the Restoration the Dissenters, ousted from Oxford and Cambridge, formed academies of their own, often beginning with a little group gathered in the household of a learned divine, much as Princeton began. One such school grew up around Philip Doddridge at Northampton. Perhaps as part of the larger philosophical revolt of the times, these schools tended to lead the way from the traditional course of study to mathematics and physical science, and to English rhetoric and literature. Dickinson and Burr had been in close correspondence with Doddridge, in quest of advice on studies and text-books, and a comparatively liberalized curriculum at Princeton ensued. To this Witherspoon added Philosophy, History, and French; the reading of Montesquieu's *Esprit des Lois*; and the study of Addison and Swift for the cultivation of a good English style.

But the index of a great teacher appears less in courses than in the subtle and immeasurable effects of his mind and personality. By this token Witherspoon was a great teacher. He insisted upon the unity and balance between "piety and literature," by which he meant the interdependence of culture and spiritual life. Said he: "Learning without piety is pernicious to others and ruinous to the possessor"; whence one can guess his probable comment on our present educational chaos. He was keenly aware of the tensions of national growth, and insisted that Princeton should prepare men for a useful part in that growth, whether in the Church, or in public affairs, or in whatever calling; and knowing the man, one is not surprised to find his pupils after the Revolution taking a leading part in all matters of public concern, especially in the middle and southern states.

In the General Assembly of 1789, 52 of the 188 ministers had been pupils of Witherspoon. Eleven per cent of his clerical graduates became founders or early presidents of new colleges, including Union College, Brown University, Hampden-Sydney, Washington and Jefferson, the University of North Carolina, and of Nashville, the forerunner of Vanderbilt University.* He taught James Madison, the younger Aaron Burr, Henry and Charles Lee of Virginia, and the literary Philip Freneau and Hugh Brackenridge. Ten of his pupils became cabinet officers, six were members of the Continental Congress, 21 sat in the Senate, and 39 in the House. Twelve became governors of states. Such a tradition of public service was already active when Witherspoon arrived, but his influence and

* Other institutions in whose origin Princeton men played an important part are Dickinson College, Ohio University, Hobart College, Hamilton College, Tusculum-Greeneville College, Austin College, and Princeton Theological Seminary.

example greatly increased its momentum, and established for the years to follow the conscious purpose of Princeton in the Nation's service. He imparted to the college an intellectual and spiritual energy which served to carry it far through the darker 74 years that elapsed until the advent of James McCosh.

That stretch of more than two generations was dull and undistinguished, except for a few illustrious personalities of teachers whom Princeton will do well to remember. The reasons for this long decline at Princeton were in part general, in part particular.

In general American culture suffered a serious abatement after the Revolutionary War. Skepticism and atheism became fashionable, with a corresponding moral decline. The tap-root of American cultivation and manners was severed by the war, and without European nourishment American life became crude and provincial. It bristled with the "spirit of liberty," which the less discerning, including undergraduates, often failed to distinguish from wilful disorder and insubordination. Against such prevailing ebb tides educational progress was gravely retarded or stopped altogether. All American colleges suffered. The matter of finance seems always to have been critical, especially after the panic years of 1819, 1837, and 1857. But withal the nation's growth in wealth and importance was sensational, even if rank and somewhat specious, and the growth of the colleges was in kind.

Princeton, however, besides all these restraints, suffered from a particular atrophy of her own, which might be described as ecclesiastical inbreeding. The living faith of Dickinson, Burr, and Witherspoon had sunk into a tradition, both understood and expressed, that the majority of both Trustees and Faculty should be recruited from the Presbyterian clergy; and the clerical Trustees usurped what now seems an intolerable control over the college's affairs. They scrutinized the minutes of the Faculty; they interfered in matters of discipline; they intruded upon oral examinations with their criticisms; they attended classes and spied on President and Faculty with a scent keen for unorthodoxy or moral deviation; they discouraged and defeated any educational reforms envisaged by such a President as Samuel Stanhope Smith, and on occasion made appointments to the Faculty over the President's head.

These seventy-four years in the doldrums covered four administrations:

Samuel Stanhope Smith	1795-1812
Ashbel Green	1812-1822
James Carnahan	1823-1854
John Maclean, Jr.	1854-1868

President Smith was Witherspoon's son-in-law, and had acted as *locum tenens* during the many years of Witherspoon's preoccupation with public affairs, always, however, under the great man's eye. He was a Princeton cleric, thoroughbred, eloquent, impressive, charming; and he envisaged a leading, liberal, and enlightened Princeton. From the age of 22 to 25 he had been busy in Virginia founding and presiding over what is now Hampden-Sydney College. At Princeton he supervised the reconstruction of Nassau Hall after the war. He taught belles lettres, ethics, theology, and religion on a heavy schedule and served as clerk of the Board of Trustees and treasurer of the college. At the same time his studies in anthropology, among the first to apply evolutionary ideas to man, gained him a reputation in Europe. He had a talent for raising money, to which even the Trustees could not object. He was the first in the country to establish the study of chemistry in the liberal arts course. He foresaw the rise of science, and introduced a scientific course leading to a certificate of achievement. He enlisted John Maclean, Sr., trained in Scotland, London, and Paris, to teach physics and chemistry, one of the first attempts after the Revolution to resume the cultural resources of Europe. The two men labored together in adding richly to the scientific collections and apparatus.

But for all his gifts and vision, and partly because of them, President Smith had a hard time. He was handicapped all his active life by a latent and sometimes virulent tuberculosis. In 1802 Nassau Hall was gutted by flames that started, probably, from a defective flue; but the students were blamed and Smith described it as marking "the progress of vice and irreligion." Several suspected students were unjustly suspended.

Though Smith was respected and liked by the undergraduates, serious riots arose in 1800 and in 1807. They both sprang from what seemed to be unmerited suspensions. The first riot expressed itself with firing of pistols, rolling of stones through the halls, and banging of brickbats against doors and walls. It subsided only on the President's threat to dismiss the college. The second riot was more serious. The Faculty refused to hear remonstrances from committees of the students, as unlawful "combinations." After a partly enforced vacation the remonstrance was renewed with no success, and 125 students were suspended. Though Princeton was applauded for its severity by other institutions who were suffering from the same spirit of "insubordination," the matter was unwisely handled and Princeton suffered for it. The Trustees blamed the President for the state of "irreligion," and one of them thus spoke for the rest: "We mean to make the Faculty do their duty by executing the laws, and if they do not we shall in the fall proceed to employ men who have the firmness and ability to do better." In such conditions the morale of the college naturally wilted and sank.

Enrollment fell off and income declined. In their dismay the Trustees considered changing the college into a theological seminary. They and the Church in general distrusted Smith's advanced opinions and policies, especially in the direction of science. Though the college survived, out of this distrust was born Princeton Theological Seminary, which, through common trustees, dominated the affairs of the college for many years after its foundation in 1812.

As a measure of economy the Trustees dropped two of the professors—one had resigned not long before—and only Maclean, the ablest and most effective teacher of the lot, was left. But he taught chemistry, and in 1812 they asked for his resignation also, and shortly after made Smith's resignation inevitable. He lived on for seven more years. Old, sick, and in debt, there was nothing left for him but to contemplate the ruins of his visions and plans for Princeton.

During the next forty years the college made little progress, while other institutions in the land were keeping pace with the nation's growth. The curriculum remained inflexible and almost unchanged since Witherspoon's day. Much of the teaching was uninspired and uninspiring. Discipline was as unreasoning and unsympathetic as ever. From five in the morning till nine at night, the undergraduate's life was uncomfortable and dour. But the hidden cause seems to have been fear, partly unconscious, on the part of the reverend clerical administration—fear of the increasing tendency to physical science and criticism, perhaps skepticism, which might undermine their security and the spiritual security of mankind. They seemed also to interpret the insubordination of the undergraduates as a symptom of such infidelity. But the more severely they punished, the worse the disorder.

President Ashbel Green, who had strongly disapproved of Smith for his "laxity," found himself in a continuous state of nerves over explosions, pranks, and even desecrations, culminating in the big explosion of 1814, which did damage to Nassau Hall. It was followed by sundry expulsions and suspensions of no salutary effect.

Again, in 1817, in protest against various hardships, the undergraduates barricaded Nassau Hall and defied the administration. Unable to identify the ringleaders, the Faculty proceeded to dismiss suspects, but this only irritated the rioters to further outrage. An undergraduate respects justice more than anything else, so at injustice his most vehement resentment breaks into flame. Many of the students, bored by the intolerable disorder, left college. The "rioters" were even summoned into the courts, to the indignation of their parents. Again in 1823 an unjust suspension started more trouble, with organized remonstrance followed by further suspensions. By this time it was clear that the college had seriously lost reputation, especially in the South, whence it had hitherto drawn strong and steady support. Enrollment in 1827-28 declined to 71. Funds were dwindling, and the Trustees tried to balance the budget by reducing salaries, thereby wrecking the Faculty.

As the end came in sight, the canny mind of John Maclean, Jr., son of the ill-treated teacher of chemistry, brought the reprieve. In 1827 he produced a plan to reorganize the Faculty. And the year before, he had been instrumental in the forming of the Alumni Association of Nassau Hall with the avowed intention of rallying the graduates to the support of their college. By this time they had attained to high places as governors, senators, representatives, judges, and college presidents. Their interest in the college, thus enlisted and revived, saved the day.

Hitherto no building had been going on except Philosophical Hall—hallowed by Joseph Henry's experiments but since razed to make room for the Chancellor Green Library—and its duplicate, Stanhope, whose modest dignity and fine proportion are at last beginning to win the appreciation they deserve. East College rose in 1833 and West in 1836, to meet the needs of an enrollment that grew with the rapidly rising population and wealth of the country. In 1847 came the old chapel, of cruciform design, to the scandal and dismay of many who sniffed the taint of Newman and Popery. In 1837 the old Halls of the Whig and Cliosophic Societies were erected in the form of Ionic temples, eventually replaced in marble in days of the Halls' decline.

As yet there were no formal athletics, but the dreary monotony was broken by an occasional gaudy day—celebrations of the Fourth of July, and the visit of Lafayette in 1824 to receive the diploma of Doctor of Laws conferred upon him some 34 years before. Commencements abounded with crowds, food, and oratory. In 1847 two days were set apart to celebrate the college's Centenary with high festival of procession, eloquence, fireworks, feasting, toasts, and song.

Somehow, against countercurrents of reaction, the life of Princeton proceeded in a steady, if slender, stream of enlightenment. There were the "Halls," Whig and Clio, dating from 1769 and 1770. They divided the undergraduates between them, and through their rivalry and their secrecy, they enlisted for one or the other all that contentious allegiance and energy which usurps the heart of the youth in college. In "Hall" young men trained themselves and each other in debate and parliamentary practice, in politics and thinking; and explored literature by themselves in the Hall library. The Halls took their highly significant part in forming many Princeton men for distinction in the Nation's service. Even in our time older graduates have been heard to say that "Hall" had more to do with their intellectual growth than the curriculum.

It may be. But we must also reckon with that quiet, unseen, unmeasured life which the great, or even good, teacher was daily imparting to Princeton through the medium of his subject.

There was the beloved John Maclean, Sr., already mentioned, who carried an incredible burden of teaching, acquired for the college new scientific apparatus from Europe, and won hearty response from his students, only to be dropped by a suspicious Board after a few years.

And there was Henry Vethake, called as professor of natural philosophy and chemistry in 1817, allowed to resign in 1821, and recalled in 1830 as part of Maclean's plan for restoration, only to leave again after two years.

Without due memorial is Philip Lindsley, who, but for the mistrusting Trustees, could have done for Princeton all that was sorely needed in his time and have become one of her great Presidents. Beginning as tutor in 1807, by 1817 he was Vice-President and acting President in 1822. He was actually elected President in 1823, at the zero hour. But hostile Trustees and the general wreck of both finances and morale were more than he would undertake, and he left Princeton to become President of the University of Nashville. Meanwhile he had gained not only strong influence over the undergraduates—he was the only one to whom they gave respectful attention during their riots—but his reputation had spread abroad through the educational world. He was elected President altogether thirteen times by various institutions, including the University of Pennsylvania.

In his inaugural address at the University of Nashville he gave utterance to proposals for higher education, based not only upon his intelligent use of experience, but upon the noblest precedents of the past, which, like Wilson's of latter day, would have given Princeton complete leadership in educational progress. Proper recreation, especially athletic, for the orderly release of youthful energy; dignified self-help; comradeship of teacher and taught; a sustaining, invigorating atmosphere of inquiry and refinement—all these he foresaw as he envisioned the future of the college.

Robert Patton taught classics for two years early in Carnahan's time. Trained in Göttingen, he organized at Princeton a philological society, put at its disposal his then unmatched collection of ancient and modern classics, and led a revival of literary interest among the students. Alas, it was short-lived, for the Trustees reduced his salary and he resigned. Similar was the case of Evert Topping in Maclean's regime, who made bold to relieve the dull and often disorderly gerund-grinding of his Greek classes with discussion of literary values and thus roused his charges to a lively response. But Maclean would have none of it, and Topping resigned.

But the greatest of all who kept Princeton alive through the mid-century was Joseph Henry. He was born of humble origin in 1797. His only formal education he got at Albany Academy; but genius educates itself. His tastes, at first literary, at last settled strongly in the direction of science, and his publications spread themselves over a great area of that field. His real fame is reared upon his discoveries in electricity and magnetism—discoveries which anticipated, indeed partly realized, telegraphy, and foreshadowed radio. When he came to Princeton at 35, he was at the height of his powers and in full career of his inquiries. His reputation was already high and far-reaching. Friendly and modest, he gave himself freely to the undergraduates, who were fascinated by the man and his revelations, and quite unaware which was which. For really great teachers, like Witherspoon, McCosh, and Wilson, educate not only by the usual means, but by a direct radiation of their greatness, which induces an energy and elevation in lesser minds without the medium of words—like the inducted currents in Henry's coils of wire.

After fourteen fruitful and happy years at Princeton Henry accepted a call to head the new Smithsonian Institution. Twice Princeton tried to win him back, and in 1853 actually elected him President; but, except for a few occasional lectures, he would not leave his great work in Washington in the interests of pure rather than applied science. In later days he came to know Lincoln. Each recognized the other's greatness, with warm admiration. "He is so unassuming, simple, and sincere," said Lincoln.

Other luminous points in the twilight of Princeton were the distinguished Stephen Alexander, who taught astronomy from 1833 for 44 years; and Albert Dod, who, by all accounts, was a winsome, effective, picturesque teacher of almost anything. Besides teaching mathematics, architecture, and political economy, Dod was exercised in theology and literature, and was a brilliant preacher. The younger Maclean began with mathematics, but as convenience demanded, turned his hand to classics. Today the versatility of these men, especially of Henry, at first seems amazing; but our wonder is qualified when we remember that the content of their instruction was neither so rich nor profound as, by grace of research and specialization, it has since become. Yet their very versatility gave their instruction a certain philosophical breadth and gravity which most of our modern specialists have lost.

John Maclean, President from 1854 to 1868, had been practically throughout James Carnahan's administration the real dynamo of the institution. He conceived no great ideas, was not an impressive man, and was regarded by undergraduates with mingled affection and amusement. But he was a good manager. It was he who at 27 saw the need of organizing the alumni in support of the college, and devised the plan which saved its life. He was energetic in financial campaigns in 1830, 1835, 1853-54, and 1855, and pressed these last two for the founding of scholarships and new professorships. He appreciated a great scholar like Henry, yet he firmly maintained the ecclesiasticism which had long prevailed in the place. He would allow no changes in the old inflexible curriculum. He encountered heavy discouragements, such as the panic of 1837, the second burning of Nassau Hall in 1855, and the Civil War, and met them all with fine courage. He proceeded at once with the restoration of Nassau Hall to essentially its present form. Though feelings ran high in the Halls and on the campus as the issues of 1861 became more acute, Maclean kept the college on an even keel by such moderation that more excited partisans accused it of indifference to "the Cause." When war broke out, one third of the three hundred students left, and a large number from the South entered the Confederate army. It is painful to think of the cruel severance of friends between the two sides in those hard days.

Forty years later, at the Commencement of 1901, two grizzled veterans of the Confederacy were called forward by their old college to receive, amid loud acclaim, the distinction which the call to arms had so untimely forestalled. Said the *Alumni Weekly*: "A notable feature of '61's reunion—in fact a notable incident of this Commencement—was the conferring of the Bachelor's degree upon two Southern members of this class who had left college before Commencement in their senior year and joined the Confederate Army. They were Thomas Helm and John H. Odeneal, of Mississippi, and nobody could be received more heartily into the fold of Princeton alumni than these two gallant sons."*

The old disorders seem to have subsided with time, and superfluous undergraduate energy escaped in the form of "horn sprees," wherein groups abroad at night shattered the peace with raucous tin horns. Then, in 1858, baseball made its advent and games with outside nines began; and the next year students and Faculty together managed to produce a rude gymnasium. In 1869 occurred an event which is brought out and dusted off every autumn—the first intercollegiate football game, which Rutgers won.

Maclean had other worries. In 1843 the first Greek-letter fraternity appeared, followed in time by nine others. Afraid of their effect upon undergraduate life, Maclean, as soon as he became President, moved for extirpation. It was a difficult and delicate business, but at the end of ten years he believed that Princeton was rid of them. Some of them, however, lived underground well into McCosh's time. That indomitable Scot, fully convinced of their evil effect, fought them to a hard finish against certain influential alumni, but with a majority approval of undergraduates.

Maclean was worried, too, about the apparent conflict between science and religion, a conflict which became more critical with the appearance of *The Origin of Species* in 1859. About all he could do was to consider the orthodoxy of candidates in making his appointments. His choices did not altogether redound to Princeton's good, for the men best qualified to teach were not necessarily Presbyterians. Yet he had reason for complacence in pointing out that during his administration the endowment had increased nearly $500,000, and that most of it had been devoted to scholarships and professorships. And in spite of the war the enrollment had not declined.

* June 15, 1901, page 797.

But now, in 1868, just a century after Witherspoon, Princeton needed another great and enlightened leader; and, perhaps unwittingly, she found him. James McCosh, a professor in Queen's College, Belfast, had already won high favor in America during his lecture-tour in 1866. He had distinguished himself as a courageous liberal in the ecclesiastical excitements in Scotland and Ireland. But one wonders if, in choosing him, all of the Trustees could have been aware of what was in store for them. He was familiar at first hand with the educational ways of the Scotch, English, and continental universities. He was to shake Princeton out of her provincialism, and it was ominous that in his inaugural he spoke prophetically of "a university."

He was in his prime at 57, and he took over much as the great Richard Bentley in 1699 took over at Trinity College, Cambridge, in its like need. "It's the will of God," he once argued over some domestic question. "Indeed," replied his sainted wife, "I'll be thinking it's the will of James McCosh." And the will of James McCosh it was during his administration. It was always "me college." The Trustees found him indomitable. So did the Faculty, and he cannily played off one against the other. One of his "bright young men" had the courage to oppose him in a faculty meeting on one occasion, and of course was crushed. The young man was pretty indignant and humiliated. The next day McCosh met him and said: "Ye were perfectly right in your contention yesterday, but I had me way." The Trustees, exasperated by his dominance and their own helplessness, moved, on another occasion, to a vote of mild censure, led by Dr. William M. Paxton. McCosh assumed deep humility, and said: " 'Now no chastening for the present seemeth to be joyous, but grievous: nevertheless afterward it yieldeth the peaceable fruit of righteousness unto them which are exercised thereby.' Dr. Paxton, will ye lead us in pray-er?" And that was the end of that.

But his power of will, his shrewdness, and his energy were reinforced by an inscrutable Scotch humor and an irresistible Scotch charm. One of his students in after years said that he was "the most beautiful human being he ever beheld," an opinion well borne out by the surviving portraits.

Like Dr. Johnson, he "had not patience with folly and absurdity." At a meeting of his famous discussion circle, open to any from juniors to professors, someone made a fatuous remark, which was followed by a flippant speech from another. "Silence!" roared McCosh; "Ye're na better than an atheist." Then, glancing at the first speaker: "But that's better than a fule." Dean William F. Magie used to recall that when he first returned from Germany, McCosh summoned him to these discussions, and without warning said: "Mr. Magie, ye'll lead the discussion." So the young tyro caught at his first thought, and suggested the question whether our ideas of design in the universe are innate or inferred from experience. "Very good," said Dr. McCosh. "Ye'll find it in Lucreetius." A seminarian then solemnly cited Genesis: "God created man in his own image, in the image of God created he him." Whereupon McCosh roared: "Be still, Sir; ye'll not bring the holy Word of God into a philosophical discussion."

During his administration of twenty years (1868-1888) the college emerged from quaint but stodgy paternalism into a semblance of the Princeton of today. McCosh was a great builder. In his time came Halstead Observatory (1868); a gymnasium (1870), on the present site of Campbell Hall; old Dickinson (1870), where the tower of the Firestone Library now stands; Reunion (1871); Chancellor Green Library (1873); the School of Science (1875), superseded by the new library; Murray (1876); Witherspoon (1877); the purchase of Prospect as a President's house (1878); Edwards (1879-1880), "to be let at a moderate cost" to refute the perennial notion that Princeton is a rich man's college; and Marquand Chapel (1882). The Museum of Art was also begun. Of these twelve buildings, only seven remain. Whatever architectural regret they later came to provoke, in their day they were timely. McCosh also did much to improve the setting of the college, realizing from Old World experience the cultural importance of such matters. He designed the grounds "somewhat on the model of the demesnes of English gentlemen."

He was criticized for spending too much on brick and stone, though he recognized full well their minor importance. Said he: "I proceeded on system, and knew what I was doing." He indefatigably sought the means, which, in the enthusiasm of his advent, came almost without asking. "I could not walk up Broadway without some one coming up to me and saying, 'Do you not want so and so?' " During his administration the college received nearly three millions. The Faculty increased from 16 to 40, the students from 264 to 604.

He revised the course of study by rearing on the old foundations an increasing breadth of choice for the upperclassmen. Classics, mathematics, English, and the philosophical subjects were retained for all, and he labored throughout his term to extend the array of advanced subjects. His paleozoic critics were dismayed, while others, in the allure of Harvard's license, thought he did not go far enough. Criticism never daunted him. He even engaged in formal debate with President Charles Eliot of Harvard on the soundness of free election of courses.

He developed the school of applied science, conceived in Maclean's time, and launched with a professorship the four-year course in engineering. He engaged a professional librarian, who catalogued the library, made it more accessible, and brought it up from a meagre assortment to high rank among American libraries of the time. He established fellowships for graduate study which attracted an increasing number of students, especially in philosophy and science. Among them were promising recruits for the Faculty.

At all times, both in word and practice, he declared his faith in teaching through intimate and personal contact—that basic conviction which from the beginning has been the core of the Princeton tradition. To him buildings and courses were less than men, and men in groups less than the individual man; hence his chief concern was the Faculty. "Is he alive?" he would ask about any candidate for a post. Well could he distinguish the teacher-scholar from the mere pedagogue. Somehow he failed to enlist Basil Gildersleeve, Princeton 1849, the greatest Hellenist America ever produced; and to keep John B. McMaster, the historian. ("And why did ye not tell us ye were a great man?" said he, years later.) But the roll of young men he did choose was an earnest of life and eminence for Princeton through a generation to come. It included such names as Brackett, Young, Hunt, Scott, Osborn, Winans, Marquand, Fine, and Magie.

As in his earlier days in Scotland the object of his utmost endeavors was the individual parishioner, so now it was the individual student, whose welfare depended upon the life of the college. He labored in every way to raise its moral and social level, and to this end first attacked its "barbarous practices," especially hazing. No story more entertaining was ever told than his account, in his farewell address, "Twenty Years of Princeton College," of the adroit way in which he first put the proud Chancellor Green in his place and then frightened a hazing gang into a written apology and promise of good behavior; or his story of meeting head-on a rising rebellion of the student body with such strategy that in the end "the threatening cloud passed away."

He resumed Maclean's warfare on Greek-letter fraternities, and with the help of Professor Lyman Atwater and one courageous undergraduate they were finally exorcised.

At first he gave encouragement to athletics, which were now entering upon the intercollegiate stage. But he was troubled by the preoccupation and excesses that soon infected them, and the distraction from the proper interests of the college man. He feared lest "your strutting college heroes may consist of men who have merely powerful arms and legs." His son, a first-rate hurdler, he once facetiously introduced: "And this is me son, Andrew, whose brains are in his heels." Andrew in time became an eminent surgeon.

The old practices of spying by the Faculty were abandoned. Suspects always had a hearing, and cases were judged in conference between Faculty and an elected committee of undergraduates. In all ways the relations of teachers and taught became more open and intimate—a state of things attained and enhanced by the help and influence of Dean James O. Murray.

Without paternalism or sentimentality or condescension, both Dr. and Mrs. McCosh convinced each student of their sincere personal interest in his welfare. Naturally his pupils were proud of him and loved him. Nor did this regard on their part inhibit a sort of affectionate interplay which seems to have cost him no dignity. One spirited youth, passing the open door of McCosh's lecture-room, shouted: "Hey Jimmy!" and fled. "I take no notice of that vulgar fellow," said McCosh, and resumed his lecture.

Above all and in all that he did the ruling consideration was spiritual. Convinced Presbyterian that he was, there was in him none of the old ecclesiasticism that beset the earlier Princeton. In his baccalaureate of 1872 he contrasted faith in Christ with faith in doctrine. His generosity and tolerance, though viewed askance by more sclerotic minds, exerted a liberating influence throughout the college. He accepted evolution as a part of Christian truth. "Ye'll not teach the young men that evolution is false," said he to his Faculty; "tomorrow ye may wake up to find that it is true." At an interchurch convention some venerable Anglican in his prefatory remarks assumed that all present could agree upon the Apostles' Creed. "Huh!" grunted McCosh to his neighbor, "I'll not descend into Hell with the Episcopaylians." But this of course was in fun. His whole life and teaching were devoted to asserting the transcendence of the spirit above all specialized knowledge, ordering and illuminating it as but a part of the whole Truth one and single.

From the beginning McCosh envisaged Princeton not as a mere college, but as the material out of which he hoped to construct a *Studium Generale*, "a university of the highest order." This vision he was able to realize only in part. But at his retirement he could say: "The college has been brought to the very borders. I leave it to another to carry it over into the land of promise." The momentum which he gave Princeton kept up well into the next century, and was resumed and augmented under Woodrow Wilson.

Dr. Francis Landey Patton's administration ran its course through the expansive nineties. If at first some objected to him as merely another minister in the Presidency, it was characteristic of the man that all objections quickly melted under his irresistible charm and utterance. He was one of the most skillful public speakers of his time. He was master of all the legitimate devices of the art. He deployed, but never misused, a goodly measure of histrionic talent. It is said that in his youth he aspired to become an actor, but his mother intervened. He exercised a lively and pointed wit. But beneath all the art and technique was a strong and consistent conviction and a vigorous and agile mind, whose training in the law and in theology provided a well-ordered frame and shapely design for all that he had to say.

He had ideas. Like McCosh he called for the teacher-scholar: "The professor who has ceased to learn is unfit to teach." He proposed an extension of self-government among the undergraduates, and much closer participation of the alumni in the college's affairs; in fact, a much freer circulation of ideas among all members of the college body. But the first in order should be the development of a Department of Politics, including, of course, History and the study of Society. In this procedure he was but giving extended form to a tradition strong at Princeton since Witherspoon's day.

It was again a period of raw and rapid overgrowth in the country at large, and, like country, like college. Everywhere, even in remote corners, young men and their parents were caught by the lure, and it became the fashion to "go away to college," more to gain social technique and make the right friends than to lay hold upon an abundant intellectual life. Patton, quite aware of the situation, remarked that most students then swarming into college seemed to regard education merely as "a process of being sprayed with culture." During his administration the enrollment rose from 604 to 1,237.

Money seemed to be easy, especially for material expansion. The college grew, but with the immature growth of a stripling through adolescence. Buildings followed in rapid succession—Dod, Brown, and Alexander—in the same restless riot among bad imitations of historic "styles" which prevailed the country over. At last the late Gothic of the Pyne Library pointed the way to something better. Cope and Stewardson had set the course at Bryn Mawr, by their skillful adaptation of Tudor Gothic; and through the influence of Professor Andrew F. West, a splendid precedent was set at Princeton in 1896 by the building of Blair Hall. It proved a style becoming to the terrain and climate and unseen genius of Princeton, and was an outward omen that Princeton was returning from the temporary and never too congenial influence of German *Wissenschaft* to the more humanistic English tradition. Klauder and Day, who succeeded Cope and Stewardson, were no slavish imitators; they strove in every way to adapt Tudor Gothic to present-day needs, and to express in their designs the charm and spirit of the place, of which they were keenly aware. Hence the fairly consistent architecture which is now the outward embodiment of Princeton. Some there are who regret that building at Princeton has not developed from the plain precedent of Nassau Hall; but such development, if consistently extended to meet present needs, ran risk of a dreary monotony, incapable of the cheerful variety and ingenious adaptation of structure which now cast the spell of the place upon all who pass by.

Dr. Patton, able and fascinating, was framed by nature more for the contemplative than the active life. While the college boomed, standards fell, courses multiplied without systematic control, lecturing took the place of intimate teaching, discipline relaxed, students cunningly plotted their easiest way by "gut" courses and syllabus, hazing revived, and intellectual pursuits fell into abatement and low price. It was the time when Princeton got the name of "country club," to which some of her purblind critics still cling. Intercollegiate athletics rose to an absorbing prestige, with a shocking apathy of conscience.

But there were able men among the Faculty who were dismayed at the drift of things. Such were Murray, Scott, Brackett, Winans, Ormond, Fine, West, Daniels, and Woodrow Wilson. And two significant events came to pass which should have proved to the disheartened that the old vitality was only waiting for the right man to rouse it anew.

One of these events was the Sesquicentennial in 1896, planned and managed chiefly by West. It lasted more than a week, with lectures by foreign scholars, a round of social events, an anniversary sermon by Patton and an ode by Henry van Dyke, a symphony concert, fanfare and pageantry of undergraduates and alumni, the conferring of honorary degrees, President Grover Cleveland's appeal to young men to enter public life, Wilson's famous historical oration, "Princeton in the Nation's Service," and the proclamation by President Patton that the College of New Jersey should henceforth be known as Princeton University. What satisfaction this would have given McCosh, could he have lived to hear it. This elaborate celebration roused Princeton not only to a new sense of her great past, but to new effort. Funds were raised, under West's direction, to build Blair and the Pyne Library, and to endow fellowships and new professorships.

The other and more important stirring of the old life was the establishment of the Honor System. Back in 1872 the students had first moved in this direction, but the administration had failed to take wise advantage of their sentiment. Discontent with supervisors of examinations continued, however, especially in the minds of the many men from the South. The honor system had succeeded in southern institutions; then why not here? In 1893 the *Daily Princetonian* made the move and the Faculty followed it up. In spite of rare violations, which have always received severe penalties from the students themselves, the system is jealously cherished now after nearly sixty years. No doubt it has entered deeply into the affectionate pride of every Princetonian, especially when he considers the wistful envy of other institutions which shrink from this venture in idealism.

Patton made an abortive move for a law school, and was more successful in his efforts to build up the Department of Politics. Evidently the pleas of Wilson and Cleveland had not been ineffectual. But the provisions for graduate study, though strongly urged by West and the Faculty, roused in Patton no enthusiasm. Seminaries in the Pyne Library, however, proved seed-plots indeed. In the classical seminary the collection has slowly grown into one of the best equipped implements in the world for advanced study of the classics.

At last in 1900 the Graduate School, under Dean West, was organized; but even before that West had obtained from Cope and Stewardson plans for a great Gothic Graduate College to stand on the present site of McCosh, Dickinson, and the Chapel. Be it noted that this location was exactly what Wilson afterwards proposed, with the intent that graduate and undergraduate in close proximity might mingle, as members of one household, to their mutual advantage. But money was not forthcoming, and fifteen years were to pass before the dream materialized, this time unfortunately a good half-mile away.

Besides the Faculty, other saving forces were very much alive. Outsiders had long since observed a peculiar intensity in the devotion of Princeton men to their college. It savored of romance and chivalry. Something about the place, something sweet, warm, friendly, and ancient, abiding nowhere else in such measure and still remarked by even casual and inadvertent visitors—this subtle influence has ever laid strong hold upon young men who have spent here their most susceptible years.* Compared with alumni of sundry other institutions, they are not, and have not been, men of great wealth; but they have responded with

* Doubtless the spell was upon Mark Twain when he wrote to Laurence Hutton: "Princeton would suit me as well as Heaven; better in fact, for I shouldn't care for the society up there."

every effort to the needs of their college in so far as these needs were made clear to them. The depressions in 1893 and 1907 occurred just at critical moments. But the readiness was there.

When in 1902 it became clear to Dr. Patton that his retirement was expedient, he did perhaps his greatest service to Princeton with his advice to the Trustees that inclined them to the choice of Woodrow Wilson as his successor. For the third time Princeton was to renew her vigor and expand under the impact of a great personality. It proved a brief administration of but eight years (1902-1910), yet this was enough to repeat, if not exceed, the renaissance under Witherspoon and that under McCosh.

Wilson like many others was discontent with the deepening chaos of higher education generally. With the expansion of knowledge, courses were multiplying and specializing without control. Students were crowding the colleges in ever mounting numbers. Instruction took place more and more by lectures. Passing became a matter of a bit of intensive cramming, and standards fell. So did respect for the university's legitimate claim upon a student's effort. Athletics and social life took its place. Many teachers, especially those trained in Germany, felt little concern or responsibility for the student as a human being, and the gulf between teacher and taught grew wide, with consequent disorder and insubordination. While these conditions were general, they were especially acute in so segregate an institution as Princeton.

But Wilson was not discouraged, for many were the auspices in favor of easy reform. As an undergraduate in the great days of McCosh, he had known and loved the college. He had for twelve years been a member of the Faculty, sharing discontents and ideas with at least a dozen colleagues upon whose sympathy and support he now could count. He was aware too of the ancient vitality of the place—of its charm, its homogeneity, its tradition of public responsibility and spiritual values, which had been strong from the beginning.

All the changes he made at Princeton, or would have made, were not a mere "program." They were the consistent outgrowth and development of his conviction that real teaching, as distinguished from mere imparting of information, is a matter of close impact of personality upon personality; that "study is a part of life itself"; that education is not to be valued for its own sake, but as equipment for service in the world. His two addresses on Princeton in the Nation's service, one at the Sesquicentennial in 1896, the other at his inauguration as President of Princeton in 1902, may be taken as his Credo on the matter.

Naturally the first undertaking was the reorganization—or organization—of the course of study, and the raising of standards. This work, involving long discussion and delicate adjustments, took less than two years. Courses were reduced in number, brought to bear upon basic and essential matter, and uniformly shaped to three hours a week. A plan was laid down for the four undergraduate years. It began with required fundamentals and expanded towards free reading in senior year. It met with nation-wide acclaim and imitation.

Meanwhile Wilson was moving forward on the wave of warm support by Trustees and Faculty to the "preceptorial system" (unlucky name). Nearly fifty young men were found and drawn from widely different academic origins to Princeton by the hope that Wilson held out to them of escape from the impediments to teaching and scholarship which had generally overtaken American higher education. More strongly were they drawn by the genius and personality of Wilson himself, and by the amenity of the place. The community of life which sprang up through the whole college, the new enthusiasm for learning with which it tingled, the fellowship of student and preceptor springing up into lifelong friendships, were something new in this generation. And yet not new in the world. For all of Wilson's achievements and proposals at Princeton, as he himself declared, were only matters of old common sense whose revival was long overdue, like the householder in the parable who brought forth out of his treasure things new and old.

The accession of many young scholars did much to raise the power and, in time, the prestige of the Faculty. But Wilson was also in search of immediate mature reinforcement of the staff, and the coming of such men as Thilly, Fetter, Capps, Abbott, Munro, and Conklin greatly enhanced its distinction.

Only one who lived and worked hard at Princeton through the four-year renaissance from 1905 to 1909 can conceive the full release of energy, the happy freedom, of that time. It could not last, they feared. Nor did it.

As far back as 1896 Andrew West had begun to discuss the matter of a graduate school and college, and, as we have seen, plans were drawn for a splendid quadrangle on the campus. Wilson and West were then agreed that the graduate school should, both in fabric and fact, be a closely organic part of the whole institution, with freest interplay of association and influence from professor to freshman. They were agreed on many other points—on the importance to liberal education of a beautiful setting, on the elevation of standards of scholarship, on the classics properly taught (and both men were favorite teachers of undergraduates) as an indispensable basis of liberal education. But the rift, which began imperceptibly and widened progressively, was essentially a rift of personalities. West was charming, persuasive, energetic, a master of the expedient, talented and refined, of excellent taste, a humanist but not a profound scholar. Though he always had a care for the beauty and fitness of externalities, he was not superficial. Neither was he submissive. Wilson too was charming, persuasive, energetic, a humanist and a man of good taste, but in a matter of integrity of principle he was inflexible. He loathed a quarrel but would not default where he saw what ought to be done. Perhaps the very likeness of the two men made their dissension the more intense. For Wilson was far the greater man, the idealist-genius, surprised and grieved at the stupid failure and slowness of his fellowmen to see and do what was so obvious to him.

West's scheme for the graduate college had been postponed by the setting up of the preceptorial order. It was now to be further delayed by a grander proposal for the reorganization of undergraduate life in residential colleges. This was not, as sometimes represented, aimed at the clubs, though it did involve a change in their alignment with the course of undergraduate life. It was the fulfilment of Wilson's vision for Princeton, fifteen years before, as a "community, a place of close, natural, intimate association . . . of young men with older men, . . . with veterans and professionals in the great undertakings of learning, of teachers with pupils, outside the classroom as well as inside." Wilson was no doubt right in his confidence that the necessary money would be forthcoming.

At first the proposal met with general favor and even enthusiasm. Many members of the Princeton family—Trustees, Faculty, and alumni—realized that it marked an advance far ahead of all other American higher education. But it was new and unaccustomed. Some questions were asked. Then a few heads were shaken. Then the opposition of conservatives and vested interests, chiefly led by West, grew. In October 1907 the proposal was withdrawn and Wilson seriously considered resigning. He was encouraged, however, by devoted friends not to give up his purpose, but to wait until he could win the wholehearted support of both the University and the public which surely awaited him.

Meanwhile the real issue of the President's authority over the Dean of the Graduate School became more and more acute. West evaded that authority in various ways, soliciting funds and drawing luxurious plans for a Graduate College, which he now proposed to build on its present site, a good half mile from the campus, where his control of it might be more independent of the administration. A gift of $500,000 was offered on condition of that location. Wilson could accept no such dictation of "money." The gift was withdrawn. The storm that broke rose into a mad fury, and reverberated far beyond the bounds of the University. Was education in this country to escape from the thraldom of wealth and fashion and rusty conservatism? Wilson, with strong backing both in Princeton and at large, fought the "little Princeton party," as he called them, and seemed about to win, when, on May 18, 1910, old Isaac Wyman, Princeton 1848, died and left the Graduate College no one knew how many millions (it afterwards proved to be less than one). West by the will was appointed a trustee of the estate.

Shortly after, to some callers at Prospect, Mrs. Wilson was apologizing for a worn spot in the upholstery. With wry humor Wilson remarked: "Looks rather like a tottering administration, does it not?" In the autumn he resigned from the Presidency.

It was an old story of the idealist-genius outstripping his time: success at first, then final defeat, then ultimate ironical triumph. And it is a tale full of strange ironies.

Not many years later both Harvard and Yale carried into effect Wilson's idea of the residential college, the idea which Princeton had rejected. If this was galling to many at Princeton, they might find a bit of comfort in observing that both Harvard and Yale, larger, surrounded by urban dreariness, hemmed in with professional and vocational schools, needed the reconstruction more than did Princeton. Princeton, on her hill, homogeneous, *en famille*, mostly unprofessional, with her intimate teaching, already enjoys in part some of the benefits which the scheme might have conferred—benefits indeed which she owes to Wilson himself.

Although at Princeton the reorganization might have signally marked the culmination of Wilson's service to the University, it was not essential to his real service. This was a subtler matter. For he imparted to Princeton an intellectual and spiritual momentum which are still strong, a clarified purpose and vision still clear at the end of forty years. Visitors from outside in Wilson's day, including one from Oxford, used to remark that Princeton, unlike other colleges, was united in the common purpose of her teaching, and was going about to accomplish it.

Meanwhile, there apart on its hill, stands the Graduate College, an isolated model of the residential colleges by which Princeton might have been the first to profit, had this precocious project not intervened.

It is all the mode nowadays to review the history of mankind, to generalize from such a review, to diagnose the present case of society, and even to prophesy. This is natural enough in an age so ripe. Our learned seers and prophets discern in human history recurrent cycles of civilization, rise and fall, systole and diastole, "withdrawal and return," like the cycles in nature or in the life of an individual. To some they appear to rise in a spiral, to some they lie on an indifferent level, to some they descend, like Dante's corkscrew, to the bottom of Hell.

Institutions in their course are subject to the same cycles, and pass through periods of intense stretch and effort and strife and attainment into a calmer phase of appropriation and adjustment of what has been attained. Such seems to have been the case of Princeton as she entered upon the twenty years of the administration of John Grier Hibben.

Two years of interregnum under the titular Presidency of John A. Stewart, senior Trustee, and the acting Presidency of Dean Henry B. Fine helped to reduce somewhat the temperatures generated by the strained tension of the Wilson regime, and to prepare the way for more deliberate if less exciting years. It was time to appropriate the enormous energy and adjust the high direction which Wilson had imparted to the institution, to put into logical effect the great ideas which he had left with it. The Hibben administration from 1912 to 1932 was the flowering and harvest of Wilson's planting.

Mere statistics measure the outer growth:

	1911-1912	1931-1932
Enrollment	1,543	2,554
Faculty	166	256
Endowment	$5,194,861	$24,679,436
Budget	$831,538	$2,870,415
Faculty & Departmental Expenses	$395,604	$1,551,134
Land	540 acres	900 acres
Campus	62 acres	120 acres

The growth of endowment represents chiefly the devotion of the alumni through the Graduate Council, especially in the campaign for $14,000,000 after the First World War. It also includes the bequest of $6,000,000 from Henry C. Frick. The finances of the University were in wise and conservative hands and suffered comparatively little from the crisis of 1929.

Hibben, though a cleric, labored under no ecclesiastical formalism. He was a man of warm and generous instincts, concerned with the individual case of every member of the Princeton household, and no measure can be found of the kindness and sympathy which he and Mrs. Hibben spent in a thousand unknown ministrations. The University was their parish.

The most obvious sign of growth was in brick and stone. Cuyler, Holder, and Palmer Stadium were finished, and the Graduate College was dedicated in 1912. But on May 14, 1920 old Dickinson and the Marquand Chapel were burned. It was not until 1924 that work was begun on the new chapel, and it took three years to finish it.

But never in all her history was Princeton the scene of such Aladdin magic as unfolded itself during the last twelve years of the Hibben administration. In 1920 was dedicated the beautiful but simple War Memorial Chamber in Nassau Hall. Then followed in 1921 McCormick, completed in 1927; in 1922, Pyne, Henry (Class of 1904), Foulke (Class of 1905), Baker Rink, and the Faculty Houses in College Road; in 1924 the Isabella McCosh Infirmary, Laughlin, 1901 Dormitory, Eno Psychological Laboratory, and the beginning of the Chapel; in 1925 the Faculty Houses on Prospect Avenue; in 1926-28 the new quadrangle of the Graduate College; in 1927-28 the Engineering Building and the Frick Chemical Laboratory; in 1928 Lockhart, Walker, 1903 Dormitory; in 1929 McCarter Theatre and Dickinson Hall; in 1930 Fine Hall; and in 1932 Joline. In the meantime, in 1927, the great Chapel had been finished and dedicated with high ceremony, including the singing of Bach's Mass in B minor by the Bach Choir of Bethlehem.

Many administrative measures were devised for the better condition of undergraduates and their relations to the Faculty. Besides the new Infirmary a new Department of Hygiene was instituted; personal advisors were assigned; the Bureau of Self-Help and the Bureau of

Personnel were developed; the Senior Council collaborated with the Faculty in administration of discipline; a Council on Undergraduate Life made up from Faculty, Administration, and students was formed, and the affairs of the Clubs underwent repeated revision; a Student-Faculty Association in the interests of religion was created. Required daily attendance at a chapel service was done away with in 1915, and in time the Westminster, Procter, and Catholic chaplaincies were established. It was the cherished and oft reiterated purpose of President Hibben to build a University Center as a common meeting-ground of students and Faculty, similar to those at certain larger and less homogeneous institutions. In fact plans were actually drawn for such a center to replace Reunion Hall. All of these efforts were, of course, only corollary to Princeton's traditional concern for the individual student.

Throughout the administration the Faculty was drawn into closer and closer relation with the President and the Trustees in conducting the University's affairs. Perhaps the most important of these liaisons was the Committee of Three, elected by the Faculty to confer with the President and to pass upon all changes of status in the Faculty. The Advisory Council of the chairmen of the various departments was also called by the President to consider matters pertaining chiefly to scholarship. The three Deans, of the Faculty, the Graduate School, and the School of Engineering, were added to the Curriculum Committee of the Trustees, and three members of the Faculty were added to the Committee on Honorary Degrees. Rules defining rank and status of the Faculty were formulated, a system of retirement, pensions, and insurance was created, and salaries were increased.

It was but natural that right after the excitement of Wilson's day the institution as a whole should somewhat have relaxed its efforts. For a year or two it was disposed to drop back into step with other institutions rather than keep the lead it had won. But the men who had joined the Faculty during the first two decades of the century would not have it so. A committee of eight was appointed to review the Preceptorial System. Their report led to a renewed realization of its importance to Princeton, and to a revival of its ideals. It is a costly method, and a method not always appreciated by novices. It therefore needs constant and watchful protection against false economies, compromises, encroachments by increasing prestige of examinations, and the decline of intelligence and devotion on the part of the teacher. But the new generation seems to have caught the living conception from its predecessor, and to be imparting to it new life.

In scholarship general tendencies of the times asserted themselves: the Classics slowly declined in spite of a gallant last-ditch Conference on Classical Studies organized by Dean West in 1917; Greek was dropped as an entrance requirement in 1918, Latin in 1930, and one degree of Bachelor of Arts established for all graduates except in Engineering. Princeton adopted the College Board examinations for entrance. Qualified students were admitted to courses advanced beyond those provided for their year in college; and any who could might graduate in three years.

But the most significant improvement was the so-called Four Course Plan, launched in 1924 and much applauded since by imitation in other places. It was delicately adjusted to give a student more freedom in his reading, especially in junior and senior years, converging upon a particular subject, and terminating in a thesis and a comprehensive examination at graduation. A standard higher than the ordinary was required for this special work. At first a storm of uninformed criticism broke upon the plan, but wisdom was justified of her children, and the renaissance of both teacher and student was refutation enough.

In the course of the Hibben administration three important schools rose within the University: the School of Architecture (1919); the Industrial Relations Section (1922) under the direction of Professor J. Douglas Brown; and the School of Public and International Affairs (1930), founded in the direct Princeton tradition of training for public service, and now fittingly distinguished by the name of Woodrow Wilson. None of these developments in scholarship was an innovation, but each was the logical issue of intentions which had long been intrinsic in Princeton.

The First World War disrupted the University's progress as had the others. Even before the American declaration of war, many members of the University went into service under other flags. In 1917 President Hibben put at the Government's disposal all the resources of the University—laboratories and dormitories, grounds and refectories. At various times during the war Princeton accommodated a Students' Army Training Corps, a Naval Training Unit, a Government Ground School for the Aviation Corps, a Pay Officers' School for the Navy, a School for Instructors in Physical and Bayonet Training, and a School for Y.M.C.A. Secretaries. In the laboratories, partly under members of the Faculty, research in sound ranging, gas warfare, radio, and medicine went forward. Out of the war grew the Department of Military Science and the Reserve Officers Training Corps in Field Artillery. Altogether 6,170 members of the Princeton family were in the service and 151 gave their lives. From such solemn and devoted sacrifice Princeton turned again, sobered and dedicated anew, to her long task.

It was a great administration, great by inheritance, if less picturesque than others. "Horsing" went by the boards unlamented in 1914, and the dangerous class rushes in 1915. Athletics came under stricter regulation. Distinguished visitors brought a holiday now and then—members of the French Academy, President Warren G. Harding in dedication of the Battle Monument, and the brave Cardinal Désiré Mercier of Belgium, whose figure was thereafter emblazoned in the great window of the north transept of the Chapel.

In the general railroad strike of April, 1920, President Hibben proffered the railroads the help of volunteers under careful regulation. A large number of students offered themselves, possibly as much in hope of adventure as of service. Though they were not gone long, they brought back some vivid bits of experience as firemen, brakemen, and switchmen, and hearty letters of appreciation from the railway officials to the President.

In 1932 President Hibben, in the fullness of years, honor, and affection, resigned his office. For a year Edward Duffield, of the Board of Trustees, acted as President. Then from the Faculty was chosen Professor Harold Willis Dodds to guide Princeton through a new administration. He was not an alumnus, except for a Master's degree in 1914, nor a cleric, though of clerical family. He had won his doctorate at the University of Pennsylvania. He had taught at Purdue University, lectured variously, served as electoral advisor in Nicaragua, as advisor to the Tacna-Arica Plebiscitary Commission, and as Secretary of the National Municipal League and editor of its *Review*. He was 43. He had been teaching Politics at Princeton for eight years, and in that interval he had become deeply imbued with the best in the spirit and inheritance of Princeton, and as definitely aware of it as if he had been bred therein—perhaps even more so because of his wide experience elsewhere. For his administration has been a consistent and energetic realization of that spirit and inheritance in the life and work of the University. In his own words it set out to be "a logical development and improvement of essential elements in our long-established program." Thus, both in speech and action, he has often and earnestly declared his conviction that the best teacher is a scholar, and the best scholar a teacher; that in all teaching the first consideration is the individual human being and his highest intellectual and spiritual welfare; that the Liberal Arts, combining Science and the Humanities in just proportion, constitute the indispensable discipline for a free and enduring democracy ("It is clear that our vexed world will not be saved by the purely vocational mind"); that among all members of the body academic the circulation of ideas should be as free from social and traditional obstructions, and as vigorous, as it can be made; that an institution must ever be on its guard against "statism" (for "he who pays the piper can call the tune"); that education and scholarship steadfastly look for their praxis and fulfillment in service, especially public and national service. All of which goes to make up the perennial unwritten constitution of Princeton.

To these ends it has been a hard-working administration with its morale high, abounding in those unseen, unrecordable successes which form the real history and solid fame of an institution of learning. Perhaps for this reason, when war intervened, it found Princeton attuned and alert beyond most other institutions for the supreme demand.

Princeton's abiding concern for the individual student continued to project itself variously. Enrollment in the university and in its various groups tended to restriction of numbers. Preceptorial teaching was kept in constant repair. The designs of the new library were slowly evolving with the intention of making it a place of easy and natural intermingling of students and teachers in their common quest;

and such an instrument of closer personal association in learning it has already proved to be.

To the same end artificial barriers which with the years had become set and obstructive were one by one eased or removed. Old classifications which had in countless instances thwarted the growth of individual talents were broken down, and the circulation of the whole body academic released and quickened. This therapy, already begun in the Hibben administration, applied itself in sundry ways, from qualification for entrance to graduation. Candidates for Princeton were no longer screened merely by the mechanical process of set examinations, but their records, talents, and personal fitness came more and more into account. "We are cutting new doors in the academic walls which divide departments," said the President; and indeed new doors also penetrated the old blind walls that set off class from class, year from year. Many courses once open only to seniors or juniors were made accessible in lower years. Qualified freshmen were freely admitted to courses in upper years, and the way made open for such as could claim it by their own abilities.

The Four Course Plan was so ordered through the broad antechambers of the earlier years that the senior found in it a happy and welcome release for his own enterprise, and an escape from the *malaise* and manly weariness of having for so many years been told just what to do. It was even found profitable to require of exceptional seniors only three courses in the first term, and none at all in the last term, that their energies might be free for the shaping of a thesis, a work in which they took happy creative satisfaction. In these conditions some studies were produced, especially in politics and literature, which deservedly attained publication.

Besides the Four Course Plan, three other instruments were efficacious in this liberalizing process—the School of

Public and International Affairs, the Industrial Relations Section, and the Divisional (now Special) Program in the Humanities, first operative in 1936. The President, who considered his office one of leadership rather than command, continued to reiterate the conceptions of university discipline already mentioned and the needs for more scholarships and endowment. He also pressed for "cross-department fertilization" toward some common methodology and synthesis of the Sciences and the Liberal Arts; in short, for free circulation between all parts of the academic life. He observed with just satisfaction: "I know of no university of first rank whose best scholars give as much time to undergraduates as they do at Princeton."

Indispensable to the success of such intentions has been the high morale of both Faculty and students, and the devotion of such men as Eisenhart, Morey, Gauss, Russell, Heermance, Taylor, Duane Stuart, Root, Munro, Corwin, Kemmerer, Bender, Spaeth, Baldwin Smith, Brown, and many more. The function of the clubs in the undergraduate world was subject to periodic readjustment. Such devices as the Student-Faculty Association, formed in 1930, for practical service within and without the campus, all made for closer comradeship throughout the academic household. Undergraduates seem to have grown less "collegiate," less standardized in pose and opinion, and much more hospitable to education; and to have acquired a higher and more mature independence of judgment.

In the eight years of this administration before the war, the intellectual resources of Princeton expanded in many directions—so many in fact that they admit here of little more than a bare and incomplete list.

The Industrial Relations Section, inaugurated in 1922 as "a clearing-house of research material for students of governmental policies, employers, and trade-unions," was a pioneer of its kind among American universities. In little more than 25 years it has become a center of consultation, not only for the many various elements of industry in the United States, but for those of many foreign nations. In the University it has served as an instrument of instruction, not through courses, but by providing guidance, materials, and field visits, especially in the preparation of senior theses. Its accumulation of special studies, reports, periodicals, and bibliographies has risen to about 300,000 items, and is available, by consultation and correspondence, to all the world concerned. The Section has also published many studies of its own. Its September week-long conferences at the Graduate College, inaugurated in 1931 and held every year since but two, are limited to 100 representatives from widely varied functions of industry. Modeled after the "preceptorial" idea, close and intimate, "away from the noise and distraction of the city," they offered precedent for the design of the Bicentennial Conferences. There men of many industries ponder such subjects as pensions, unemployment benefits, and stabilization of employment, in sessions which permit no accurate measure of their influence toward the solution of the perplexed and delicate questions which beset industry today. To the conference has been added an annual seminar for 40 younger men carefully selected from the personnel staffs of various companies. The Section's endowment of $360,000 by the Rockefellers in 1938 was increased later by $460,000 contributed by 65 industries and eight national trade-unions. All told, the Section enjoys the cooperation of some 900 organizations.

The School of Public and International Affairs, established in 1930, offered a focus of study to upperclassmen in the four departments of History, Politics, Economics, and Modern Languages. By 1939 it had grown to independent departmental status with provision for graduate work; by 1941 it had acquired a building of its own; and in 1946 received the fitting title of the Woodrow Wilson School of Public and International Affairs. It has since received an endowment of two million dollars. Under its paramount purpose of liberal culture it trains men "in the independent investigation of the problems of the day," requires "intensive practice in written and oral exposition and deliberation under the modern 'conference' method," brings students into personal contact with men of affairs, and provides for travel, residence, and study in foreign countries under guidance and supervision. The topics of the conferences are of wide range but clear focus, and appropriate practical experts from outside take a leading part in them. They are designed to duplicate as far as possible the process of affairs in the world at large, and to impart "a clinical reality" to studies in the social sciences as well as a sense of social responsibility.

Within the School, the State and Local Government Survey has made studies which have led to the enactment by the State of New Jersey of important laws relating to municipal affairs. Also within the School, the Office of Population Research has produced important studies in demography and fertility, and published quarterly the *Population Index*. Clearly the School has been, and continues to be, at one time an instrument of culture for qualified students and a useful assistant to the Government and the public.

In 1941, out of such precedents, sprang the Bureau of Urban Research, "a medium for the coordination of information and research in the many different fields that have to do with cities."

Perhaps the most original undertaking of the administration was the Special Program in the Humanities (art, history, philosophy, music, religion, literature ancient and modern). Beginning with advice on courses in freshman year, it becomes a pyramidal—or rather an hour-glass—

scheme for capable men, converging upon a thesis in the fullness of their course on a subject of interdepartmental scope. Its sponsors devised it with utmost care as an exceptional opportunity for exceptional students and "an antidote to the dangerous trends of modern education." It was described by certain outside investigators of education the country over as "the most significant plan of study" they had found. It clearly pointed the way to the "New Plan" of 1947. No doubt it serves as a strong point of resistance in sustaining the Humanities through their present low estate until they come again into their own.

Two new departments, beginning in embryo, sprang into lusty life: the Department of Music, procreated in 1934, and the Department of Religion, in 1938. The Department of Oriental Languages and Literature, reinforced by the great Garrett Collection, and attracting students and scholars to its six-week summer conferences from all quarters, energetically pursued its humanistic purpose of illuminating the civilizations of the East through history, fine arts, religion, language, archeology, and literature. The International Finance Section on the Walker Foundation, with its resources in the Benjamin Strong Collection, made and published studies of cartels, and, by invitations from the governments of Turkey and Cuba, made economic surveys in those countries. A five-year discipline in "Creative Arts"—drawing, painting, sculpture, music, and writing—was inaugurated in 1939, not in any hope of producing masterpieces, but for the insight which practice adds to theory and exposition. A program of studies in American Civilization, drawing upon the resources of at least eight departments, was launched in 1942.

The scholarship of the Thirties and early Forties was prolific also in other forms: the excavation of the Agora in Athens, arranged in 1929 through Professor Edward

Capps and conducted by Professor T. Leslie Shear till the war intervened; the excavations at Antioch, 1932-1937, at the invitation of the French Government in Syria, in association with the museums in Baltimore and Worcester; the excavation of the Church of St. Martin at Angers under Professor George H. Forsyth, Jr., 1933-1938; the magnificent Index of Christian Art from the beginnings to 1400 under Professor C. Rufus Morey, begun in 1918 and by 1950 grown to 450,000 cards and 80,000 photographs, recording 35,000 monuments; the Museum of Historic Art, greatly enriched by the canny acquisitions of Professor Frank Jewett Mather; the monumental edition of the writings of Thomas Jefferson in fifty projected volumes, begun in 1943 under the editorship of Dr. Julian P. Boyd, with editorial responsibility assumed by the University (assisted by a subvention of $200,000 from the New York Times Company) and the full publishing burden assumed without subsidy by Princeton University Press; the geological expeditions to various regions of the earth, especially the general region of northwest Wyoming and southern Montana, and the establishment of the Princeton Camp at Red Lodge, the cynosure of students from all quarters. The Library too has added wealth to wealth, particularly in the Garrett Collection of Persian, Turkish, Arabic, and western European manuscripts; the de Coppet Collection of manuscripts and books relating to Napoleon; the Rollins Collection of Western Americana; the Parrish Collection of Victorian Literature from Scott to Barrie; the John H. Scheide Collection of manuscripts from the eleventh to the sixteenth century; the McIlwain Collection of books on medieval history and culture; and the Adler Collection in graphic arts. The Library has also the curatorship of the almost matchless Gest Oriental Library.

Through the last three or four decades Princeton has put forth a certain centripetal attraction for various enterprises in the pursuit of knowledge and the arts. All of these have in one way or another reinforced her potential. The most illustrious instance is the Institute for Advanced Study, founded in 1933 in closest mutual interchange of resources with the University. Auxiliaries from without also took form and direction, such as the Advisory Councils (1941) of competent alumni and others to take counsel in the affairs of each department, and the Friends of Music (1941).

But now for the fourth time in her history Princeton's peaceful growth was arrested by war. She began to feel the tension as early as 1937. At Commencement, 1940, in the shadow of Nassau Hall, the President recalled Princeton's glorious service to the nation in the past, and said: "Today we of this generation reaffirm our allegiance to the Government of the United States and of New Jersey. Come what may, as on former occasions the University pledges its full cooperation with our government in its program of national defense, and promises that its whole organization, men, facilities, and equipment, are again at its disposal as it may require them."

The temper of the place was naturally restless, but it was serious. There was no hysteria, nor any of that falsetto patriotism which Dr. Johnson calls "the last refuge of a scoundrel." But from the moment of Pearl Harbor the effort was total and practical. In response to the University's offer, twelve problems of defense were assigned to her laboratories. Twenty-three new courses bearing upon the war were set up in different departments. A year-round schedule went into effect. The work was accelerated so that men might win their degrees or finish as much of their course as possible before being called. In the year 1943-1944 there were no less than six Commencements. Machinery was devised to make inventory of the war resources of the University, of individual men and their special aptitudes, and to give them the information and advice they sorely needed in a time of such excitement.

Courses for special training in flying, field artillery, and naval service were instituted. As the war progressed Princeton undertook "the biggest job in her history." Her resources for feeding, lodging, housing, and teaching were at the disposal of five different schools for the service:

The Army Post Exchange School, which occupied the buildings of the Graduate College from July, 1942.

The Naval Training School, from October, 1942, to October, 1944, which trained 8,500 officers.

The Army Specialized Training Program, from April, 1943 to April, 1945, which served as a model for similar schools elsewhere, and was the first to instruct in the Army Area and Language Program, especially in Arabic and Turkish.

The Navy College Training Program, from July, 1943.

The Naval School of Military Government, instituted in October, 1944.

Princeton did her utmost to keep in touch with the members of her family in the service. The War Service Bureau set up in 1943 followed the career of each absent undergraduate, and was ready with advice looking to his return. Book lists and books of their own choosing were sent to the men at the front. The Program for Servicemen met returning veterans and helped them individually to a readjustment. Three out of four came back to finish their course.

A total of 9,792 Princeton men altogether were in the service; 353 gave up their lives.

Among instruments devised to meet the situation, none distinguished Princeton more than the so-called Personnel Index, established by the University and the Graduate Council as a clearing-house through which each alumnus could find his proper place in the service. The Index was compiled by detailed questionnaires. In 1943 it proceeded in reverse to guide the alumni back to civilian life. To this end it established contact with many prospective employers and enlisted the help of alumni the country over.

In 1943-1944 about 3,700 men overcrowded the campus. Included were over 600 civilians in the regular course who were disqualified for service by juniority or physical defect. The burden of teaching for the Faculty, or what was left of it, increased by half; but throughout the ordeal the courses in liberal arts, much shrunk, kept running. As the President observed in 1942, the militant false ideologies only confirm us anew "in the belief that attention to technology must not lead our nation to neglect the values of the will and of the spirit to which a liberal arts education is directed. We may confidently anticipate a revival of interest in these values when the war has been won."

Plans for Princeton in the peace to come began in 1942. By July 1, 1946, the college returned to its normal schedule, if not, as yet, to normal conditions; for some 4,000 students, veterans and all, overran the campus. In spite of crowding, the University made only the slightest possible temporary concession to numbers of her time-tested ideals of training. The air was full of projects and programs as she entered upon her Bicentennial Year. Two in particular sprang from the main branch of tradition. One of these was the inauguration in 1945 of 21 invitation graduate fellowships in the social sciences and humanities. These bear the appropriate name of Woodrow Wilson, appropriate in their purpose of attracting men of talent and ability into the profession of teaching and scholarship.

The other project was a New Plan of Study, which for four years before its inauguration in 1947 underwent continuous process of refinement through a long succession of committee meetings, councils, and symposia. It was less a new plan than a new adjustment of an old plan to the needs of freshman and sophomore years. On paper it was symmetrical and well-proportioned, "a mean between two extremes of regimentation and unbridled individualism," "an educational pyramid, with exploration of the major fields of learning as the base, divisional concentration as the converging sides, and departmental concentration as the apex." In short, a rebuilt house of learning. But the test of a house is living in it, and upon moving in Princeton has found certain alterations necessary.

Always more important than the house is what goes on inside. Whatever her habitat, Princeton's inner life is insured by her old faith in the ultimate spiritual value of all learning.

If we pause to look back a century or more to the Princeton of the early eighteen hundreds, we cannot escape satisfaction at her latter-day growth in stature, in wealth, in scholarship, in beauty, in reputation, and in cosmopolitan breadth. Now and then some are heard to lament the changes, the influx of aliens, loss of the old intimacy, the decline of humanistic culture. The old days had their own virtues, no doubt. But anyone whose life has been merged with the life of Princeton for the last generation or more must be aware that these changes, for better or worse, are but incidental to something more persistent, more intrinsic. For he feels still the old subtle charm, compelling a loyal, even romantic devotion in the hearts of her servants and children; yet, in reinforcement of this charm, a resolute concern in the welfare of nation and world, and ultimate insistence that spiritual values transcend all others.

CHAPTER II

Concatenation Accordingly

THE design for the Bicentennial Year unfolded gradually. As finally carried out, it presented an architectural effect of many harmonious details ordered in one harmonious structure. Towers of similar form rise to varying heights toward the highest of them all; and clustered among them are numerous halls and oriels, niches and shrines, the whole gathering itself up in a mass energy of both tradition and purpose toward the great observance of June 17.

It had its formal origin in a small committee, afterwards three times increased, appointed by the Trustees on April 20, 1944. As finally constituted, Walter E. Hope '01 was its chairman, Whitney Darrow '03 its vice-chairman, and Col. Arthur E. Fox '13 its secretary. On November 6, 1944, the Faculty selected an Administrative Committee which was to work in closest association with the Trustees' committee. Out of these grew a numerous ramification of committees and deputies in the hope of distributing the work of preparation as widely as possible throughout the Princeton family, and enlisting in the effort all its branches—Trustees, Faculty, undergraduates, alumni, and devoted friends.

Everybody at the time was keenly aware of the unfavorable auspices. The war was still on, though moving toward a conclusion now in sight. Many of the Faculty, students, and alumni were still in the service. The minds of men generally were still preoccupied with more urgent matters. In a world so disordered an assembly of the learned from all parts was impossible.

But with the end of the war in 1945 many of the auspices so untoward at first were turning into unusual promise. It was a time for civilization to take inventory, and to form and weigh ideas for reconstruction. For ideas are genetic in civilization, and universities are genetic of ideas. What time, therefore, could be more opportune for a bicentennial commemoration than this? And moreover let it be a commemoration distinctly in three tenses—a reverent review of the glorious past, a sober examination of our present state, but above all a high and practical vision for the future.

In some such way the conception of the Bicentennial grew in the minds of those who planned it. Its first focus was the anniversary of Princeton's birthday, October 22, 1746, the date of the signing of the First Charter. This, of all days, was to be Princeton's high feast-day. In accord with the traditional way of celebrating academic anniversaries, it should crown a climactic week or ten days of conferences, entertainment of delegates, lectures, gala and spectacle, academic procession and ceremony, and conferring of honorary degrees. Academic routine could easily be suspended for a week or so. After the excitement was over it would readily resume its even course, and probably soon forget the occasion and what it was about.

But the peculiar opportunity of this anniversary, the pressing thought for the future, not Princeton's future only but the whole world's, persisted in the minds of the Committee, and would not confine itself within the narrow dimensions of one "gaudy" day only, or even a gaudy week. Why not a gaudy year?

This idea, startling at first, grew more and more to seem inevitable. There were misgivings of course. Could celebration keep up for a whole year, and not sink into apathy and anticlimax? Could the University, already overburdened with returning students, reconstruction, and the inroad of veterans, spare the energy necessary to its success? And there were more material difficulties—disorganized transportation, scant supplies, limited means of entertaining visitors. But with the support of Colonel Fox, the greater conception of the Bicentennial celebration overcame all fears and finally prevailed; and as it became more familiar, it turned all misgivings into lively enthusiasm. Its intention ceased to be mere celebration or display. Rather it should be so devised that Princeton might attain to a clearer, more impelling realization of herself by a long and deliberate contemplation of the forces that have made her what she is; and to reinforce, as she may and can, such effectual energies as the Nation and the world can put forth in the construction of a new age of peace. To this end a whole academic year was none too much. Let the succeeding events of the Bicentennial Year intermingle with the daily routine of the University's life throughout its duration; let these events keep reminding members of the Princeton family so often and so long of Princeton's past, present, and future, as to enlarge their idea of her greatness, and deepen their loyalty; let the year in its course call together at intervals many of the world's best minds in intimate and unrestrained conference on matters of critical importance to our present condition and our future; let it recognize at large the high achievement of this generation in arts and science, in statecraft and religion. Interspersed with all these salient events let us arrange many appropriate and incidental reinforcements—exhibitions, recitals, concerts, lectures, anniversary sermons, memorials, dedications. And since a measure of play is essential to true learning, let us now and then pause for occasional frolics and interludes. Thus was everything ordered, as Goldsmith says, in a concatenation accordingly.

Such was the Bicentennial Year as preconceived by its directors, and such in the event it proved to be. Every onlooker at any part of the year's progress seemed to be curious about the concealed mechanism which gave it movement and order. They were the more curious because it was so perfectly concealed. Events involving the most complicated arrangements, the most exact timing, passed as naturally as dawn and sunset. To all appearances there was no mechanism. Yet behind the scenes in constant and vigorous action moved an elaborate organization of the whole Princeton world, reinforcing itself from the outside with the support of press and radio, with the Government both of State and Nation, the embassies, other institutions and learned societies, business big and little, and individual scholars the world over. Disappointments, miscarriage of plans, strikes, cancellations, unforeseen hitches, sometimes desperate, sometimes funny, were bound to occur, and often did; but when they did the audience in front was not aware. Just credit for all this achievement would distribute itself far and wide among the host of willing collaborators, including more than 200 members of local committees, and more than 350 people whose efforts made the conferences a success, besides a double score of lecturers, preachers, editors, and authors. But the necessary courage, ingenuity, and propulsion of leadership, as usual in such undertakings, issued from a few men such as President Dodds, the late Walter Hope, Colonel Fox, Whitney Darrow, Professor Sherley W. Morgan '13, and Dean J. Douglas Brown '19.

In January, 1946, the conception of an appropriate Bicentennial Year was embodied in the following announcement and sent to more than six hundred universities and other cultural institutions throughout the learned world, and to the press:

Bicentennial Announcement

We, the President, the Trustees, and the Faculty of Princeton University, send cordial greetings to our colleagues in institutions of higher learning throughout the world.

The University year, 1946-1947, will bring Princeton to the end of its second century and to the beginning of its third. It is therefore fitting and proper, as we observe this Bicentennial Year, not only to rejoice in the success which Providence has given to scholarly efforts in the past, but also to take counsel with other scholars in preparing jointly to meet the tasks lying beyond this crucial moment in history.

Since the days of Witherspoon and Madison, Princeton has dedicated itself to the ideals of freedom in thought and spirit. In eighteen hundred and ninety-six, on the occasion of our Sesquicentennial Celebration, the voice of one of Princeton's illustrious sons, Woodrow Wilson, gave expression to a deep sense of national obligation in the phrase "Princeton in the Nation's Service." On the eve of its third century, Princeton University rededicates itself to those ideals.

And now, in this our Bicentennial Year, the grave crisis in human affairs which confronts us transcends all national bounds and imposes new and pressing obligations upon the World of Learning. Wise men must speedily take earnest counsel lest the world's tragic sacrifice shall have been offered in vain. Princeton, therefore, proposes to direct its Bicentennial Celebration to the end of applying, in consultation with scholars throughout the world, our common skills, knowledge, and wisdom to the reconsideration of the fundamental obligations of higher learning to human society, hoping thus to contribute to the advancement of the comity of all nations and to the building of a free and peaceful world.

Now therefore, we, the President, the Trustees, and the Faculty of Princeton University, have designated for special observance and commemoration the Bicentennial Year of our University, from the twenty-second of September, nineteen hundred and forty-six, to the seventeenth of June, nineteen hundred and forty-seven. And in due season, we shall invite representatives of colleges, universities, and learned societies of the world to participate in the ceremonies which we are planning.

HAROLD W. DODDS, *President*
WALTER E. HOPE, *Chairman of the Executive Committee, Board of Trustees*
ROBERT K. ROOT, *Dean of the Faculty*

January 1, 1946

The Bicentennial Year really began on September 20 with a radio prelude by President Dodds, Mrs. Eleanor

Wilson McAdoo, and Dean Brown. But the signal opening took the appropriate form of a special service in the Chapel on Sunday, September 22, with a full academic procession, and a sermon by The Most Reverend Geoffrey Francis Fisher, D.D., Archbishop of Canterbury.

It was a radiant autumn day. The procession, led by the University Choir, included representatives of the undergraduate and graduate students, the Bicentennial Committee of the Borough of Princeton, the Faculty, officers of administration, the Trustees, and the Archbishop. Slowly it moved across the campus through sun and shade, the varicolored hoods flashing bright against the somber black, while bystanders no doubt pondered many things as it passed. One might ask himself how ancient is this immemorial academic pageant? Why should sober men of learning every now and then yield to some instinct for picturesque display? Why this pomp and circumstance? Is it perhaps escape from what Shakespeare so shrewdly discerned as "the scholar's melancholy"? From the dusty dreariness of the daily grind? From petty frays in what old Roger Ascham called "the cockpit of learning"? What would Thomas Carlyle, the Philosopher of Clothes, have to say? Might he recall his catastrophic nightmare of the House of Commons suddenly denuded? Or one might cite Alexander Pope's not too respectful lines:

> "Broad hats, and hoods, and caps, a sable shoal:
> Thick and more thick the black blockade extends,
> A hundred head of Aristotle's friends."

All human pageantry, including academic processions, is an easy target for the irreverent, even for men as great as Pope and Carlyle and Shakespeare. But the academic procession is very ancient, and therefore must signify something serious. And on this radiant, retrospective day a thoughtful man could see in it only a symbol of the ancient

President Dodds with the Archbishop of Canterbury leaving the University Chapel after the Opening Convocation

The Academic Procession of the Opening Convocation

Nobel Prize winners at the first Conference: Messrs. Dirac and Siegbahn, Madame Curie-Joliot, Messrs. Bohr and Compton

Frank H. Knight and Trygve Lie at the Charter Day Convocation

October 19: the Academic Prc

f the Charter Day Convocation

Dinner in Procter Hall for guests of the Conference on Planning Man's Physical Environment

Conference participants William E. Rappard and Albert Einstein

Arnold Toynbee delivers a public lecture in McCosh Hall

Senator Smith, Secretary Forrestal, President Dodds, Senator Saltonstall

Gifford Beal '01 (center), with Dean Condit and President Dodds, at the dedication of his Joseph Henry Murals

tradition of learning, and the essential unity of Truth manifest in a thousand phases. As it moved out of the sunshine into the solemn shadow of the Chapel, caught up the sturdy old cadences of the processional, "O God Our Help in Ages Past," and proceeded up to the chancel, it could suggest only the focus of all truth in Him who is the Way, the Truth, and the Life.

This, properly enough, was the theme of the whole service. The President framed it thus:

> It is fitting that we should open our Bicentennial Year with a service of worship. Princeton was founded by men of deep and fervent religious conviction. . . . By this chapel service we express our respect for the purpose and spirit of our founders and signify our regard for the place of religion in the life of this University and its power over the minds and behavior of men.
>
> It is also fitting that our first Bicentennial sermon should be preached by His Grace, the Archbishop of Canterbury. When the College of New Jersey was organized we were a part of the British Empire, and our charter runs to the British Crown through the royal governor of the province. With Britain we share a common literature, a common law, common political ideals, and common religious and moral values. Together we also share a common responsibility to sustain these ideals and values against hostile philosophies of life.

In his sermon the Archbishop boldly asserted a like theme. Said he:

> In every department of its work a University should be essentially theological, imparting in each department not a fragment of unrelated knowledge but a facet of truth which takes its appointed place in a faith, a hope, a doctrine able to lift men above the confusion of their own ends and desires and passions into a controlled discipline of life and purpose, strong enough to deliver them from the bondage of created things into the liberty of the Sons of God.

He then reviewed three latter-day doctrines which have variously preoccupied the minds of men. These were humanism in the sense that man is the compass and end of all knowledge; natural science as the only means of attaining to the Truth; and the combination of these two in "scientific socialization." But no one of these is enough. Each overlooks the individual man. Each is but partial in scope, not all-inclusive. All three must conspire in the transcendent knowledge of God.

It may now be more apparent than at the time of it how well-attuned was this opening service as an overture to the whole Bicentennial Year. Not only in its externals, but in its burden and tenor, it was prelude to a certain underlying convergence of thought and aspiration more apparent as the year advanced. For the year amounted to a sort of summation of the Humanities, the Natural Sciences, the so-called "Social Studies," into a spiritual consciousness overbrooding them all. It reasserted the identity of teaching and learning as one function. It reminded us that if, by reason of the boundless scope of modern learning, we must teach the Truth in parts, yet we must teach those parts, however narrowly partial, as parts constituting a Whole.

At the close of the service, the first Convocation of the Bicentennial Year was held in the Faculty Room of Nassau Hall, and the degree of Doctor of Divinity was conferred upon the Archbishop.

After lunch a group of undergraduates went over to Prospect, where the Archbishop and Mrs. Fisher were being entertained, and quite informally presented to him the Bicentennial medal. This was the first of such presentations to recipients of honorary degrees. It seemed highly appropriate that undergraduates should perform this office in view of the Archbishop's long association with young men.

Such, then, were the auspices which inaugurated the Bicentennial Year.

CHAPTER III

Gaudy Days

FOUR convocations, besides that of September 22, when the Archbishop of Canterbury was invested with the degree of Doctor of Divinity, were held during the Bicentennial Year. The first of these, though not the most elaborate, was in many ways the most beautiful.

The official birthday of the University is October 22, for on that day, in 1746, the aged Governor John Hamilton, by advice of several substantial friends of the embryonic college, affixed his signature to the first charter, and thus brought this institution into the world. The day is therefore observed as Charter Day, and the second Convocation was fittingly called the Charter Day Convocation. It was held on the preceding Saturday, the 19th, as more convenient for all concerned. Perhaps the shift gave some comfort to the precisians who were inclined to insist upon the distinction in dates between New Style and Old Style.

At any rate it was a beautiful day—October in Princeton at its best—bright, temperate, and tranquil. And there was something about it most appropriate to the theme of the day, for on such a day the world seems to pause, and rest, and grow reminiscent. It was Princeton's own peculiar day, the day of the whole year when she thought more particularly of herself, and reviewed her hard but glorious past, closely inwoven with the history of the Nation, especially in its times of high crisis. Compared with the final Convocation in June fewer visitors from the world outside were present, and those who were felt themselves, under the spell of the place, transformed into members of the Princeton family.

Again, the Chapel lent the right and perfect setting. The procession was augmented to some four hundred altogether.

Besides the Trustees and Faculty and 23 recipients of honorary degrees, it included the Undergraduate Council, representatives of the Graduate School, representatives of the alumni and officers of the Alumni Associations, representatives of neighboring institutions, representatives of foreign academies at that time guests of the American Philosophical Society and the National Academy of Sciences, the New Jersey Bicentennial Commission, the Governor of New Jersey, and representatives of the United Nations, including members of the Security Council and the permanent Secretariat. The procession moved across the campus from Nassau Hall past Clio and Whig to the measure of a hitherto unperformed march by Beethoven played by the undergraduate band grouped about the Cannon. More than ever, with all its variety of insignia and function, did this ordered group of men represent the essential unity of learning and public service. More than ever, as it passed into the mellow depths of the Chapel, did it suggest the high common purpose upon which all varied human endeavor should converge.

After the Invocation by Dean Robert R. Wicks, the Governor of New Jersey read his Bicentennial Proclamation, in which occurred the significant sentence: "It is appropriate to observe that our problems today, as they were two hundred years ago, are fundamentally spiritual."

This observation by direct sequence anticipated President Dodds's address of the day, of which the burden was historical. In conclusion he spoke of Witherspoon as a special favorite of his, and cited a passage from that great man's lectures on Civil Society wherein he defines the advantage of civil liberty as its "tendency to put all the human powers into motion." The President added: "I can find no better definition of the function of a liberal education than is suggested by this trenchant phrase. It is to cultivate that climate of human values, and that proficiency of mind which will 'put all human powers into motion.' "

The combined Princeton Chapel Choir and Glee Club then sang the ode composed especially for this Convocation by Edward T. Cone '39. It is a musical setting of the well-known passage in Ecclesiasticus beginning, "Let us now praise famous men, and our fathers that begat us"; and in almost every word it illustrated the history of Princeton.

Twenty-three honorary doctorates, according to their divers distinctions, were then conferred upon 22 men and one woman, most of them participants in the first series of Bicentennial Conferences. Of the 23, seven were British, and six others were foreign—Danish, Swiss, Chinese, Norwegian, Spanish, and French.

The Convocation came to a close with the singing of Isaac Watts's metrical version of the Ninetieth Psalm, which has now become traditional at Princeton: "O God Our Help in Ages Past." As the volume of two thousand voices and the organ rose high into the vaulting, intoning the simple but austere old tune of St. Anne, the cheerful solemnity of the whole occasion seemed to be upgathered into a moment of high concentration in which Princeton's two hundred years, with all her struggles and failures and successes, were intensified and strangely present. Nor was it such an experience for Princetonians only. One who had come from the other side of the globe recalled afterwards "that memorable and perfect day at Princeton. I was stirred to the very soul by the dignity and beauty of that Bicentennial Convocation ceremony."

This high point in the Bicentennial Year was set in a cluster of lesser events. The night before had occurred the open and concluding session of the conference on the Humanistic Tradition in the Century Ahead, with its memorable addresses by Professor Marjorie Nicolson of Columbia and President James B. Conant of Harvard. On the afternoon of the Convocation, Princeton played Rutgers at football. During the intermission was enacted a hilarious antimasque of the first intercollegiate game in 1869, reconstructed from old photographs and other documents. Spectators recruited from the Triangle Club and the Theatre Intime and players from the soccer squad, accoutred as of the period, set the big crowd aroar.

The story of the Battle of Princeton, January 3, 1777, so carefully and beautifully retold in the Bicentennial year by Alfred H. Bill, and so closely inwoven with the history of the college, was properly recalled on the Sunday following the Charter Day Convocation. The long efforts of the State of New Jersey to establish a memorial park on the site of the battle came to happy fruition that afternoon in the dedication of the battlefield. Governor Walter E. Edge and President Dodds spoke briefly, and Dr. Douglas S. Freeman, the most recent biographer of Washington, appropriately gave the dedicatory address.

Dr. Freeman, with skill and insight, reviewed the Battle of Princeton as the crisis of the War for Independence, when Washington saved the American cause from what seemed inevitable defeat, after he had been driven southward from the line of the Hudson. He said:

> Washington was compelled to retreat and to arrange his forces in the area between the Raritan and the Delaware Rivers. When you cross those rivers on your journey to New York or to Philadelphia, I beg you, do not forget that there is one of the most decisive of all the battlefields of American history, perhaps for that matter, of world history. Who knows?

Dr. Freeman pointed out the happy omen that this critical battle for freedom ended "under the walls of the college," with all that it implies of freedom of learning and intelligence in the Nation's service. "What greater promise for the future of our America than that we dedicate this battlefield as it were to the sound of the chimes of the University." He then cited the account of the battle in the Olden manuscript with its memorable sentence: " 'Of these men who were on this field and there in front of Nassau Hall, not a man among them but showed joy in his countenance.' Joy in his countenance . . . the promise of new victory, of new Joy where the bells still sound the third centenary of Princeton."

That same afternoon, October 20, Mrs. Elizabeth Sprague Coolidge generously adorned the occasion with a recital by the Pro Arte Quartet. The program included a rendering for the first time of a quartet by Arnold Schoenberg. Mr. Schoenberg had expected to attend the conference on the Humanistic Tradition just ended, and was to have received an honorary degree at the Convocation, but unluckily was prevented by illness.

One incident, less public, added its bit of distinction to Charter Day, 1946. On the day itself, October 22, President Dodds received a message by cable from the President of the Russian Academy of Sciences, which read: "Academy of Sciences of USSR sends to Princeton University its warmest greetings on the occasion of the Bicentennial Anniversary of its scholarly activities, and wishes to the President, members, and students of the University much success in their scientific work for the welfare of humanity."

Except for this welcome message and two invited Russian delegates who turned up unexpectedly and briefly at the conference on Nuclear Science, the Committee was unable, in spite of repeated attempts, to elicit any response from the Russian institutions of learning.

February 22 has by tradition become a day when Princeton alumni turn home again to Nassau Hall. This is quite as it should be, for in 1777 the college endured its baptism of fire under the aegis of General Washington, and in 1783 was blessed with his presence and received not only his benison but a benefaction in the amount of fifty guineas. The Convocation of February 22 was therefore chiefly in the nature of a family gathering. And as the theme of Charter Day had been historical, so on this day it was Princeton of the present.

It was not inopportune that the conference on The University and its World Responsibilities had come to a close the day before, and the open meeting summarizing its ideas occurred that evening. A paper by the French Ambassador, Henri Bonnet, read in his absence, and a paper by Archibald MacLeish were in general agreement that the function of the Universities is to discover and safeguard knowledge, but if that knowledge is to serve the world in its present desperate need, the universities must attain not only to more intimate relationships with each other, but to free and fluent dispensation of their peculiar resources to the agencies of state. The university is, therefore, a most important instrument in the fashioning of peace in the world.

The late Princeton winter was true to precedent, and on the morning of February 22 the campus lay deep under a heavy, wet snow. So the procession was confined to the Chapel. It included as before representatives of the undergraduates and graduate students, and of neighboring institutions, the Graduate Council, Faculty, Trustees, and recipients of honorary degrees. The order of the Convocation was brief and simple, with the President's address on the Princeton of the present as its center of gravity.

He proposed no new departures, no experiments in novelty, for Princeton, but a fulfilment of her age-old purpose, a liberal education "that equips a person to be a competent member of a free society. In brief, it is education for freedom, a phrase that has become . . . the theme of our Bicentennial."

In the first place, it declares our aim to be the development of a competent individual. We thereby recognize that it is people we have to educate, not masses. . . . This is the reason that Princeton spends so much time and money on a plan of study which individualizes the student to a degree, I believe, quite extraordinary in higher education anywhere. Liberty, said Woodrow Wilson, belongs to the individual or it does not exist; and the same is true for education.

But an individual is not isolated. His relations with his fellows, such as those provided by the residential college, are also highly important in his education.

Extra-curricular activities work together with the classroom and preceptorial to give a young man a sense of group security, a chance to establish his worth to his fellows, to discover his own powers and limitations, at a critical period of his life, when he is torn by growing pains and biological urges which he cannot identify or understand until he has passed through them. . . .

In the training of the mind, as in education for social living, the residential college has something distinctive to offer. In such an environment "a course of study is not merely a process of acquiring knowledge, but a life." As Woodrow Wilson insisted, education of the mind does not come from words of instruction alone. It is gained from participation in a pattern of community living as well. Supplementing all formal courses of study is the prevailing intellectual climate in which the students and teachers live. It is the residential college that is most able to translate all available educational influences into a true community of learning.

The President then described in some detail the revised course of undergraduate study, and said in summary:

Having worked up from a broad base in underclass years, by senior year the boy finds himself equipped with a fund of knowledge in a related field on which his mind can play in an original way. He also finds himself in command of a methodology, a technique of thinking, which enables his mind to operate in an analytical and constructive manner on the data before him. . . . Unless a young man learns how to apply knowledge, how to mould it into fresh and original patterns, all that he absorbs is smothered in an inert "classroom compartment" of his mind, because learning is never related to the world about him.

In his conclusion, President Dodds expressed a firm belief that:

> The one indispensable weapon for America, atomic age or no atomic age, is an economically prosperous and a spiritually harmonious people united under the banner of freedom. And yet we do not find within ourselves that agreed understanding as to what constitutes freedom, why it is necessary, and how we can harvest its blessings, which we must have to be strong. Abraham Lincoln noted in 1864 the need for a definition of liberty. "We all declare for liberty, but we do not mean the same thing," he said. Fifty years later Woodrow Wilson continued the same theme: "You cannot have liberty where men do not want the same liberty, you cannot have it where they are not in sympathy with one another, . . . you cannot have it when they are not seeking common things by common means." . . .
>
> In this critical moment the hundreds of colleges throughout this land cannot stand aloof; they must help lead the way to an understanding of freedom, for ultimate human values can prosper in no other atmosphere. Let the college agree that freedom is to be its objective; let it . . . clarify its concept of freedom, and let it move to clothe that concept in deeds.

When the Choir and Glee Club together had sung Handel's fine anthem, "Let their Celestial Concerts All Unite," the University Orator, Walter E. Hope, presented the 35 recipients of honorary degrees for investure by the President. Of these, 17 were alumni. The distinguished guest of the day was the new Secretary of State, the Honorable George C. Marshall, upon whom was conferred the degree of Doctor of Laws. The Convocation ended with the singing of the traditional "O God Our Help in Ages Past."

By slushy thoroughfares the audience, or at least some 1,740 of them, made their way to Baker Rink for luncheon. After they had put from them the desire of meat and drink, as Homer says, as many more crowded in under that spreading roof to hear the address of Secretary Marshall, his first since taking office.

He addressed himself especially to the undergraduates. He observed that this moment of relaxation after the strain of war is more critical than the days of the war itself, and warned his hearers not to become mere interested spectators of events. "I say to you as earnestly as I can that the attitude of the spectator is the culminating frustration of man's nature." He referred to the indecision and insecurity of this country after the first war, which had their direct bearing upon the recent war and its endless tragedies.

> In order to take a full part in the life which is before you, I think you must in effect relive the past so that you may turn to the present with deep convictions and an understanding of what manner of country this is for which men for many generations have laid down their lives. Therefore, a deep understanding of history is necessary—not merely recent history, . . . but an understanding of that history which records the main currents of the past activities of men and which leads to an understanding of what has created and what has destroyed great civilizations. You should have an understanding of what course of action has created power and security and of the mistakes which have undermined the power and security of many nations, and above all, a clear understanding of the institutions upon which human liberty and individual freedom have depended, and the struggles to gain and maintain them. . . .
>
> I doubt seriously whether a man can think with full wisdom and with deep convictions regarding certain of the basic international issues today who has not at least reviewed in his mind the period of the Peloponnesian War and the fall of Athens.

He ended with an appeal to all young people thus prepared to follow the example of the two great Roosevelts and to take active part as workers in one of the political parties.

Compared with the high ceremonies of October and June the Convocation of April 3rd was a modest affair. But it had its peculiar quality and distinction. It was held in the Faculty Room of Nassau Hall, and its auspices were the ancient auspices of this consecrated place. Here the portraits of Witherspoon and Washington, of McCosh, Patton, and Wilson, looking down upon the small gowned group and their guests, could only remind them of the sanctity of the spot, hallowed as it is by all the extremes of faith, fortitude, and fortune that have entered into the making of Princeton. Here the college first settled for its long career. These sedate walls bore their fiery part in the very crisis of the country's struggle for liberty. Through almost two centuries they have sheltered the unrecorded and often dull routine of minds growing by contact with other minds, whether living or dead, conceiving and begetting dreams and ideas proliferous of action and life for the Nation in time to come. These memories solemnized the moment. Yet its very solemnity was pervaded with that subtle but cheerful warmth and friendliness of the place Princeton which never fails. The effect was one of pleasant dignity and informality combined. With simple ceremony the convocation conferred honorary degrees upon 18 scholars and artists, six of them foreign, including two Chinese and one Moslem.

As this festal year drew to a close, its fervor, far from cooling as some had feared, rose to a pitch wholly adequate to proper observance of the four final days. These were Saturday to Tuesday, June 14 to June 17.

The program laid down for them was somewhat like the traditional program for these academic anniversaries—the visitation, reception, and entertainment of delegates from other institutions; music, feasting, illumination, solemn services, pageantry, sports, and recognition of attainment; and other diversions of appropriate kind. But this festival season rose to far greater height by reason of the months of ascending interest which had preceded it.

This elevation was not a matter of happy chance. Said Colonel Fox, on whom, as secretary of the Executive

Committee, the heaviest burden of the year's success had fallen:

From Sunday, September 22, 1946, when the Archbishop of Canterbury opened the anniversary year in the University Chapel with the first of a series of Bicentennial sermons, to Tuesday, June 17, 1947, when the President of the United States delivered a major address from the steps of Nassau Hall, Princeton University had faithfully attempted to carry out the pledge expressed in the Bicentennial announcement: "Not only to rejoice in the success which Providence has given to scholarly effort in the past, but also to take counsel with other scholars in preparing jointly to meet the tasks lying beyond this crucial moment in history." In the days which fell between these two memorable occasions, distinguished scholars, government leaders, and men of affairs from many nations came to Princeton to take "earnest counsel lest the world's tragic sacrifice shall have been offered in vain." Through the medium of conferences and convocations and the other related events of an integrated program, a two-hundred-year-old American university has exerted its fullest effort to "contribute to the advancement of the comity of all nations and to the building of a free and peaceful world."

Thus, by careful and well-concealed design, the year had risen on lesser points of eminence to this crowning moment of welcome and greeting to the whole learned world. The first Convocation had been reminiscent and had taken place in the reminiscent autumn. But it was now June, a natural season of expectation and hope, and the prevailing tense of these closing days of the Bicentennial Year was future.

Naturally, the first to arrive at this family party were the sons of the household itself, the alumni, who gathered on Friday, June 13, and remained until Sunday. On their departing heels came the delegates. But Saturday, all day, was the day of the alumni, when they were "at home."

In the forenoon took place an event of especial interest to the graduates—the dedication of the new two-million-dollar Herbert Lowell Dillon Gymnasium. Mr. Dillon, the largest single contributor to its cost, was present, supported by a host of gleeful classmates of 1907, and expressed his warm satisfaction in this opportunity of service to his college. President Dodds then accepted the gymnasium in behalf of a grateful University, and declared it dedicated "to the harmonious cultivation of healthy bodies and sound minds."

In the afternoon the Princeton baseball team defeated Yale, 1-0, before a huge and hilarious crowd, the more with glory, since the victory broke a long winning streak of 11 games for Yale. But the weather was not promising for the campus festivities of the evening. And, as it turned out, it was perhaps as well that the original plans for a magnificent historical spectacle and pageant in the stadium had proved impracticable.

Professor Jean Labatut, well experienced in such work, had drawn up a brilliant design for this divertissement. The floor of the stadium was to have been filled with nine platforms supporting successive representations of important moments in Princeton's history, and so connected by means of lighting that they unfolded in order as nine spiral branches of the Princeton tree rooted at the open end of the stadium. A narrative composed by Booth Tarkington '93 was to give continuity to the action, and contemporary dances would have illustrated the different periods. The whole was to be accompanied with elaborate symbolic lighting, fireworks, and music, including the amplified music of the Chapel organ and the 1892 Carillon. It was to end in a whirling dance of atoms subsiding into a grand apotheosis of Te Deum in a vast vaulted cathedral of light. Tarkington was already enthusiastically at work upon the script at the time of his lamented death, May 19, 1946; and this event, with other circumstances, defeated the scheme. It would indeed have been a midsummer night's dream of overwhelming splendor.

During the year that remained, graduates of Princeton proficient in the theatre met in close council with others to devise a fitting spectacle for Saturday evening. Proposal after proposal was considered and abandoned, with the final result of a simplified diversion to be staged on the broad platform in front of Nassau Hall, with the perfect setting of that venerable façade. But as weather would have it, the performance was driven to shelter in the McCarter Theatre. The place was packed with alumni. The program of ancient Princeton song and story was happily, and doubly, entitled *Going Back.* It proved to be memorably effective.

By way of prelude the band of the Ninth Infantry, New York National Guard, gave an hour's program. Then José Ferrer '33, as narrator, and 54 members of the Glee Club, with five soloists from the alumni, took over and reviewed the story of Princeton, punctuating it with many lyric intervals. These were old songs, some forgotten, some perennial: "Free America," John Dickinson's "Liberty Song," "Yankee Doodle," "Rosin the Beau," "Mr. Indian," and "The Centennial Ode."

On Sunday morning was held a solemn Service of Remembrance in the University Chapel, this time in special memory of Princeton men whose names are inscribed on the Roll of Honor. It included an anthem "Immortales Salutamus," composed for the occasion by Joseph F. Hewitt '07 and George F. Riegel '15, and an address by Dr. Thomas Guthrie Speers '12. The service rose to a beautiful and solemn conclusion when the long procession of men, each representing his class, moved slowly up into the dim, soft light of the chancel. There each representative laid his wreath in order upon the floor of the chancel; then all stood at attention as the lingering, yet ultimate, notes of taps rose, spread far through the vaulting, and died away.

With the spell of this solemn hour upon them the graduates gathered on the front campus for the annual meeting of alumni. The spirit of the meeting, rising above its routine business, was that of dedication to the future. Said Harold H. Helm '20, the retiring chairman of the Graduate Council and president of the National Alumni Association:

> The founders and the men who made Princeton what it is today were men of faith. They worked . . . for what they believed Princeton should and would become. . . . As alumni, we are not merely a part of the future in which they believed and for which they worked. . . . We are the inheritors of that faith. . . . As this spirit of Princeton supports us through life, we, as alumni, are more and more determined to support her in return. On this solemn but happy occasion, I am sure the alumni wish me to assure you, President Dodds, that we, her sons, pledge ourselves to underwrite the future.

At this point the Bicentennial reunion came to a close and Princeton turned "Open House" to all the learned world. Luckily the weather had reformed overnight and so continued till all was done.

No inception of the whole three days' celebration could have been happier than the garden party at Prospect that Sunday afternoon under the ancient trees and athwart the garden slope laid out by Mrs. Woodrow Wilson forty years before. The warm stone walls and tower of the mansion, now rounding out its first century, seemed to shed upon the shifting throng of delegates and their hosts a welcoming benediction.

In the evening they gathered again at the newly-dedicated gymnasium to hear a festival program by the Boston Symphony Orchestra under the leadership of Dr. Serge Koussevitsky, who was forthwith to become an honorary alumnus of Princeton as Doctor of Letters. The program well suited the moment. It consisted of the Brahms Academic Festival Overture, Bach's Third Suite, and the third movement of The Testament of Freedom by Randall Thompson of the Faculty. Professor Thompson happily was present. The *pièce de résistance* was Beethoven's third symphony, the Eroica. The acoustics of the improvised auditorium by good fortune turned out to be excellent and the orchestra rose to the occasion.

And now as the order of events got under full way, turning the minds of host and guest alike from the past toward the future, it was fitting that the next day, Monday, should begin with a Service of Dedication in the Chapel. The beautiful order of service, reprinted in a following section, was prepared by Dr. Robert R. Wicks, the retiring Dean of the Chapel, and the service was conducted by him and the Dean designate, Bishop Donald B. Aldrich.

From the service the congregation had but to step across the paved area that now unites the Library with the Chapel to assist in the laying of the cornerstone of the new library building. The ceremony amounted in effect to a sort of preliminary dedication of the Harvey S. Firestone Library. There were brief remarks by David H. McAlpin '20, chairman of the Trustees' Committee on the Library, and Paul Bedford '97, who had led the efforts for the collection of funds necessary to the construction. Then Harvey S. Firestone, Jr. '20, fortified with a card of honorary membership in the Bricklayers, Masons, and Plasterers International Union, Local 3, with the help of two or three operative masons, sealed the stone in memory of his father, for whom the library is named. The stone contained, *inter alia*, copies of current magazines and newspapers, metropolitan and local, a University catalogue, the *Library Chronicle*, the Handbook and the Librarian's current report, a photostat of Woodbridge's catalogue of the library of the College of New Jersey, 1760, the Bicentennial medal, as many of the pamphlets summarizing the conferences as had been published, a photograph and biographical sketch of Harvey S. Firestone, the personnel of the architects and builders, bookplates of the Library, and a copy of the Holy Bible.

By way of conclusion President Dodds expressed the gratitude of the University to the Firestone family for the generous gift which made the Library possible, and took the occasion to say:

> The laying of this cornerstone is a climax to long years of planning. It testifies to the indispensable place of the library in the cultivation of free minds. On a foundation two centuries deep Princeton strives to uphold unswervingly the ideal of untrammeled investigation of all paths of knowledge. Books have always been and will continue to be indispensable to the pursuit of this ideal. . . . These steel girders and columns that rise above us do not represent merely another building. They do not mean solely a shelter to books to preserve them against the ravages of time, nor do they signify merely the convenience of Faculty and students in the use of the books. This much they obviously do signify. But beyond these things they signify the inestimable opportunity of intimate association with the thought and experience of the human race.
>
> Within the walls of this building the miracle will constantly occur that we take for granted, because the process is quiet and continuous rather than spectacular and instantaneous; the miracle of the imagination kindled, prejudice thrown overboard, dogma rejected, conviction strengthened, perspective lengthened. This miracle is performed by teachers and students together through the instrumentality of books, the only means by which the past can speak to the present or the present wisely prepare for the future.
>
> This library has been thoughtfully planned with one chief purpose in mind—to break down the barriers between a young man and the company of the great, and to make it easier for him to appropriate for himself that which hosts of great men, leaders in the march of human progress, have to offer. But this library, like any other, can only present an invitation and an opportunity. What students and scholars do with that opportunity is for each to decide.

Ceremonies rose to a higher pitch of state and array on the afternoon of Monday at the formal reception of visiting delegates. This occurred amid the faded but not unbecoming Byzantine splendors of Alexander Hall, which, if anything, heightened the picturesque and sometimes bizarre effect of varied academic costume from all corners of the earth. The delegates proceeded in order of antiquity, with the University of Salamanca, founded in the Twelfth Century, leading all the rest; but close behind were Paris and Toulouse, Oxford and Cambridge. On the platform sat the President, with members of the Board of Trustees and the Faculty. One by one, this time beginning with the youngest institutions, the delegates ascended the platform to be received by the President. In many cases they presented scrolls on which were emblazoned formal greetings of congratulation to Princeton, while the arches rang with repeated applause. All these presentations done, the President formally accepted them and said in part:

Your presence here is more than a gracious gesture of friendship. It is high proof of the essential oneness of sound labor, of the comity of purpose that makes scholars everywhere citizens of one world-wide commonwealth. . . .

Unless such consciousness be promptly extended to the peoples of the earth, there may not be any world at all in which disinterested learning will have a chance to prosper. Thus, while scholarship has its peculiar responsibilities to the several fields of learning, it has, by the very fact that it has succeeded in transcending the boundaries of nations, a further fresh responsibility of social leadership. Of those who have accomplished much, much is to be expected. For this reason no aspect of human endeavor is under a heavier obligation than scholarship for promotion of that intellectual awareness and that emotional temper which will prepare the peoples of the earth for "one world."

President Conant of Harvard, on behalf of the American delegates, remarked:

Princeton's distinction and leadership, never more evident than in recent years, delight us; the conferences held during the past months as part of your celebration have been significant events in the intellectual history of this country; your hospitality on those occasions and again today strengthens the bonds that bind together the scholarly world.

And Sir James Irvine, Principal of the University of St. Andrews, speaking for foreign institutions, dwelt in particular upon the Scottish tradition of democratic learning which has entered into the creation of Princeton and other American institutions, and its insistence upon the transcendent spiritual values that lend to scholarship any permanent value it may have.

Late that afternoon the day's formalities resolved themselves into an informal interlude of a garden party at the Graduate College. In that lovely "hortus conclusus," sheltered by gray walls and gables and towers lifting themselves high into the June blue, a free and more intimate mingling of delegates and hosts was inevitable. In that setting and in such a climate of weather and mind, passing formality could only deepen into personal acquaintance, and acquaintance into friendship. Quite unawares perhaps, auspices were thus perfected for the happy and genial serenity which pervaded the high proceedings of the following great day.

For the Bicentennial Dinner of nearly 1,700 guests that evening, the gymnasium had been transformed from the concert auditorium of the night before to a huge banquet room. Mr. Hope, as chairman of the Bicentennial Committee, was the presiding genius of the occasion; which is to say that it was permeated by the cheerful warmth and dignity of his presence. Bishop Henry Knox Sherrill, Presiding Bishop of the Episcopal Church in the United States, said grace.

At length, the feast now finished and the chairs pushed back, the speeches began. Mr. Hope spoke of John Witherspoon and how he and the college were early involved in the struggle for independence; said he: "This was a natural consequence of the fact that Princeton had its origin in a demand for greater liberalism and for the training of greater men, not only for the ministry but for service to the state."

He then proceeded to his duties as toastmaster and felicitously introduced in order the speakers of the evening. These were:

President Dodds
The Honorable H. Alexander Smith '01, United States Senator from New Jersey
His Excellency, Alfred E. Driscoll, Governor of New Jersey
Robert Gordon Sproul, President of the University of California
Douglas Southall Freeman, Biographer and Historian
Field Marshal Viscount Alexander of Tunis, Governor General of Canada
Mildred McAfee Horton, President of Wellesley College
Charles Seymour, President of Yale University
The Honorable Herbert Hoover

President Dodds, readily complying with the toastmaster's delicate admonition to be brief, pleasantly concluded: "I am saving my remarks, in which I shall completely reconstruct the whole system of higher education in the United States, for tomorrow morning! I beg of you to attend. In the meantime I shall only repeat what I tried to say this afternoon: how gratified and encouraged we all are by your presence here, and to say, God bless you, every one."

Senator Smith, who was chairman of the United States Commission for the Bicentennial, spoke for the Government:

As we close these Bicentennial celebrations, the Government of the United States, which this commission represents, is proud to join in this great world-wide expression of international understanding. God grant that this year of fellowship between thinkers and doers of all nations may have made a significant contribution to the building of a free and peaceful world.

Governor Driscoll spoke of Princeton's part, from the beginning, in the Nation's service, especially during this year of celebration, "by saying to scholars from America and foreign lands, 'Come, let us reason together, for by reasoning together we shall find a way of peaceful salvation.' Once again the State of New Jersey salutes its historic friend, Princeton University, in whose history and accomplishments and achievements it is justly proud."

President Sproul, speaking for state universities and colleges said:

> Through the years Princeton University has steadfastly fought for high standards of teaching and research, for loyalty . . . to university ideals and for that intellectual freedom which is the *sine qua non* of the matchless values of university life. It has done much to justify the claim that if we want to keep education in America, we must keep the endowed universities, . . . because it may, and probably will, require colleges and universities of all kinds, working wholeheartedly together, to make good that guarantee.

Dr. Freeman, whom Mr. Hope designated as representing the ancient tradition of the South at Princeton, asserted that one of Princeton's glories is the proper balance which she has maintained between natural science and the liberal arts. Names like the elder Maclean, Stephen Alexander, Henry, Guyot, and the open-minded McCosh established her distinction in science. "But Princeton, the mother of moderation, would not be herself—wise and just in her determination of values—if she did not recognize what science is not, what it cannot do, and what it must allow to other expression of the human mind through the liberal arts."

At this point the speaking gave way to a musical interlude by the Marine Band, and to a little ceremony which is likely to remain vivid in the memory of that evening when the rest has long grown dim. This was the presentation of the Bicentennial medal to Mrs. Thomas J. Preston, the former Mrs. Grover Cleveland, and to Mrs. Woodrow Wilson.

Mr. Hope called to mind Sir James Barrie's recollection of Miss Ellen Terry, loveliest in her day, when all young men of imagination proposed "in some such frenzied words as these: 'As I can't get Miss Terry, may I have you?' " It was much the same, said Mr. Hope, fifty years ago, when Mrs. Preston, as the young bride of the retiring President Cleveland, came to live in Princeton, and the entire college, including himself, fell in love with her, and have been so ever since. One of the distinguished guests afterwards wrote that the great moment for him of the whole Bicentennial came when at long last he beheld Mrs. Preston. "When I was a very small boy," he wrote, "she was a bride in the White House. She has been a lovely legend every since. Her appearance at the dinner on Monday evening was for me as a child's dream come true of seeing the Queen. Nor was there disillusionment, for she is surely still a beautiful and charming lady."

By another reminiscence of fifty years Mr. Hope reminded the older guests of the thrilling figure of Woodrow Wilson, then in the prime of forty, at the Sesquicentennial, as he delivered his historical and prophetic discourse, rededicating Princeton to the Nation's service. Said Mr. Hope: "You will understand with what pleasure we welcome here tonight that gracious lady, Mrs. Woodrow Wilson, who was ever at his side during his years of trial and strain, and whose companionship and sympathetic understanding did so much to sustain him."

As the speaking was resumed, Viscount Alexander paid a glowing tribute to the Americans who had fought under him in the Mediterranean campaign, and to General Eisenhower, "my old chief and friend," as the designer and director of the "great allied battle-fighting machine controlled by a supreme direction," which proved a battle-winning factor. This led him to speak of the happy relations over the years between Canada and the United States.

President Horton then expressed the gratitude of women's colleges to Princeton in these words:

> You train a good many of our professors. You employ a good many of our graduates. . . . You publish the books of some of our professors. You establish policies which we imitate as far as our slender resources permit. You establish devices for increasing your resources which we slavishly imitate without the same results. Need I say that you train our husbands very well, and you have set a standard for civic leadership for which we are deeply and sincerely indebted.

Mr. Hope, then inquiring what a family party would be without father, pointed the indispensability of Yale to Princeton's birth two centuries since, and presented President Seymour, who had generously absented himself from the felicity of a Yale Commencement a while to grace this occasion. Said he:

> We have to insist in all honesty upon Yale's responsibility for Princeton. It is a historical duty. We have also to confess that the responsibility is traceable very directly to the dissatisfaction of Yale alumni with the way in which their own alma mater was being conducted. . . . I take some personal share in the responsibility of Yale for Princeton because curiously enough it was the regime of my own great-great-grandfather at Yale, Thomas Clap, which gave rise to this dissatisfaction. . . .
>
> The two institutions have complete community of purpose—service to the public welfare by the fostering of the liberal arts ideal, taking the form of a college at the heart of a great university of comprehensive and advanced learning. . . . But our great duty goes far beyond getting them [our students] ready for a livelihood. It is to prepare them for life in a democracy by teaching them how to think freely, intelligently, and courageously. The institution that holds fast to this ideal, refusing to be diverted into interesting but distracting bypaths, best serves the interests of the nation. And for the examples set by Princeton over the past two centuries, we of Yale are deeply grateful.

The last speaker, the Honorable Herbert Hoover, was presented as "incomparably the world's best-informed man, with the unique ability to put that information to effective and immediate use." Mr. Hoover, with pleasant overtone, but no less serious import, pointed to the astonishing attainment of the country in two centuries: "It teems with millions of comfortable farms and homes, cattle and hogs. It is equipped with railroads, power plants, factories, highways, automobiles, and death warnings. It is studded with magnificent cities and traffic jams." Withal it has set up ten thousand schools, and a thousand institutions of higher learning attended by two million students taught by a hundred thousand professors. All this has been the work of "a God-fearing people under the blessings of the right-wing system of freedoms." What of its future?

> I am confident that the two million youth under your guidance and inspiration are the best and most promising body of future leadership this country or the world has yet seen. . . . Out of your labors there is rising a greater host of efficient, morally and patriotically inspired men and women, with a better understanding of their public responsibilities, than any generation and any nation has yet possessed. You are contributing not only to the American people but to the whole world. You are performing an exacting task requiring not only knowledge, but patience, tact, and vision. Yours is indeed a glorious mission, magnificently performed.

And so, with three lusty stanzas of "Old Nassau," came to an end a very agreeable evening of good cheer, pleasantry, gratulation, good sense, and high increase of happy auspices for the morrow.

> Early before the world's light-giving lamp
> His golden beam upon the hills doth spread,

town and college were astir. The dawn, almost the earliest of the year, gave promise of perfect weather for this high day in Princeton's calendar. It was cool and calm and bright, rare even for June, that supposed month of rare days. To a townsman walking abroad in the early forenoon the familiar place seemed unfamiliar. Nassau Street was empty of traffic. The whole place was swept and garnished. Guardians of the law in their horizon blue seemed to be everywhere. Barriers blocked the wonted ways. Many strangers, some in odd and unusual array, hurried about to find their appointed places. Academic costume has its vagaries the world over, it seems. Yet somehow in the course of these two eventful days even the strangers seemed in good measure to have become assimilated to the place and to be a part of it. Such is its mysterious and powerful spell. In spite of any alteration it was still Princeton.

As sun and excitement rose higher, everybody became more aware of the arrival somewhere south of the town of the President of the United States and other distinguished men who were to adorn the occasion. The Presidential train brought, besides the President, Mrs. Truman, Miss Margaret Truman, Chief Justice Frederick M. Vinson, and General Dwight Eisenhower. The party included also relatives, aides, and members of the White House staff. It was met by President Dodds, Mr. Hope, Governor Driscoll, and Mayor Minot C. Morgan Jr. '35 of Princeton.

For everyone it was holiday. To be sure, the whole scene was haunted throughout by a cloud of secret service men, helpers, camera, radio, and television operators, pressmen, and police. These were indispensable. But they were as unobtrusive as ghosts. No one noticed them. And the whole progress of events moved as by a spontaneous agreement and natural order. Thus everyone was carried along by the informal-formal spirit of the day and rose with it to the higher moments. As the Governor said afterwards, "I repeat my statement of the other day: for the first time since the election last November I truly enjoyed being governor."

Cloister, court, and archway slowly filled with black gowns and gorgeous trappings as a thousand persons who were to walk in the procession found their assigned places.

Forty-three foreign nations were represented and 42 of the United States. It was a lively and picturesque backstage.

As on previous occasions, the procession was to move in climactic order, from lesser to greater distinction. It was marshalled in this sequence:

The Undergraduate Council
Representatives of the Graduate School
Representatives of Alumni Associations
Representatives of Alumni Classes
The Graduate Council
The Faculty of Princeton University
Delegates of Universities, Colleges, and other Educational Institutions
The Bicentennial Committee of the Borough and Township of Princeton
The New Jersey Princeton Bicentennial Commission
The United States Princeton Bicentennial Commission
Recipients of Honorary Degrees
The Trustees of Princeton University
The President of the University and the President of the United States

Representatives of the oldest universities, Salamanca, Toulouse, Paris, Oxford, Cambridge, and St. Andrews, waited in a group together. By this time, well aware of their ancient commonalty, they were chatting like old associates. The representative of the University of Toulouse happened to be a Princeton man who had taken his Doctorat ès Lettres at that venerable institution. Looking back down the line, he spied Harvard in 34th place and Yale in 42nd. He had often suffered under the condescending pride of seniority in his Yale and Harvard acquaintances. But now, with gentle disdain, he pointed out their humbler position and said to his ancient coevals: "Voyez-vous, donc, en bas là, Harvard et Yale; des bébés véritables, des enfants—O là, là!" This raised a laugh.

The long procession moved through bright sun and soft shadow, from Holder Court, down through Campbell

Archway, then eastward toward Alexander, thence northward between Holder and the Presbyterian Church to Nassau Street, till it reached the great FitzRandolph Gateway directly in front of Nassau Hall. Here it entered a vast and crowded theatre that spread in wide semicircle over most of the front campus. Along the broad and shady walk through a standing audience of five thousand it advanced toward the spreading platform and the seats in front of it. And behind the whole spectacle rose the grave and shadowy mass of Nassau Hall, nursing her memories and adding to them as she looked down upon a spectacle the like of which she had never seen before.

As the procession drew towards its more interesting end, waves of applause rose higher and higher with the arrival of each celebrity, until the crescendo reached its top pitch with the appearance of the President of the United States. It was holiday with him too, as all could read in his cheerful smile.

Halfway up the walk his eye suddenly fell upon the radiant small figure of a little girl, daughter of one of the class secretaries, who stood with her mother at the edge of the crowd, wide-eyed and absorbed. The picture was irresistible on this festive morning. The President dashed out of the line and heartily shook hands with her to the hilarious delight of those around her, and to her own deep embarrassment. But some day she may enjoy a bit of complacence when she hears: "Granny dear, do tell us again about the time the President shook hands with you!"*

* It was also a marked day for two other children. General Eisenhower caught sight of a small boy desperately maneuvering to get a snapshot of him. He stepped out of line, flashed his irresistible smile as he posed, then said: "I hope you got a good one, Johnny!" The youngster rushed home, and burst breathless in upon his mother with "O Mom! General Eisenhower is a *very* great man. He knew my name." And when a small miss saw the eminent bearded figure of Cardinal Tisserant being invested with his hood, she sprang up in high excitement: "See, Mummy; they're giving Santa Claus a degree too!" Earlier in the day two workmen paused

At last the long line of "Aristotle's friends" were settled in their places, and the final cadence of Elgar's "Crown of India" by the United States Marine Corps band died away among the elms. A hundred people were seated on the great platform in high sunlight against the deep shadows of Nassau Hall and the noble white Princeton banner which hung over its entrance.

When was there ever such an assembly of notables? Beside the President of the United States and former President Hoover, there were such as General Eisenhower, Field Marshal Viscount Alexander of Tunis, Admirals Chester W. Nimitz, Ernest J. King, and William H. Leahy, Chief Justice Vinson, Judge Learned Hand, Messrs. Warren R. Austin, Bernard Baruch, and John W. Davis, Governor Driscoll, the Presidents of three great sister universities, Dr. Albert Einstein of Princeton, men illustrious in scholarship and poetry and the arts, in the Church, and in business.

Yet there was conspicuous precedent in Princeton's history for an occasion so superlative. One's mind ran back 164 years to the Commencement of September 24, 1783, when Congress was sitting in Nassau Hall. A stone's throw yonder, in the old church, were assembled, with the College and the graduating class, many of the high dignitaries whose public office had brought them hither—members of Congress which had adjourned in honor of the day, seven signers of the Declaration of Independence, nine signers of the Articles of Confederation, eleven signers-to-be of the Constitution, the French Minister, Marquis de la Luzerne, and, above all, General Washington himself. It was a day abounding with inflated oratory now out of fashion.

---

to notice in a detached way the academic stir and pageantry. "What's all the fuss, Bill? Who are all these guys?" "Who them? They say they're goin' to give 'em the third degree."

Yet these two high moments in the life of the college, so many years apart, were in strange agreement. Both occurred at the end of a desperate but victorious war against tyranny. Both were graced by the presence of the men who had led our armies over a long, rough, and tortuous road to final triumph. In both, the minds and hearts of all present were engaged with the problems of peaceful reconstruction; and foremost among them was the fashioning of a new Union to ensure that peace.

The very thought recalled the memorable words of another Chief Justice, Edward Douglass White, uttered impromptu on this very spot back in 1912, and here in the midst of this illustrious assembly now eternized in perennial bronze:

> I could not but think that if the great and noble men whom this institution necessarily recalls, the founders of our country, were here today, as, thanks be to God, they may be invisibly to us, what joy would fill their hearts as they saw the evidence of love of country and of respect for its institutions marked by the presence of the President of The United States and by the invitation, not to me personally, but to the Chief Justice, and also by these ceremonies.
>
> I could see them here, Washington and those who founded our institutions, and hear them say "Behold, we have not lived in vain. The love of the country which we founded remains, the institutions of freedom which we established are not passing off the face of the earth, but, safe in the hearts of its people, the mighty nation which stretches from ocean to ocean will preserve and transmit them to those who are to come as a priceless blessing for the maintenance of the freedom and the liberty of mankind."

The order of service was simple and obvious: the Invocation by Dean Wicks, the singing of "America," the address by President Dodds, the traditional Watts-Wesley hymn, "O God Our Help in Ages Past," the conferring of honorary degrees, the address by President Truman, the National Anthem, the Benediction by Dean Designate Aldrich, and the Recessional. The whole Convocation lasted about an hour and a half.

President Dodds in his address, "Education for Freedom," maintained the need of liberal education today, not for an élite as in the past, but for a democratic society. "It is a good heritage, this liberal arts tradition, well able to serve the republic today as it did yesterday." But it is suffering from certain dangers and defects. It is threatened by the world's loud clamor for vocational training. It is in danger of atrophy from the selfish notion that its aim is the social prestige or intellectual satisfaction of the individual, not the responsibilities to others which it lays upon the educated man. The colleges themselves are also at fault. They have found it easier to transmit information than to develop minds. To this they are driven by the overwhelming crowds of students, lack of funds, and energies unequal to the task. They therefore occupy themselves with overhauling of courses of study, not with the processes of genuine teaching. They are in a present confusion which must be resolved before they can serve their generation as they should.

Received knowledge is inert knowledge, useful so far as it goes, but no substitute for first-hand knowledge. More crucial than the new arrangements of course material is the development and application of teaching methods which will train the mind constructively as a proficient and creative servant of one's personality.

It is our business to train scholars rather than pupils.

I mean future lawyers, doctors, statesmen, and business men; for sound methods of scholarship are the methods of clear and imaginative thinking in any field or occupation. In the realm of life as well as books, one's thinking must meet the criteria of scholarship if one is to come out with the right answers. . . . Facts and their critical appraisal must be supplemented by active imagination, in short, by creative thinking. Training for scholarship is equally fruitful in the cultivation of emotional awareness in art and literature, in the development of taste and the appreciation of beauty at its best, and finally in the acquisition of canons of what is ethically right or wrong for the individual and for society.

Furthermore we have spent vast resources on instruction in the physical sciences to the neglect of the humanities. And our study of the humanities has deteriorated, has lost its humanity, from preoccupation with the scientific and historical method, with man in the mass and the species in course of evolution rather than as the individual.

Since you cannot divide a man when it is mankind that you are studying, liberal education must take him as he is, a self-conscious individual who is, within limits, master of his fate and thus is able to circumvent prophecy. Science and history strive to be impersonal, but life is incorrigibly personal.

Objectivity destroys superstition. Must it destroy faith also? Over the centuries the answer of liberal education has been No. A student's spiritual growth remains today, as yesterday, an acknowledged chief concern. We have never repudiated this responsibility, nor do we dare do so, but we have often been indifferent to it. . . . Unless the net influence of the liberal arts college is in support of ethical values and of religion from which such values stem, it is not keeping faith with its public.

The private college and university is best able to protect liberal education from those influences which would break it down; indeed to guard freedom of thought and study from the corruption of political influence and the despotism of a majority only too ready to do all our educational thinking for us.

The theme of our year's celebration has been education for freedom. Since the administration of President Witherspoon, who in colonial days against Tory opposition turned the College of New Jersey into a hotbed of liberty, there has been no division here on the basic proposition that the chief mission of the liberal arts and sciences is to nourish freedom.

"A kind of liberal education," it has been said, "must underlie every wholesome political and social process." Of course there are millions of ordinary people who have never been in college but who have absorbed the great lessons of a liberal education. But we cannot rely on such self-inspired people alone. Our society must

Secretary of State Marshall delivers the Alumni Day Address

Presenting Bicentennial Medals at the Geology, Paleontology and Evolution Conference in the Princeton Inn

The Undergraduate Conference in session

Guests of the Conference on Planning Man's Physical Environment prepare for a national network broadcast

Television camera and sound crews at the Final Convocation

The Front Campus on June 17 as the Fin

ation brings to a close the Bicentennial Year

President and Mrs. Dodds and Mr. Hope receiving guests at Prospect

The garden party at Wyman House of the Graduate College

Laying the cornerstone of the Firestone Memorial Library

Dr. Koussevitsky and the Boston Symphony Orchestra in Dillon Gymnasium

Dinner guests: Admiral King, former President Hoover, Governor Driscoll

The Bicentennial Dinner of June 16

see to it that a constant leaven of humane learning infuses and permeates its whole system, and the agency best adapted to supply this leaven is the college of liberal arts and sciences.

At the Sesquicentennial in 1896 Grover Cleveland pleaded for more men of liberal education in politics devoted to the public welfare; and Woodrow Wilson affirmed his faith in the American college.

He condemned any tendency in the academic person to "proud aloofness and lofty superiority," which holds "the services of mankind at arm's length while we read and make scholars of ourselves." "We are not put into this world to sit still and know; we are put here to act," he said, and these words might well be carved over the doorway of every college in America. Were he to return to Princeton today I believe that he would discover in the evolution of our general plan of education through the intervening years the unfolding in modern ways of the educational philosophy to which he so fully committed himself while he was President here.

Princeton enters her third century with certain convictions as to what she wants her future to be. We shall be zealous in strengthening our graduate schools and we shall continue to stress the college as the element which alone gives meaning to a university. We shall uphold the banner of the general as the only safe foundation for the particular. We shall strive for quality rather than quantity; we have no illusions of grandeur that bigness will satisfy. We shall resist the pressure to be large in numbers, for we believe that we can best serve our democracy by remaining small. As a residential university, we shall emphasize the community of students and teachers, believing that the life of the campus is a potent supplement to formal study and instruction. We shall continue to accept and discharge as well as we can the broad responsibilities of the American college towards all those aspects of human personality which it has taken as its domain. We shall always see to it that our students represent a democratic cross-section of American youth, geographically and with respect to economic circumstance. We shall strive to develop mental proficiency as I have defined it, and to this end work to maintain the highest scholastic standards, but we shall not forget that moral proficiency must be cultivated as well. We shall seek to advance learning as well as disseminate it. We shall remember that we were founded by God-fearing men and we shall strive to communicate to our students the sense of duty that made our forebears strong. . . .

As she crosses the threshold of a new and fateful age, Princeton will strive to meet any challenge, to dare any adventure to preserve her integrity and to further her enduring purpose. Proud as we are of our history and grateful for the strength our heritage brings to us, we know that to rest on it can lead only to decay and destruction. We intend to be the progenitors of a stronger Princeton, not merely the beneficiaries of generations that went before us.

After being invested with the degree of Doctor of Laws, President Truman spoke not only to the six thousand men and women there present but by radio to an unseen audience of six and a half million. He observed that since Grover Cleveland's plea of fifty years ago, the colleges have responded with a steadily increasing number of trained men and women devoting themselves to the public welfare. But, with the Nation's new and grave international responsibilities, and the magnitude and complexity of the Government's business, the need is greater than ever. Many specialists are available, but "we need men who can turn a group of specialists into a working team, and who can combine imagination and practicability into a sound public program."

The Woodrow Wilson School of Public and International Affairs of this University was established with this purpose in mind. It seeks to prepare students for public careers. It is significant that the School bears the name of a statesman whose concept of civic duty contributed so much to the Nation and to the world.

The business of government suffers from a low scale of salaries, insufficient to attract executives from private life to public service. And the high executives are not supported by an adequate number of administrators specially trained for careers in the Nation's service. This last deficiency calls for the planned cooperation of universities with the Government in providing special training for public careers.

The President then spoke of universal military training

as essential to security in the reconstruction of a war-torn world, and described the bill just submitted to the Congress, which had been prepared by a distinguished commission of which President Dodds was a member. In recounting the benefits to the individual of such training he said:

> The experience of living together and fulfilling a common responsibility should strengthen the spirit of democracy. It will be an experience in democratic living, out of which should come in increased measure the unity so beneficial to the welfare of the Nation.
>
> We must remember, above all, that these men would not be training in order to win a war, but in order to prevent one.

In conclusion President Truman dwelt upon the higher obligation which lies upon all institutions of learning to serve all nations in the cause of lasting peace.

> The course has been charted. The Constitution of the United Nations Educational, Scientific, and Cultural Organization states the basic truths by which we must be guided. That Constitution reads: "Since wars begin in the minds of men, it is in the minds of men that the defenses of peace must be constructed."
>
> The construction of the defenses of peace in the minds of men is the supreme task which our educational institutions must set for themselves.
>
> This Convocation is a symbol of what our educational institutions can do in the cause of peace. It marks the end of a great series of conferences, attended by scholars from all over the world, who assembled here for free discussion of the most challenging problems facing men today.
>
> The special significance of these meetings is that they restored bonds in many fields of learning between our own and other lands—bonds which had been impaired by the war. The resumption of meetings of scholars, business men, religious leaders, and government officials is evidence of our conviction that the peace must "be founded, if it is not to fail, upon the intellectual solidarity of mankind."
>
> Free and inquiring minds, with unlimited access to the sources of knowledge, can be the architects of a peaceful and prosperous world.

> As we gain increasing understanding of man, comparable to our increasing understanding of matter, we shall develop, with God's grace, the ability of nations to work together and live together in lasting peace.

With the Recessional the great throng dispersed. Delegates, hosts, and friends of Princeton, all formality now dissolved, gathered in various happy and unpremeditated groups for luncheon in the University dining-halls. At Prospect the very distinguished guests sat down to lunch.

General Eisenhower was presented to Mrs. Preston and seated next to her at the table. He may have failed to hear her name, for, as the story goes, he asked her if she had ever lived in Washington.

"Yes, for eight years."

"And where did you live?"

"In the White House."

"The White House!"

("I suppose," said Mrs. Preston in telling the story, "he may have wondered if I were the housekeeper.")

"Perhaps I ought to explain, General Eisenhower, that I was then Mrs. Grover Cleveland."

Then, at his evident confusion, "But, General Eisenhower, our hostess surely would not have done me the honor of a place next to you, if I had not had some such right to it."

Still her same unerring, lifelong consideration for others!

And now the great Bicentennial Year was at an end; "the most distinguished academic ceremony I ever remember attending," said the President of another institution. And the representative of a British University wrote in retrospect:

> I was particularly impressed by the spirit of Princeton and the stress laid upon spiritual—indeed the Christian—values of your university's life. The occasion will always remain as one of my

most treasured memories and it was not only a great privilege to be with you, but also a great inspiration. I felt myself wishing that I could renew my youth and live in your stimulating atmosphere for a prolonged period.

By nightfall the old town was empty and very quiet. The next day it rained—hard. But no one cared.

CHAPTER IV

Landings on the Stairs

FROM time immemorial the world has insisted that the proper place for the scholar is the high and lonely tower. Thence he can to advantage overlook the world and draw his conclusions. And many have observed in scholars a cat-like instinct for high places. But the true scholar, for the sake of his scholarship if no other, refuses to be confined all his days in a tower. He must needs come down into the street at times, mingle with the crowd, make acquaintance with men and women to authenticate or correct his conclusions. But on the stairway between the tower and the ground, he meets other scholars going up and down between their towers and the street. And they pause in pairs or groups on the landings to compare notes and release the pressure within their own minds.

The Bicentennial Conferences were just such landings on the stairs. Coming when they did, after long confinement in the tower by seven-year disorders in the street below, they offered a timely release of pent-up ideas. They pooled ideas conceived in the most remote towers of this rambling Mankind-Castle; they comforted and heartened with personal contact the lonely watchers so long constrained; and at the end, they sent them on their way revived and fertile with new enterprise.

The series of sixteen conferences extending from September to May formed a sort of catena or chain in which were set the other events of the year, some more, some less conspicuous, and which gave a continuity and progress to the whole course of the year and saved it from anticlimax. These conferences were indeed the most original and distinguishing part of the entire Bicentennial Year. They dramatized the whole commemoration. They took advantage of just the moment in the world's affairs when it was of first importance to pause and take "earnest counsel." As the President said in advance: "Princeton is convinced that men of learning who in time of war were able to devise new methods of destruction may well, in conferences occurring throughout the Bicentennial Year, by taking counsel together and addressing themselves to the problems that confront us, make even more significant contributions to human society in a peaceful new world than they made to the destruction of the old."

The conferences, too, were pragmatic. They turned what might otherwise have been a chiefly commemorative, brief, and spectacular affair into extended action looking to the future. They thus embodied what has always been the actuating spirit of Princeton training and culture, a culture to be attained not for its own sake, but to be transmuted into useful service. It was thus that the conferences were conceived in the minds of the Faculty Committee, and especially in the mind of their chief designer, Dean Brown. For these men clearly saw that the celebration might be turned to good use in helping to recover the momentum lost in the war. "American scholarship," said Dean Brown, "should not only make up for ground lost in our own country during the war, but must assume a much larger proportion of the total task of advancing learning throughout the world."

Both the conception and the program of the Conferences grew slowly. A gathering of scholars on an academic anniversary was nothing new. It was obvious, if not conventional. At first, when the Bicentennial plan was limited to a few days, or, at the most, weeks, ending on Charter Day, the notion of nine or ten conferences on subjects as yet undetermined, beginning in mid-August or early in September and running till Charter Day, briefly prevailed. But as the conception of the Bicentennial expanded into the compass of a whole year of jubilee, the conception of the conferences also expanded and defined itself accordingly. It found a sort of focus in the device, "One Truth in One World." At last, after much expatiating, conferring, and revising, the following schedule of sixteen conferences was drawn:

SERIES I

1. September 23-25: The Future of Nuclear Science
2. September 28-30: Chemistry and Physiology of Growth
3. October 3-4: Engineering and Human Affairs
4. October 7-9: The Evolution of Social Institutions in America
5. October 11-14: The Development of International Society
6. October 16-18: The Humanistic Tradition in the Century Ahead

SERIES II

1. November 13-14: University Education and the Public Service
2. December 17-19: Problems of Mathematics
3. January 2-4: Genetics, Paleontology, and Evolution
4. February 19-21: The University and its World Responsibilities
5. March 5-6: Planning Man's Physical Environment
6. March 25-27: Near Eastern Culture and Society
7. April 1-3: Far Eastern Culture and Society
8. April 22-24: Scholarship and Research in the Arts
9. April 25-26: The Role of the Undergraduate in University Life
10. May 12-14: Secondary Education in the Years Ahead

This list of subjects is by no means encyclopedic; nor was it intended to be. Some subjects appear to overlap others. No doubt at the end of the year the Committee thought of revisions in the list which they might have made. But when all is said, the subjects provided plenty of room and incentive for the very sort of discussion which its designers sought to provoke. And the subjects stood arrayed as well-disposed points of out-thrust and of prophetic augury for the future.

The history of Princeton is punctuated by repeated insistence upon close personal contact as essential to the best teaching. Conference rather than indoctrination has ever been its preferred process. Especially in these last nearly fifty years of preceptorial teaching the idea of skillfully conducted conference has dominated its training. Thus the ideal preceptorial conference—stimulating, personal, interrogative, regenerating—permeated the design of these Bicentennial conferences. Experience in the Princeton Industrial Relations Section also entered into the plan. Annual conferences of leaders in industrial matters held at the Graduate College, in a beautiful though not luxurious setting, detached for a season from affairs, relaxed and drawn into closer intimacy of mind with mind over the breaking of bread, generating ideas by contact, in a place whose genius peculiarly fosters such conditions—such experience virtually predetermined the form of the Bicentennial conferences.

And this idea became a gratifying reality in the conferences themselves. Of one of them it was written: "The conference was not made up of lectures to auditors, but of discussions among equals. In one way or another, almost every member was a distinguished teacher. As such he was fully aware . . . that the teacher and learner are one; that Socrates was a better teacher than the oracle at Delphi; that the framing of the right questions is the first step toward the right answers." Old Alcuin, the best teacher of his day a thousand years ago, would surely have applauded, with his "Sapienter interrogare docere est." It was the director of the conference on Engineering who said in retrospect that it was the common hope of all the conferences to raise, define, and illumine important questions—"a hope that was amply fulfilled."

Thus the design took shape. The conferences, if they were to be intimate, must be limited and restricted. Not more than 120 were to be invited to each. Of these probably less than 100 would attend. As it turned out, about 1,000 in all attended the conferences. The largest number at a single conference was the 120 at the conference on Scholarship and Research in the Arts, but these were divided between the sessions on fine arts and those on music. The smallest number was 35, at the conference on the Role of the Undergraduate. Besides the participants, two or three recorders and representatives of the press were present at each. But the number in attendance, within such limits, mattered little.

It is true that the groups were not homogeneous. They were by no means purely academic. Many men of business and public affairs took part. Philosophers mingled with men of science, artists with journalists and librarians. Neither were they all American. Men from 26 other nations engaged in the discussion of the various conferences. Learned men not only from Canada, England, and France, but from Italy, Holland, Denmark, India, Mexico, Sweden, Lebanon, the Vatican, Russia, Turkey, Egypt, China, Puerto Rico, Switzerland, Rumania, Scotland, Spain, Poland, Czechoslovakia, Brazil, Iraq, Iran, and Jerusalem, were present at different times. Yet their centripetal concern for the subject before them made for ready intimacy one with another, and for free discussion, and thereby for a sense of the real commonalty of interest in one world.

The design of these conferences differed from that of the ordinary academic conventions of specialists. In those the various members report on their special findings, while the larger, more transcendent implication of their combined discoveries goes unconsidered. But in these, however minute the specialist's scrutiny, its greater import was paramount, and free discussion was the order of the day. As Dean Brown observed, they were to differ from the usual specialists' convention as a preceptorial conference differs from a lecture. At the same time they were to lose nothing of the authority of the specialist in his own field.

The adjustment of these two intentions into a single concept and program for each conference was no easy matter. It involved a very careful selection of directors for each conference, men capable of both the idea and the execution. And each of these directors, possessed of the idea, endeavored with equal care to embody it in the choice of his helpers, in compiling his list of guests to be invited, and in framing his program. Furthermore, he or his assistants had the most delicate task of presiding over each session of his conference, an office which called for all he had in him of alertness, consideration, tact, and decision. It is not in mortals to command total success in such an undertaking, but in the present instance they deserved it; for by all accounts the conferences attained to a high degree of the achievement which their sponsors had preconceived.

Nor were they unmindful, from long experience in these matters, that certain physical conditions are essential to the success of such discussion—withdrawal from the roar of traffic, above its smoke and stir, fair and happy surroundings in safe retreat and unpretentious comfort, warm and sincere hospitality—circumstances peculiarly happy at Princeton. To realize them fully, members of a conference were required to live together for the two or three days of its duration in "a little scholars' community," as Woodrow

Wilson called it, accepting no hospitality or entertainment, however urgent, from friends outside. Such requirement had precedent as far back as the symposium of Plato—perhaps much further. Long ago men discovered the strange concomitance between the breaking of bread at a common board and the release of mind and spirit for higher flights; and such concomitance was a necessary condition of the best success of these conferences. Even Plato's precedent of a literal symposium of mildest sort was not overlooked, and provision was made for potables that cheered and enlivened the wits without inebriation.

Partial exception to the strict segregation was allowed when members of certain conferences, such as the one on Scholarship and Research in the Arts, were allowed to accept invitations to dine at the undergraduate clubs. Such an exception was permitted for the glimpse it gave members of one aspect of undergraduate life and, in turn, for the hour's familiar converse with eminent men which it gave the undergraduates.

The dignified yet comfortable setting of the Graduate College was in close accord with the design of the conferences; as one guest put it, "a fitting frame for scholars from all parts of the world." As such it served for the First Series. The Second Series enjoyed the somewhat less academic but no less comfortable environment of the Princeton Inn.

On looking back one member wrote: "The informal talks at meal times, or during the afternoon walks across the golf course, or ranging far into the night, cannot be captured in print. The conference did not settle the great issues. But in many minds it raised them, creating an extraordinary impression that so much had been said and thought that weeks, not days must have elapsed." And all the time the concealed and intricate mechanism, indispensable to the success of the conferences, was running so smoothly and quietly behind and beneath that members were unaware of it except on afterthought.

The plan left wide room for variation between conference and conference according to subject and personnel, yet a certain uniformity of program was practicable and expedient. Since conference rather than indoctrination was the intent of the plan, not more than half of the time of any session was allotted to the speakers, and the rest devoted to carefully regulated discussion. Inevitably such discussion rose to various degrees of temperature, boiled over the limits of the session, and flowed on at table or in the lounge at all hours. And if its conclusion, like the conclusion in *Rasselas*, proved a conclusion in which nothing was concluded, the main object of the inquiry had been achieved. Some have thought that the best preceptorial hours end with a question mark. It is a notion older than Plato.

The program of the conference on The Humanistic Tradition in the Century Ahead is a fair specimen of those laid down for all.

FIRST DAY

Approaches to the Humanistic Tradition

First Session: Approaches to Humanism
Chairman, John W. Dodds
Speakers, Howard M. Jones, Leo Spitzer

Second Session: The Historic Approach in Humanistic Inquiry
Chairman, George H. Sabine
Speakers, Hajo Holborn, Louis Gottschalk

Third Session: The Aesthetic Approach to the Humanistic Tradition
Chairman, Salvador de Madariaga
Speakers, George Boas, F. O. Matthiessen

Fourth Session: Permanent Elements in the Humanistic Tradition
Chairman, Charles W. Hendel
Speakers, Werner W. Jaeger, Jacques Maritain

SECOND DAY

Contemporary Impact of the Humanities

First Session: The Possibilities of Adult Education
Chairman, Baron Lindsay of Firker
Speakers, James R. Angell, Robert M. Hutchins

Second Session: The Powers of Practising Artists, the Popular Arts, and the Press in Developing Humanistic Culture
Chairman, Lyman Bryson
Speakers, Francis M. Taylor, Archibald MacLeish

Third Session: The Responsibilities of Institutions toward the Humanistic Tradition
Chairman, Frank Aydelotte
Speaker, Reinhold Niebuhr

Fourth Session: The Effect of Democratic and Totalitarian Thought upon the Humanistic Tradition
Chairman, Ralph B. Perry
Speaker, W. H. Auden

THIRD DAY

The Humanities in an Expanding World

First Session: Social Studies in the Humanistic Tradition
Chairman, Walter W. Stewart
Speaker, Robert M. MacIvor

Second Session: Science in the Humanistic Tradition
Chairman, Harlow Shapley
Speakers, Richard H. Shryock, Wolfgang Köhler

Third Session: The Humanistic Tradition in "One World"
Chairman, Christian Gauss
Speakers, Ernest J. Simmons, Chi-Chen Wang

FINAL PUBLIC MEETING IN MC CARTER THEATRE
Chairman, Harold W. Dodds
Speakers, Marjorie Nicolson, James B. Conant

Besides the program an exhibition of 150 books by various participants in the conference was set up at the Graduate College.

The dramatic structure of this program is apparent. It unfolds in three tenses. It served to keep in line discussions which, on a subject of this sort, are only too prone to deviate and run astray. "No topic was exhausted. . . . The topics were so arranged . . . that in one sense this was a single 18-hour conference with adjournments after each of the twelve parts." And yet the discussions were insured from cramp or confinement by the diversity of the participants, who included presidents of colleges, teachers and specialists in history, philosophy, literature both ancient and modern, music, psychology, fine arts, theology, education, astronomy, archeology, and sinology. Many subjects were drawn into the range of vision—art, teaching, science, political facts and theory, morals, Greek tradition, Christian tradition, international peace and understanding, education and its present disorder, but all with consistent focus upon the one matter in hand, the humanistic idea.

The design and procedure of this conference were generally those of the others, with proper allowance, of course, for variation according to their subjects. Most of the programs carried with them certain accessories: daily broadcasts by radio and special exhibitions or recitals of appropriate material. The appointed recorder of each conference and the selected correspondents of the press were resident members of the conference. Most of the conferences ended with an open meeting in which a chosen speaker, or speakers, summarized the proceedings, and were sometimes able to convey what was less tangible, the convergent direction of the conference which passes mere reason. The proceedings of each conference, except that on the Role of the Undergraduate, and that on Scholarship and Research in the Arts, were afterwards issued in pamphlet form, a pamphlet for each conference; but the authors of these pamphlets are almost unanimous in their despair of transmitting the real essence of the conference, the growing intimacy, the release of intellect, the fertile impact of mind upon mind, the humanizing of matter inanimate and remote through a kind of companionable incarnation. These were, as one observer remarked, "the intangible results—the stimulation, the cross-fertilization necessary to carry a man's imagination from one stage to another in an area of research, the sense of added confidence that comes from discovering other pioneers who share the same beliefs and hopes for the future." Such matters, intangible and immeasurable, constitute the hidden soul of these encounters, and are as incapable of record as the hidden but essential history of a university.

Though the conferences varied widely in scope and temper according to their varied subjects and personnel, yet by their close and continued intimacy the human basis established itself as it rarely does at the usual learned convention. Through all their variation one may discern signs of a commonalty which may be read as a good omen in this latter-day chaos of education. A dozen men were participants in more than one conference, some of them as far removed from one another as the Chemistry and Physiology of Growth from the Humanistic Tradition.

A correspondent who "covered" the Second Series, a Princeton graduate of 1930, saw and felt in the conferences "the relatedness of human knowledge." "Scientists," said he, "heard from humanists and *vice versa*, and such high specialists in the vineyard of knowledge as geneticists had to make their work intelligible to paleontologists and evolutionists." Many of the figures of world renown were included in those who took part in more than one conference. Notables who had come overseas to attend the conference on Nuclear Science, for example, reappeared in Princeton three months later at the conference on Mathematics.

All the conferences appear to have felt a certain tension between concern for their special subject in itself, and concern for its relation to the affairs of man at large. Yet, the conferences on Mathematics, on the Chemistry and Physiology of Growth, on Genetics, Paleontology, and Evolution, on Scholarship and Research in the Arts hardly glanced over their boundaries at the surrounding world, and waxed prophetic only of future possibilities in their own field. Such preoccupation was perhaps natural and necessary in subjects of this sort.

Even within the high and close mystery of Mathematics took place one of the most exciting of the conferences. Over 80 participated, and of these, 13 had come from abroad representing nine different nations. Above the manipulation of theorems, equations, and problems the discussion sometimes emerged—or deviated—into spirited debate on the nature of axioms, proof, formal systems, and logic. But the intention of the whole conference was toward unification of mathematical studies, by bringing together "a small and diversified group of capable and active workers," and it ended in a consciousness of success. It was "the first international gathering of mathematicians in a long and terrible decade." And the human value of this most abstract subject asserts itself in the director's observation: "The manifold contacts and friendships renewed on this occasion will, we all hope, . . . 'contribute to the advancement of the comity of all nations and to the building of a free and peaceful world.' "

The conference on the Chemistry and Physiology of Growth kept strictly to its own boundaries, but within these it seems to have made a wide and complete cycle, for its record concluded: "We had thus come the full turn of the wheel. The problems of the synthesis of proteins are intimately conjoined with those of the action of the glands of internal secretion. And both these, together with the many other aspects examined during the conference, comprise the background and the hopes for the future elucidation of the fundamental problem of growth." And the members are said to have left Princeton in high hopes of discoveries in this field during the next century.

The conference on Genetics, Paleontology, and Evolution combined three closely related fields of inquiry and moved in the direction of a synthesis of biology and geology. And though it kept well within its bounds, it did, like most of the men in conference met, especially the scientists, cast sober and disturbed glances into the world beyond. For thus its director, Professor Glenn L. Jepsen, reflects at its conclusion:

In terms of organic evolution the recent war had been another intraspecific struggle, but with a new and catastrophic twist which gave a bewildered society new cause for examining its social modes and its delegation of responsibilities. Forces which in nature contribute to stability and progress had been released at rates that threatened civilization's continuity at its most critical and uncontrollable point, the genetic thread between generations, the chromosomes.

The more than two billion of us received a cumulative total of less than half an ounce of chromosomes from our ancestors who had preserved this precious thread with almost no change for 50,000 years or more. We can contribute only the same slender fiber of heredity to our descendants. For them our temporary custody of it is important. It bears the principal sum of man's physical evolution and hence carries the potentialities for cultural attainments from the past to the future.

Society, after the atom bomb, has become somewhat more aware that biological man and ethical man are not in separate provinces of thought, that science and the interpretation of science are in one scholastic world. The facts of atomic fission could lead to the fusion of knowledges into social wisdom.

The engineers, "priests of the machine," at first occupied themselves for a day with their cult of natural resources, materials, transportation, conversion into energy. But the conference assumed more and more a humanistic tone, as it took note of the individual worker and the individual engineer, both of them losing their individuality in the collective economy which has submerged them in the rise of Big Industry, Big Government, and Big Unions. What, then, is to be the right training of the engineer, whether for a practical career, or a career of research, or, for what transcends and should determine both, his service to human society? Social scientists and social engineers have not yet found the answer. Which led Ralph E. Flanders to his extraordinary conclusion of the conference.

For three hundred years or more, he observed, the engineer has been molding the discoveries of science into usable forms, both destructive and constructive, until he has now reached the point where he can no longer evade moral responsibility. Our problem is twofold: "To establish a free productive society, and to maintain peace in a free world." The first is the task of the "social sciences," the second, of the "political sciences." The touchstone of a true science is its ability to predict, an ability which the social and political "sciences," for all their industry, have not yet achieved as have the physical sciences. "Where can we find the Newtons and Einsteins of social phenomena?" There is Spengler with his predestination of the cycles; there is Pareto with his cold analysis of human motives, and their capability of manipulation regardless of moral consideration; and there is Margaret Mead, whose study of aborigines shows how men may be molded to any form, evil or good. All this concerns the engineer, whose labors are, or should be, for the welfare, not the destruction of mankind.

If society can be molded, who is skillful or wise enough to undertake the task? "I wish to suggest that, in the essential content of the Bible and in Christian ethics derived from it, we have something which is more in the nature of social science and social engineering than we have been accustomed to think or admit." Not by authority or revelation, but on the basis of human experience through many generations. "We have here the terms on which societies live or die. . . . They are the fundamental data of human well-being. They can be defied only at our peril." Therefore the facts of the spiritual life must be ingrained in the oncoming generation. Otherwise "the world is headed for decay and destruction."

On the last day of the conference, October 4, in the lobby of the John C. Green School of Engineering, new murals depicting the life and discoveries of Joseph Henry were presented and dedicated. These were both painted and presented to the University by Gifford Beal '00, winner of the Abbey Award, by which he was allowed to choose both site and subject.

The conference on the Future of Nuclear Science was, from both its subject and its position at the beginning of the whole year's series, the most conspicuous of all. It was conspicuous too in its personnel. Sixteen representatives from ten foreign countries took part. Of the 77 participants 11 were recipients of the Nobel prize. The roster shows such names as Bohr, Compton, Joliot, and Conant. Besides professors of physics, mathematics, chemistry, philosophy, and astronomy, it included directors of large commercial laboratories, administrators in education, and directors in scientific departments of the Government.

It began, rather surprisingly, with education in science, even in the secondary schools; proceeded to minute particularities of nuclear science; but on the third day confronted the question which more or less openly haunted all the conferences throughout the year. In this instance it was called "Physical Science and Human Values." The discussion had reached the point of defining the foundations of freedom in science, and an English participant was just uttering the opinion that freedom in science might awaken a people's mind to the possibilities of general freedom, when "Pat he comes like the catastrophe of the old comedy"—in walked two advisors of Andrei Gromyko in the United Nations Atomic Energy Commission, M. G. Mescherjakov, of the Leningrad Radium Institute, and Victor S. Vavilov, of Leningrad University. Mr. Mescherjakov spoke extempore to the effect that diversities in ideologies only reflect diversities in nature, but one fundamental point, a common philosophy of nature, remains. "I consider the unifying idea of this natural philosophy as a symbol of the unity of the world. I think that in our troubled times this is a very hopeful sign."

But the conference as whole seemed agreed that a common philosophy of science is not enough to save the world. As in the other scientific conferences, phrases were heard like "believing in a certain spiritual reality and covenanted to the service of this reality"; and "intelligence can be given a meaning only in terms of the individual." There was talk of the proper evaluation of "absolutes," of intellectual rehabilitation, of the question of values. "Here is one of the most important arenas for the exercise of intelligence, in purging and educating our values." "We scientists have become very conscious of the fact that our efforts eventually will lead to results which are apt to modify the living conditions of mankind. . . . Our conscience is awakened and we hope that these modifications will be for the good and not for the worst. . . . We poor scientists . . . will have to understand human behavior." And the veteran astronomer, Henry Norris Russell, called for a new Hippocratic oath for the physicist: "New powers of life and death are in our hands, and we must use them soberly, advisedly, discreetly, and—so far as in us lies—in the fear of God."

The conferences on the Near and the Far East were embarrassed by the wealth and variety of their material, but their programs were most economically devised to enlist just such special subjects as would best carry a general significance.

About 60 participated in the conference on the Near East. Of these, 12 came from such countries as Turkey, Egypt, Iran, and Iraq, together with prominent diplomats from Washington. The art, literature, culture, religion, and politics of Iran, Turkey, and the Arab lands were all brought into focus, with appraisal of their present status and vitality, and of the enlightenment they can lend to our own civilization.

Pendent to the conference was an exhibition of Arabic, Turkish, and Persian manuscripts from the incomparable Garrett Collection in the University Library.

The conference director, Professor Philip K. Hitti, announced that Princeton was the first to recognize the importance of these subjects by establishing a program of Islamic studies for undergraduates as well as graduates, whereby they may acquaint themselves with the culture of the Moslem peoples.

The conference was afterwards described as something more than a mere conference—"a unique experience." Perhaps nothing in the way of formal utterance distinguished it more than Professor William Ernest Hocking's comment at the end. He said in effect:

> No one who has entered the Arab world of today can have failed to note two things: the suffering of spirit which comes of the historic crisis, with its demand for change, and the extraordinary freshness and vitality of the spirit of this great people. That vitality will use the social and industrial technics which it finds most pertinent to its life. Like China, it will have impulses from the Soviet type of organization and from our own; and like China it will not take them as ideological opposites, with an either-or requirement, but will create its own synthesis if it is allowed to do so. While we

talk of the "dignity of man," let us remember that here in the Arab world, in spite of a hundred obstacles, the dignity and poetry of the human spirit reaches a new height.

The conference on the Far East was confronted with a field so vast that instead of trying to "survey mankind from China to Peru," it confined itself to China. Even so it suffered dichotomy of program into Chinese Art and Chinese Society, and the two parts ran simultaneously for the three days of the conference. The upshot of the disquisition on Chinese art seems to have been a demand for new criteria and methodology in such studies, especially in relating them to Chinese history and philosophies contemporary with the works of art.

As for Chinese society, its ancient twofold composition of government and masses has been broken up by the rise of the proletariat, soldier, and business man. But certain safety checks still persist—the long-inherited sense of family and the ancient instinct for stability. "Moderation, a capacity for social cooperation, and a resilience in the face of hardship are virtues for which the Chinese people have long been distinguished." America, therefore, would be wise to support the moderates of all classes, both revolutionary and reactionary, in the orderly rebuilding of China.

Perhaps the most illustrious distinction of this conference among all the conferences was the display of five exhibitions of Chinese art. These were:

1. A loan exhibition of bronze ritual vessels, representing a span of a thousand years, many of them very rare and beautiful, from a score of public and private collections. Half of them had never before been exhibited.

2. The famous collection of nearly 500 paintings gathered by Dr. DuBois S. Morris '93. In honor of its Bicentennial Year Dr. Morris generously presented the collection to his Alma Mater. The presentation was formally made at

the concluding dinner of the conference in Procter Hall. The donor's son, DuBois S. Morris, Jr. '33, speaking on behalf of his father, dwelt on the faith in which the collection had been formed, that art as a basic human means of expression must be a medium of profound sympathy and understanding between nation and nation.

3. A collection of "rubbings" from engraved stones arranged as far as possible in chronological order from the second to the twentieth century. Of these many are as yet undated and call for the attention of scholars.

In passing it may be well to mention here two of the several studies that were nurslings of the Bicentennial. The University Press had just issued in time for the anniversary Professor Rowley's description of the Morris Collection under the title *Principles of Chinese Painting*; and his study of the development of style in the portrayal of the human figure, based on the historical evidence of the rubbings, was already in preparation.

4. An extraordinary collection of rare illustrated books and manuscripts from the National Peiping Library, which had been lodged for security during the war in the Library of Congress. This was supplemented by treasures from the Congressional Library's own collection, and from the New York Public Library.

5. Of paramount importance in Chinese archeology were 125 enlarged photographs made and loaned to the exhibition by Dr. Liang Ssŭ-ch'êng. They represented not only primitive cave sculpture, but "elegant Sung sculptures and the first T'ang building to contain not only a date," but also paintings of Buddhist figures on roof beams, and sculptured portraits of architect and donor.

Exhibitions were also an important accessory of the conference on Scholarship and Research in the Arts. Its title would have been clumsier but more descriptive if it had read "Fine Arts and Music," for the three days were divided, two to one, between them. On the third day the disciples of the Fine Arts left the musical people to their own devices, and were carried in special bus and railway car to Baltimore for lunch with the Alumni Association of Maryland, and for the opening of the magnificent exhibition of Byzantine Art assembled in the Baltimore Museum of Art by the Walters Gallery in special observance of the Bicentennial. They were also asked by Harvard University to continue their conference for two days, April 25 and 26, at Dumbarton Oaks. They were further invited to view a special exhibition of Byzantine material at the Freer Gallery in Washington. This exhibition, likewise in honor of Princeton's Bicentennial, contained Biblical manuscripts, paintings earlier than those in the Baltimore exhibit, Armenian illuminations, and beautiful specimens of Assanian and Parthian silver.

Besides all this display of "large richesse," the committee on the conference put on view at Princeton the drawings of the desecrated church of St. Martin at Angers, made by G. H. Forsyth, Jr. '23, who for six summers, from 1933 to 1938, carried on excavations on this site and unearthed a sort of architectural history of the place from the time of Domitian to the fifteenth century, including three successive churches, of the sixth, ninth, and eleventh centuries.

Meanwhile the musicologists, after a day of conference were refreshed by an exquisite recital of Sixteenth Century Italian and French part songs under the direction of Professor Randall Thompson, in the becoming setting of Procter Hall, based primarily on Alfred Einstein's new three-volume work, *The Italian Madrigal.*

The conference on Planning Man's Physical Environment seems, by all reports, to have been the most picturesque of the whole series. It was limited to two days, which was perhaps enough considering the explosive nature of its elements, both personal and topical. Perhaps in anticipation of such outcome the committee had designed its program as an attempt to define "those diverse forces which are likely to influence man's environment in the future." This gave the conference a distinctly humanistic quality from the first. The committee had even arranged some preliminary correspondence among the members to bring the discussions into sharper focus.

The discussion clearly reflected that architecture as an art is related to almost everything else in the Universe—materials, the atom bomb (of course), human biology, human experience, culture, religion, social science, the ideal community, democracy, political control and regulation, standardization, the perennial debate between town and country, between tradition and the future, form, space, and space-time mathematics. It was inevitable that in spite of the committee's best efforts the discussion should splash about and even boil over at times. The record, however, discovers certain "areas of agreement" and specifies eleven of these which are after all pretty obvious, and remind one of certain of the more enduring conclusions of John Ruskin. But the conference rose to a climax unexceeded by any of the others in the concluding speeches in open meeting, by Robert Moses and Frank Lloyd Wright. These were both pungent and picturesque.

Mr. Moses spoke out of his turbulent experience in planning and promoting public works, bloody, but unbowed:

> Unless you have a combative instinct, a stomach for a fight, and a willingness to argue your case with the press and the people, you won't go very far in changing our American environment for the better. It will not be done by soft words, and in the process you will have to meet, on the most outrageous and unfair terms, the smooth writer, the demagogue, the reactionary, the stand patter, the glib promiser, the rabble rouser, the sloth, the fox, and the lone wolf.

Yet Mr. Moses prefers our liberty, "with all its connotations, pleasant and unpleasant, stimulating and irksome," to death of the spirit under an all-powerful government.

What we all need is free trade, not necessarily in goods, but in brains. The worst barriers are those of stupid prejudice. The best imports and exports are ideas, even if they are at variance. . . .

Before we abandon our present civilization, with its manifest imperfections, and return to the caves and huts of our ancestors, I suggest that we exhaust the tenets of faith and religion, the arts of diplomacy, the sanctions of law and economics, the dictates of common sense, and the fundamental decency of the average man. . . .

The improvement of our environment . . . depends upon leadership, and leadership is partly a matter of education and partly a God-given quality which has little relation to anything we can analyze or control. It is peculiarly fitting that Princeton at its Bicentennial should be the scene of this discussion, because Princeton has a splendid and unbroken record of training for public service, to which that great educator, political scientist, executive, and evangelist, Woodrow Wilson, so often referred.

Mr. Wright, after declaring that Princeton had long been his favorite university, dwelt upon the present disease of our education and society. Our education is so split and disintegrated that it is like "a man facing a brick wall counting bricks; we mistake the counting for the reality—and so lose or ignore . . . the nature and wherefore of the wall as a wall." Education has lost any organic conviction. Our economics and politics have failed also. Our disease is urbanism and the spirit is dying of standardization and habituation. "There can be no real separation between Religion, Philosophy, Science, and the Art-of-Building. They are one or none."

The only remedy is freedom of the individual. "Under the watchful care of the people themselves, government must take its place down *under*, not up above the right of the individual to be himself."

This conference was embellished with three special exhibitions: one illustrating the work of Frank Lloyd Wright, Robert Moses, Tony Garnier, and Alvar Aalto; another demonstrating the psychology of vision from the Dartmouth Eye Institute; and a general architectural exhibit in McCormick Hall.

The conferences on University Education and the Public Service and on The University and its World Responsibilities, though three months apart, formed a kind of logical sequence in which the second was a natural corollary of the first. The first was distinguished by the directorship of the late James V. Forrestal '15, who generously saved out of his very busy life the two days and more which he thus gave to the service of his University.

A leading question of this conference rose out of the present need in public service not for more specialists, statisticians, economists, lawyers, sociologists—we have almost enough of them—but for more "generalists," men who by character and intelligence and sympathetic understanding of human nature are able to transcend the operation intrusted to their management and direct the specialists with wisdom and best effect. But how to find and train such generalists?—that is the question.

It was inevitable that Woodrow Wilson's voice should be reinvoked: "What a man ought never to forget with regard to a college is that it is a nursery of principle and honor." The present claim of the humanities and social studies in the discipline of "generalists" was reasserted, not, however, without an expression of wistful but hopeless regret for the Classics of other-day liberal education. The official report found it significant that an ardent advocate of the humanities as the best training for a public servant was not a professor of Classics, but himself a British career public servant (Sir James Grigg of the International Bank for Reconstruction and Development). And an eloquent plea for the Social Sciences came from the head of a large insurance company. Perhaps the highest reach of the conference found utterance in the words of Donald Stone, Assistant Director of the United States Bureau of the Budget:

> Must we not in short view the aims of the university from the standpoint of what it can contribute to sustaining and supporting a society in which democracy and freedom can flourish, and in which people can find opportunity for self-development? Does this not mean that the principal goal must be to develop in oncoming generations the highest qualities of character? Would not any lesser primary goal lead to an undermining of our civilization as well as to individual frustration and bitterness because tomorrow's leaders would lack not only a synthesis of knowledge, but a synthesis of life without which there can be no realization of their higher potentialities.

As for the conference on The University and its World Responsibilities, widely divergent views found utterance at first, but as the conference proceeded, as in many of the other conferences, basic agreement became more apparent. It was observed that the university's proper function is to promote and establish what Dr. Johnson called "community of mind" the civilized world over. This function was pretty well performed by the medieval university, but has been much interrupted by the rise of nationalism, and impeded at least by the modern expansion and disruption of encyclopedic knowledge into a thousand specialties. What, then, is a university's business in restoring the world's community of mind?—for the active life is as proper to the university as the contemplative. It must begin with some sort of synthetic order within itself. The humanities, the social, and the natural sciences must be reconciled, with just regard and cooperation between them as essential parts of liberal education for a new and free world. To this end the universities of the world must come to know each other and work together, and to this end the present United Nations Educational Scientific and Cultural Organization (UNESCO) is a powerful instrument.

The participants were agreed at least in their sense of present dangers to civilization—in fact were quite as jittery as certain members of the other conferences. Dr. Arnold J. Toynbee, more conscious than most of the cramp and sickness of the times, still ventured to envision a new cultural equilibrium for a unified world in which Western Christendom will be fused with the four other surviving civilizations.

The conference on The Evolution of Social Institutions in America also carried on in the flickering light of present and future uncertainty. There was talk of Federalism and States' Rights, of organization of industry and labor, of political, economic, and social democracy, of the meanings and realities of "free enterprise," of trade unions in a free society, of the place of the United States in the world economy. Though the conference at first was disposed to a certain measure of cheerfulness, it somehow "slipped into an aura of doubt" of our national adequacy to fulfill our opportunity as a preferred nation in the world today, and "closed on a note of pessimism that at best left a policy stalemate and at worst cast a long shadow of despair."

The third day of the conference, on the Church, passed into different hands. It pondered the diversity of sects within the unity of the body politic, the right relation of the Church to the national culture and to the State. On the last particular the eminent Professor Emil Brunner of Zürich drew interesting conclusions to the effect that:

> The State, being merely an instrument and not an end in itself, must never claim to be the dominating principle of human life and never should be considered as supreme value.
>
> The Church can be true to her function, her mission to form a community of believers, insofar only as she renounces any at-

tempt to organize herself in a form similar to the State as an institution with coercive power, and to dominate the State so that she is able to use the coercive means of the State as her own.

Of course the atom was not overlooked, and one member drew from it three possibilities of choice for the future: either one world or none; one hundred per cent democracy or none; one culture or none as the basis of world government. "There must be a common man, a common religious faith."

The last conference of the year was devoted to Secondary Education in the Years Ahead. Most of the members were delegates from twenty different associations of teachers, schools, colleges, and boards of education; but there were also four members from England and two, a bishop and a journalist, from the Empire. There were 73 participants altogether.

Such conferences are only too prone to reason high of such matters as objective tests, courses, age-levels, credits, ingenious devices and tricks for the class-room, projects, "teacher preparation," "vocational training," segregation;

> And find no end, in wandering mazes lost.

But this conference proved its power to rise free of such details and set a direct and definite course under such questions as Whom to teach? Who shall teach? What to teach, and to what ends? As its director remarked afterwards, "There were times when an actual sense of spiritual elation seemed to pervade the conference to prove to us that we as teachers must possess 'a quality that goes beyond and makes for more than citizenship, a quality that transcends nationalism and inter-nationalism, a quality that can persuade students that they are the children of God.' " He was quoting words called forth on the second day of the conference by the remarks of Sydney H. Wood, of the British Ministry of Education.

Beneath the whole conference seemed to run the assumption, sometimes uttered, sometimes implied, that religion in its purest sense must underlie all concepts and practice in education. The discussion really began, however, with a distinction between equality of opportunity and identity of opportunity. It is equality of opportunity rather than the other which truly consists with democratic education, wherein both the average student and the exceptional student receive each their due attention and care. To this end a teacher is committed to a tireless quest for talents; and these are by no means revealed merely through the usual "tests." Tests within their limits may be useful, but they may do much damage by superinducing a kind of hopeless determinism in the mind of both teacher and student. But hidden depths of character far beyond the sounding reach of tests may await discovery, and it takes a teacher who is a sympathetic and intelligent humanist to find them.

> The teacher's responsibility is immense. His personality, sincere and unashamed, working more by unconscious principles than by conscious precepts, is the only thing that will enable him to develop the talents of those entrusted to him. His success will depend to some degree on technique, but far more on observation—real understanding from small signs which way the talent is tending, or whether it is being stunted—and on faith in the power of every child to grow into what God meant him to be, for only by keeping close to Him can he develop the talent of his pupils along the lines which He has laid out for them.

These were the words of John T. Christie, of the Westminster School, London. In short, there is something highly spiritual, even apostolic, about this calling of the teacher.

The question, What shall we teach, and to what end? is like unto the first. Our present schemes of education are not schemes, but chaos, because they are the result of expediency or fashion or chance or notions, instead of

The Procession to the Official Reception of Delegates of June 16

Entering Alexander Hall to the accompaniment of the Marine Corps Band

Inside Alexander Hall: the presentation of greetings

The Academic Procession forms in Holder Court

Delegates of older institutions at the Final Convocation

Presidenti

Mrs. Harry Truman, Mrs. Thomas Jex Preston (widow of Grover C

t Prospect:
President Truman, former President Hoover, Mrs. Woodrow Wilson

President Truman and President Dodds

Recipients of honorary degrees in the Final Procession

Conferring honorary degrees at the Final Convocation

At Prospect: Admiral Leahy, Viscount Alexander, Mrs. Vinson, Mrs. Eisenhower, Chief Justice Vinson, Miss Truman, General Eisenhower, President Truman, President Dodds, former President Hoover, Bishop Sherrill

The final honorary degree of the Bicentennial Year

conviction. This disorder is partly the result of vastly increased specialization and the more and more minute subdivision of all knowledge, but even more of the want of a community of conviction and belief among men, strong enough to impress its unity upon any scheme of studies.

> Unless the quiet study of the thinker and the work and planning of the educator can weld into a new unity religion and nationalism, social stability and social differentiation, science and metaphysics, and national loyalty and internationalism, the splitting of minds will continue and destroy the last sparks of European culture.

And for that matter, of the whole world, for "every educational problem, when deeply considered, is seen to be a problem of humanity."

Thus the conference moved nearer and nearer to its final consideration of religion in education, as the only hope of restoring order and unity to our present chaos.

> Matters essential to the understanding of the culture of the Western World may not be eliminated without imperiling our most precious heritage. More emphasis on science, in which our age is already adequately, perhaps unduly interested, will not serve. The merit inherent in Christianity and in classical studies, with their contribution to an understanding of values above particularism, nationalism, and mere contemporary standards, must be conserved.
>
> The independent, non-sectarian day schools, . . . realizing that our scientific knowledge has outstripped our moral and ethical development, are increasingly accepting the responsibility which rests on all schools of making religious and ethical teaching the heart and center of school life.

If comparison is allowable, perhaps the conference which attained to the largest scope was the sixth and last of the First Series on The Humanistic Tradition in the Century Ahead. This conference, like most of the others, set out with rather wide divarication of ideas and definition; but as it proceeded the focus of discussion cleared; and though the conference by no means ended in agreement, it precipitated certain ideas regarding both the past and the future of human civilization, none too cheerful, and closed more in resolution than in hope.

From the beginning it was plain at least that the subject is focal for many other convergent subjects—history, philosophy, art and aesthetics, physical science, politics, theology, and religion—subjects which draw their meaning and authenticity from the humanism of the individual, as the stars in *Paradise Lost* "in their golden urns draw light" from the sun. No room here for a summary of the abounding spate of ideas during those three days. But Jacques Maritain's observations on the Permanent Elements in the Humanistic Tradition offer perhaps a fair specimen.

He remarked that the humanistic tradition as we have it is a complex of Greek and Roman antiquity, medieval Christianity, and the revelation of Man and Reason in the Renaissance. He analyzed the tradition into nine elements:

1. Affirmation of the dignity and value of the individual, and the equal rights of all men.
2. Consciousness of the value of reflection and introspection.
3. Development of scientific thought as the means of man's mastery over matter and nature.
4. Recognition of justice and law as essential to human society and safety.
5. Longing for freedom.
6. Awareness of the superiority of internal over external forces, material pressure, or coercion.
7. A sense of the universality of reason.
8. A sense of the sacredness of truth and its power to liberate men.
9. A sense of the superiority of delectation over mere usefulness, of wisdom over science, of contemplation over transitory action.

Of these only 1, 3, and 5 are emphasized today, and all the first five, though recognized, are in danger; 2 and 4, in spite of lip-service, are despised by many; the last four (6-9) have been discarded. The humanistic tradition is at stake and a terrible "crisis of growth" is upon us. Our materialism and "mass" civilization are the poison from the bursting of the Nazi abscess; and the only cure involves a reconciliation of anthropocentric reason or rationalism with theocentric reason, in love for man, for the people, and for God.

This analysis, presented on the third day, hardly suggests the tortuous course of the conference from the beginning. Miss Marjorie Nicolson in the final open meeting traced that course in most diverting fashion. She heard above the dissonance two contrapuntal voices. At first the conception of man in the light of tradition against the conception of man as a proper object of socio-scientific manipulation in this new Atomic Age. According to the second the "humanities" as a discipline have proved barren of salvation. This bifurcation extended into the consideration of humanism and art. Some were for letting popular bad taste have its head undisciplined. Great art has always risen out of the people. Others agreed with Artur Schnabel, the distinguished pianist, when he remarked: "If somebody wants art, he must come to it. Art does not descend."

Besides Mr. Maritain's decisive voice, others had been inconclusive, or asserted the triumph of Science over Humanism or the sociologists' patronage of Humanities. Miss Nicolson detected a note of defeatism in the conference, ominous in this new Atomic Age, and said in conclusion:

> We shall not preserve the Humanities in the next hundred years, unless we really believe in them more than we seem to do. . . .
>
> We fear that the world may be destroyed by Man's ingenuity—and there is something that we can do about it. There is every reason for us to labor with all our might to prevent such human stupidity. Yet as we labor, we can be more faithful to the gallant heritage of our humanistic past.

President Conant, in the concluding speech, preferred to limit his definition of the humanities to "the study of the art, literature, and general philosophy of previous ages." Admitting the exclusive and aristocratic tendencies of such disciplines, and their unacceptability to a democratic populace, he pointed out, however, that the humanities are indispensable to a democracy, and that the present situation demanded of the humanists such courage and imagination as they have never before exercised.

Such were the Bicentennial Conferences, at least so far as a brief review can reproduce them; which, after all, is about as near the original as a pressed flower, or a half-tone of the frescoes at Siena. Those volatile essences, those subtle shades of personality, escape and leave behind at best only a memory which in turn will not subdue itself to the written word.

One effect of the conferences was expansive. The presence and actual participation of so many minds from other countries tended to enlarge the scope of all members, and reverse the tendency of the active human intellect to contract its field of vision. The conference proved an antidote to the dangers of creeping specialization. Without sacrifice of definition and exactitude, it tended to a more encyclopedic sense of the subject in hand. This tendency was more evident in some conferences than in others, but it can be observed in all. It is illustrated by the remark of a professional musician who found his conception of music had been enlarged by listening to the discussions concerning the fine arts. And, if we may shift the image, the conferences relieved the congestion of scholarship superinduced by the war, reduced its muscular spasm, and restored its circulation.

But the effects were also intensive, as various members testified. "I don't think," wrote one, "that I have ever had three days of such intense intellectual excitement, and such rich provender for thought and discussion. . . . Though we never came to a complete agreement . . . I think we all realized to the full what it is to live in a truly humanistic atmosphere." And another: "This was real food, more real than what we take in our run-of-the-mill university life. Never, indeed *never* before, have I seen so many great minds gathered in an endeavor to define the anxieties of our period, and so much collective sincerity at work in criticism of the defects of our civilization." It was perhaps inevitable that the members, for a season detached from repetitious routine, should feel as if years of growth had passed in that short interval, and should go forth teeming with fertile ideas.

In several cases these propagations took, or will have taken, more permanent form as books by the members. The greatest writings of the world have had essentially an oral origin, and it is a natural sequence that the discussions of these conferences should have generated and nourished material for ultimate publication. However, the freedom of the conferences was in no wise to be embarrassed or impeded by such an intention, for the original plan provided that "the emphasis will be on interchange of ideas, rather than on producing a permanent record." Yet the list of books with their roots in these conferences cannot be compiled perhaps for many years. Indeed it very likely never can be completely determined.

As one reviews the memoranda of the conferences, not the least striking effect expresses itself only in human terms. Beneath and through all of them, even the most scientific, the human value of their discourse in terms of life and spirit is discernible as basic and ultimate. One can recognize in this tendency a wholesome antidote to whatever is left of the German conception of "pure" dehumanized *Wissenschaft*. For ideas and knowledge live only as they are incarnate. Furthermore the conferences were most fruitful in the actual personal acquaintances and friendships which sprang up in their close retreat.

Concomitant with this tendency—perhaps in logical sequence of it—the records seem to exhibit a sort of convergence of the conferences, as if from 16 different points in space lines emerged towards concentration in one point. From the various conferences the lines proceed to various lengths, some farther than others. This appears in their groping for a common sense of values, for a more encyclopedic conception of their subject, for a philosophic transcendence above mere details, for a conclusive inference, a consensus, a synthesis. In one or two instances the members touched upon something like an ultimate and over-all credo. But the tendency is significant, for it reflects clearly our growing sense of our confusion, and the instinctive thrust forward in search of a new community of mind, larger and more conformable to our vastly expanded knowledge than that which the world has known, which will bring in a new intellectual and spiritual order necessary to the material order of the world.

"It will be years—perhaps generations—before the complete effect of these sessions can be assayed. It is certain only that ideas are spreading from Princeton in concentric circles of influence throughout the colleges and universities of the world."

Princeton in the Nation's Service thus becomes Princeton in the Service of One World.

CHAPTER V

Theme with Variations

THE Bicentennial Year was conceived by its designers as a single structural unit. Its unity was both architectural and dramatic. Two main plots or themes, the Conference and the Convocation, ran in perfect harmony together throughout the year, and were often linked together by common personnel and dates. Many participants in the conferences received degrees at a convocation immediately ensuing; and sometimes the final open meeting of a conference, as in the conference on the Humanities, so closely preceded the Charter Day Convocation as to be essentially a part of it.

But these two dominant themes were reinforced and diversified and embellished in many incidental festal ways—banqueting, illumination, exhibitions, recitals, spectacle, lectures, sermons, radio, publications, including a dozen books on the history and various aspects of Princeton.

And here it is fitting to record the medal struck to commemorate the Bicentennial Year. The design by John R. Sinnock, medalist to the United States Treasury, was selected from several submitted by various artists, and is the refined result of much discussion and criticism. The obverse shows Nassau Hall in relief with the dates, 1746-1946; the reverse bears the seal of the University surrounded by a wreath of ivy. The medal was presented to all official guests and delegates who attended the ceremonies during the year.

No one present at any of the concluding events on the front campus will forget the superb great banner of white damask which hung full length from the third story of Nassau Hall to the platform floor and displayed the arms of the University applied in orange and black velvet.

During the ceremonies it threw into relief the great moments of the day as the sombre gloom of the stone walls could not have done. But its value was more than scenic, for it seemed at times to come almost to life as the concentered embodiment of the history and perennial spirit of Princeton. The banner was designed and presented to the University by Stephen F. Voorhees '00, chairman of the Committee on Physical Arrangements and Decoration.

Memorable also was the illumination of the cupola on Nassau Hall, whose ancient and beautiful dignity cannot be impaired by whatever architectural splendors have arisen near at hand. There it shone against the night sky, symbolic of the light which had gone forth from that spot for well-nigh two centuries. And in each window gleamed a candle (nowadays more safely electric) after the ancient Princeton custom on festive nights, symbolic also of the myriad luminaries that have caught their flame at this source and carried it forth into the world. For this apotheosis the University is grateful to the United States Army. The Headquarters of the First Army in New York sent down three powerful anti-aircraft searchlights, with an officer and men to operate them.

Music also lent its high utterance to the spirit of the year, sometimes by way of exalting convocation or conference, as in the Bicentennial Anthem by Mr. Cone, the program of old French chansons and Italian madrigals by Professor Thompson, the recital by the Pro Arte Quartet, the organ recital by Carl Weinrich for the musicologists, and the noble concert by the Boston Orchestra. The year was further adorned by two Bicentennial organ recitals by Mr. Weinrich, and four recitals by Princeton alumni: John Kirkpatrick '26, pianist; George Newton '29, baritone; James Sykes '30, pianist; and Joseph Hawthorne '30, violist. These four recitals were sponsored by the Friends of Music at Princeton, who also lent their auspices to the Bicentennial Anthem by Mr. Cone, and to the concert by the Pro Arte Quartet. They also provided a symposium on November 23 for the performance of chamber music by Mr. Cone, Carter Harman '40, and Andrew Imbrie '42.

Besides the exhibitions incidental to the conferences already described, others quite independent of any event were arranged, such as the Bicentennial Exhibition in the International Business Machines Building in New York; the exhibition in Princeton of Princetoniana, including sources for Professor Wertenbaker's book, *Princeton 1746-1896*; and the exhibition from May 30 to June 22 of the Laura P. Hall Collection of prints and drawings bequeathed to the University by the late Professor Clifton H. Hall. By no means least was the exhibition, "Two Centuries of Princeton History," arranged and shown by the New Jersey State Museum in Trenton. This included Peale's portrait of Richard Stockton, Princeton 1779, son of the signer and a trustee; a manuscript and portrait of William Paterson, Princeton 1763, once Governor, and the godfather of the city of Paterson; the manuscript of the inaugural address of James Madison, Princeton 1771, as President of the United States; early catalogues of the college library; books from John Witherspoon's library; and the manuscript of Woodrow Wilson's address, "Princeton in the Nation's Service."

This exhibition furnished but one of the many instances in which her neighbors rose with hearty and generous readiness to partake of Princeton's festal joy. Such were not only her many sister institutions, but the National Government and Army, the Government of New Jersey, the Borough of Princeton, and the half dozen or more learned societies represented at various convocations, which held their annual meetings in Princeton in recognition of the Bicentennial Year. The foreign embassies in Washington lent invaluable help in acquiring information about the universities of eastern and central Europe, and in effecting communication with delegates from those institutions.

Both the Federal and the State governments passed resolutions in recognition of the anniversary, and appointed commissions. These were in no sense merely honorary, for in many ways they were an important means of success in the great undertaking. The Borough of Princeton also took its hearty and willing part, what with police aid, *decors*, and general collaboration. For happily the old town-and-gown dichotomy has quite disappeared, and the hospitality, characteristic of the whole place as of old, went forth to welcome all visitors. In fact nothing throughout the year seems to have so captured the hundreds of Princeton's guests as the warm and considerate hospitality of her people, who with one accord threw open their houses and hearts to receive them. The Trustees and Faculty were of course busy with a thousand acts of hospitality the year through; and the whole Princeton family—undergraduates, graduate students, townspeople, and alumni—took their indispensable part in the year's proceedings and insured their success.

Through their own organization, the Orange Key, the undergraduates were tireless in a hundred minor services to the conferences and the convocations, from the supplying of ice-water and checking of this and that detail to the squiring of Miss Truman on the great and final day. Especially were they helpful in the reception and directing of delegates to all important events. They were also the chief source of comic relief so necessary to drama, especially to the graver drama of the year's high academic moments. The Theatre Intime lent high diversion in their burlesque Charter Day reproduction of the original Rutgers football game of 1869, as did the Triangle Club in its annual Musical, *Clear the Track*, on a Bicentennial theme. The

Glee Club and the Chapel Choir were on call from September to June and sang together in the Bicentennial Anthem at the Convocation on Charter Day, at the Convocation on Washington's Birthday, and in the performance of Professor Thompson's "Testament of Freedom" with the Boston Symphony Orchestra in June. The Choir sang also at the Service of Remembrance and the Service of Dedication. The Glee Club lent valiant support to the Bicentennial revue, *Going Back*, at McCarter Theatre, with its songs from two centuries of Princeton history. The group also gave a radio recital of Princeton songs for the British Broadcasting Company, in a Princeton Bicentennial Salute to Oxford University. Representatives of the BBC were in Princeton for a week arranging this program for some twenty million listeners.

This broadcast, entitled "An American University—Princeton," afterward received a special citation from the Institution for Education by Radio, for its authenticity and skillful design. It set forth both the academic and the social life of Princeton in "on-the-spot" recordings of both Faculty and students, with some interspersed glossing of local terms for the benefit of English listeners.

The undergraduate clubs were most hospitable to delegates and guests of the University, and offered them such glimpses of the undergraduate life of Princeton as time allowed.

The journalistic organizations on the campus, *The Daily Princetonian*, the University Press Club, and the Princeton Photo Service, gave invaluable if inconspicuous help to the public press by their "coverage" of special events, by interviews, and by verification of sundry details.

The Student Christian Association organized a series of six forums led by six of the Bicentennial preachers, Dean Aldrich, Dr. Emil Brunner, of the University of Zürich, Dr. T. Z. Koo, Secretary of the World's Student Christian

Association, Dr. Douglas Horton '12, Dr. Robert J. McCracken, of the Riverside Church, and Dr. John A. Mackay, President of Princeton Theological Seminary.

Perhaps the most signal part of the undergraduates in the year's drama was their organization of the conference on the Role of the Undergraduate in University Life, on April 25 and 26. It was instituted by the Orange Key under the sponsorship of the Undergraduate Council and assembled some 35 participants from a dozen eastern private colleges. It was a comparatively brief conference of a day and a half only, but it ranged over such delicate and living issues as student government and the honor system; fraternities, clubs, and social facilities for "non-members"; and the comparative claims upon a student's energies of study, religion, and extra-curricular activities.

But the older sons of the family, the alumni, were stalwart and ready, foot and shoulder, at every need of their Alma Mater during her Jubilee. It is impossible to list all their services, whether as individuals or in organization. But Alumni Day, February 22, was their special day, when 17 alumni received honorary degrees, and Secretary Marshall spoke at the Alumni Luncheon. Three more alumni were honored with degrees at the Convocation of April 3. June 13, 14, and 15 were also set apart for the traditional gatherings of classes at the highly picturesque Bicentennial Reunion.

Certain alumni in particular were inexhaustibly resourceful and tireless. The three officers of the Executive Committee, Messrs. Hope, Darrow, and Fox, the chairman of the Graduate Council, Mr. Helm, and a dozen others spent themselves without limit. Various alumni, particularly Senator H. Alexander Smith '01 and Secretary James V. Forrestal '15, were in position to serve as *liaisons* with the Government, the Army, and the Embassies. Others were in a similar position with the radio, the press, the lines of transportation, and other great organizations of business. And serve they all did with cheerful efficiency. Deserving particular mention for their major contributions to the success of the undertaking are Edmund S. DeLong '22, Wheaton Lane '25, Walter E. Johnson '15, H. Nevin Gehman '42, Norvell B. Samuels '24 and Howard Menand, Jr. '36.

Nor did the spirit of the Bicentennial confine itself to Princeton. In Cleveland on December 28, 1946, took place a gala performance of the Triangle Bicentennial *jeu d'esprit*, *Clear the Track*, and following it a Bicentennial Ball. This grand twofold occasion, mustering some 3,000 alumni of Northern Ohio and their friends—mostly friends— proved a joyous success under the direction of Sheldon S. Reynolds '28 and a corps of fellow alumni.

On May 14 and June 17, the University Club in New York gave two Bicentennial dinners arranged by Edward E. Watts, Jr. '21. The first did honor to 43 head masters and head mistresses of secondary schools in England and the United States who had been guests of the University at the conference on Secondary Education just concluded. The second dinner, immediately following the Final Convocation, entertained as its special guests 52 presidents of colleges and universities, most of whom had taken part in the celebration at Princeton.

All that the alumni did to adorn the year cannot be reckoned, so various it was in kind and extent, from the most prosaic and tiresome details of management to the four concert recitals by alumni and the brilliant exhibits incidental to the conferences.

The Bicentennial found utterance through many voices. The most obvious of these was the radio. Beginning September 20 with the overture Bicentennial broadcast by President Dodds and Mrs. Eleanor Wilson McAdoo, voices of the participants in the first series of the conferences were heard about twice a week on matters related to the discussions of the conferences themselves. Every conference but one throughout the year offered at least one broadcast and some of them carried as many as seven. Sometimes these were monologues, such as Professor William E. Hocking's remarks on "Democracy and Religion," from the conference on the Evolution of Social Institutions in America, or Secretary Forrestal's on "Managing the People's Business," which inaugurated a series of forum discussions. Sometimes the broadcast presented a round-table exchange of ideas, like a preceptorial conference, such as that on the question, "What are the Boundaries of Human Knowledge?" led by Lyman Bryson of the Columbia Broadcasting System, in connection with the conference on the Humanities. Many of the broadcasts took place under regularly established programs—"Frontiers of Science," "Adventures in Science," "Invitation to Learning," "The Next Hundred Years," and the like. One "forum" actually moved to Princeton for the conference on University Education and the Public Service, to deliver a program by four participants, which compared the American and British methods of recruiting men for posts in the Government.

All these reports on the conferences were dispensed on the great networks. But stations near by were quite as busy. WAAT, Newark, reported the opening Convocation and interviews with members of all the conferences. WPAT, Paterson, gave weekly résumés of Bicentennial news. WPEN, Philadelphia, presented five discussions, of which the one on "Nationalism and the Teaching of History," appended to the conference on The University and its World Responsibilities, proved to be among the foremost of the year. Thousands of letters brought proof of the high appreciation far and wide of these emanations from

Princeton. All of them were carried by the stations as a public service.

Public relations in general, press as well as radio, were maintained under the direction of Edmund S. DeLong '22, Frederick S. Osborne '24, Dan D. Coyle '38, and a committee of 18 alumni. They were guided throughout by the intention to give the world a clear idea of what Princeton really is and of what she hopes to be. To this end the press, including periodicals, was notified of each approaching event well in advance, and every facility was arranged for its representatives. Reporters assigned to the conferences were essentially members of the conferences and shared quarters with the participants at the Graduate College and at the Inn. They were notified of the arrivals and appointments of more important members, and thus found most desirable opportunity for informal interviews. For the Final Convocation some 200 press cards were issued, and their holders found working and sleeping quarters ready for them. In the course of the year not only men of the American press were coming and going, but British, French, Belgian, Danish, Norwegian, Swedish, Arab, Egyptian, Hindu, Australian, and Chinese journalists sojourned awhile on either general or special assignments.

In this age, reverting so rapidly to picture-writing, the photographers were almost as important as their brothers of the pen, and were entitled to equal regard. When ever did celebrities so abound? One commentator remarked afterwards that he had stocked his files for months ahead.

The 14 lectures on three regular University Foundations, known as the Louis Clark Vanuxem, the Spencer Trask, and the Cyrus Fogg Brackett Lectures, became a recognized part of the Bicentennial observance in that all but one of them were delivered either by participants in the conferences or by recipients of honorary degrees, or both.

These included: the first series of Vanuxem Lectures on five different scientific subjects ranging from a topic as special as "The Internal Secretions of the Pituitary Body" up to "The Problem of Plan and Purpose in Nature"; the second series of three lectures by Professor F. C. Bartlett, of St. John's College, Cambridge, on "Group Contact in Contemporary Society"; two Trask lectures by T. S. Eliot, poet and critic, on "Samuel Johnson as Critic and Poet"; and the four Brackett lectures on Engineering, by four different authorities, including Sir Harold Hartley of the British European Airways and John R. Munn '06.

The Bicentennial found its religious utterance chiefly through the nine Bicentennial sermons preached in the Chapel between September and May, though the religious significance of the anniversary, both past and future, was expressed or implied in most of the serious events of the year, and seemed never to be forgotten.

But the most prolonged reverberations of this year of acclaim were the publications to which in one way or another it gave rise. Of these, 12 appertained to Princeton itself. Three of these are biographical, including two on Woodrow Wilson and a chapter of the third. Four are historical, including Professor Wertenbaker's careful *Princeton 1746-1896*, newly compiled from original sources, and Alfred H. Bill's vivid and scholarly account of *The Campaign of Princeton, 1776-1777*. This last book is the best account of these matters to date, both in thoroughness and style. The five other volumes are descriptive of Princeton either in whole, or in such particular as its bells and windows. The most elaborate of them all is the magnificent *Princeton Portraits*, by Professor Donald D. Egbert '24, which is a complete catalogue of all portraits, painted or carved, owned by the University, with minute expert description and reproduction of each.

Already mentioned are two books which played an important part in two of the Bicentennial Conferences, *The Principles of Chinese Painting* by George Rowley, and *The Italian Madrigal* by Alfred Einstein. Emanating from the conferences have been, to date, the following titles:

E. P. Wigner, editor, *Physical Science and Human Values*

G. L. Jepsen, George G. Simpson, Ernst Mayr, editors, *Genetics, Paleontology, and Evolution*

Arthur K. Parpart, editor, *Chemistry and Physiology of Growth*

Joseph E. McLean, editor, *The Public Service and University Education*

Thomas B. Creighton, editor, *Building for Modern Man*

On November 8, 1946, just as the Bicentennial Year was rising to its high momentum, the great effort known as the Third Century Fund was launched at a meeting of the Graduate Council. The amount immediately called for is $20,100,000, including $13,500,000 for teaching and research, $4,600,000 for buildings, alterations, and equipment, and $2,000,000 for housing of the Faculty and scholarships. The ultimate sum, however, is $57,600,000.

In a stirring appeal to the alumni on behalf of the Fund, President Dodds asserted again the claims of both past and future in the making of Princeton. He reiterated her original declared purpose of educating men for public service, a purpose consistently upheld in her ensuing history, notably by Witherspoon and Wilson. "In her third century," he affirmed, "Princeton does not propose to deviate from her historic mission."

Princeton is at heart a liberal arts college, he continued, with certain professional schools attached.

Her plan of study is directed as firmly as ever to the individual development of the whole man, not just a segment of him. Her educational methods rest on her belief in the unity of all knowledge, the integrity of the individual, and the diversity of human beings.

This is why she maintains the preceptorial system, small classes and the independent work of upper-class years. . . . The Princeton Plan calls for high standards of scholarship for both Faculty and students, and for a teaching faculty relatively large in proportion to the number of students.

Princeton's function is education for freedom and its responsibilities. She aspires to quality rather than size; but she can no longer maintain that quality without better salaries, better living, and better equipment, for better men.

Princeton is a residential university, and her educational opportunities include a common social and intellectual life as well as formal classes and formal courses of study. . . . Her daily life on the campus is an education in freedom. It fits a democratic society. . . .

Proud as we are of our history and grateful for the strength our heritage brings us, we know that to rest on our past would lead only to decay and destruction. We intend to be the progenitors of a stronger Princeton, not merely the beneficiaries of generations that came before us.

The Bicentennial provides the occasion for looking ahead into the third century. If we are to project our vision into the next hundred years, as far as we can in our time, Princeton must plan toward a rounding out of its present framework and a strengthening of its fundamental elements. To that end, the Trustees, Faculty, and officers of the University have surveyed the University's immediate needs and its needs in the longer range, both of which must be met if we are to maintain Princeton and develop it into the kind of institution we want it to be. . . .

We must plan with soundness and with courage if we are to affirm our faith in the Princeton Plan of education and in the nation to whose service Princeton University has since 1746 been committed.

One act by way of affirming that faith is the allocation

of $2,000,000 of the Fund to the School of Public and International Affairs, and the dedication of the School, in the Bicentennial Year, to the memory of Woodrow Wilson. Since its beginning in 1930 it has worked primarily with undergraduates; but with new resources, it is now training graduates for high service in the Government.

And so, the long Year of Jubilee over, Princeton might pause to take some account of it and of herself as expressed in its course of events. Had she fulfilled her intention of making clear to the world what she is and what she assumes as her proper service? Letters poured in from all sides full of appreciation. They remarked on the invisible, noiseless, but faultless mechanism by which conference and convocation moved easily along their plotted courses. The many guests, now friends of Princeton, had been cheered by the warm hospitality of the place. They clung to lingering recollection of high moments during their visit, and some carried with them a new image of Princeton as a living and dedicated institution of distinct character.

Wrote one, the son of another University, in admiration of the Year's program: "It seems to me precisely the way in which a great university should summon the past in facing the future."

And another: "You gave me, for the first time, a real glimpse of the workings of a University which I have never fully appreciated before, but for which now I have the greatest respect."

And another: "The Bicentennial Year has enlarged the stature of the University within and without."

And another, a European: "Your celebration left me with a feeling of the fellowship of nations."

And yet one more: "Princeton has made a great contribution to international understanding, and I hope it will help us along the road to world peace."

Princeton gained much from her Bicentennial Year. Withal she profited by an accumulated consciousness of herself in three tenses: as she was, is, and shall be; growing not by change of nature, but by a characteristic fulfillment of her potential from the beginning, into an ever more powerful agent of enlightenment in the nation and in the world.

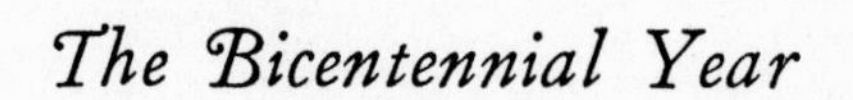

The Bicentennial Year

1

Calendar of Events
in the Bicentennial Program
1946-1947

September 20. Broadcast, CBS: "Bicentennial Year." President Harold W. Dodds, Dean J. Douglas Brown, Mrs. Eleanor Wilson McAdoo.

September 22. Service Inaugurating the Bicentennial Year. Bicentennial Sermon: The Most Reverend and Right Honorable Geoffrey Francis Fisher, Lord Archbishop of Canterbury. University Chapel, 11:00 a.m.

September 22. First Bicentennial Convocation, to confer the degree of Doctor of Divinity upon the Archbishop of Canterbury. Nassau Hall, 12:15 p.m.

September 23-25. Conference 1, Series I: "The Future of Nuclear Science." Graduate College.

September 23. Broadcast, ABC: "Nuclear Energy on Trial." 10:10-10:30 p.m.

September 24. Broadcast, CBS: "Application of Artificial Radioactive Tracers to Chemistry and Medicine." 6:15-6:30 p.m.

September 24. Open Session of Conference 1: "The Observation Problem in Atomic Physics." Niels Bohr. Frick Auditorium, 8:00 p.m.

September 25. Open Session of Conference 1: "The Scientists' Role in International Relations." M. S. Vallarta, H. N. Russell, and H. A. Kramers. McCarter Theatre, 8:30 p.m.

September 26. Vanuxem Lecture: "Cosmic Radiation." Professor Patrick M. S. Blackett, University of Manchester. Frick Auditorium, 8:00 p.m.

September 27-30. Conference 2, Series I: "Chemistry and Physiology of Growth." Graduate College.

September 28. Broadcast, CBS: "Chemistry and Physiology of Growth." 2:30-2:45 p.m.

September 29. Broadcast, CBS: "Foundation of Science." 12:00-12:30 p.m.

September 29. Bicentennial Organ Recital: Carl Weinrich. Procter Hall.

September 30. Open session of Conference 2: "Quel est l'usage des glandes surrénales?" C. N. H. Long. McCarter Theatre, 8:30 p.m.

September 30. Broadcast, ABC: "Abnormal Growth." 10:15-10:45 p.m.

October 1. Vanuxem Lecture: "The Internal Secretions of the Pituitary Body." Dr. Herbert M. Evans, University of California. Frick Auditorium, 8:00 p.m.

October 2-4. Conference 3, Series I: "Engineering and Human Affairs." Graduate College.

October 3. Broadcast, CBS: "Engineering and Human Affairs." 6:15-6:30 p.m.

October 4. Dedication of the Joseph Henry Mural. Engineering Building, 4:30 p.m.

October 4. Open Session of Conference 3: "Engineering and Human Affairs." Ralph E. Flanders, McCarter Theatre, 8:30 p.m.

October 6. Broadcast, CBS: "America's Place in the World Economy." 1:00-1:30 p.m.

October 7-9. Conference 4, Series I: "The Evolution of Social Institutions in America." Graduate College.

October 7. Broadcast, ABC: "Democracy and Religion." 10:15-10:45 p.m.

October 9. Open Session of Conference 4: "The Ecumenical Movement in its National and International Significance." Henry P. Van Dusen. Summary of Conference. Chester I. Barnard and Charles H. McIlwain. McCarter Theatre, 8:30 p.m.

October 11-14. Conference 5, Series I: "The Development of International Society." Graduate College.

October 13. Bicentennial Organ Recital: Carl Weinrich. Procter Hall.

October 14. Broadcast, ABC: "One World or Two?" 10:15-10:45 p.m.

October 14. Open Session of Conference 5: "Is an International Society Possible?" Isaiah Bowman. "Next Steps in the Development of International Society." E. L. Woodward. McCarter Theatre, 8:30 p.m.

October 16-18. Conference 6, Series I: "The Humanistic Tradition in the Century Ahead." Graduate College.

October 17. Broadcast, CBS: "Are the Ideas of Nationalism and Humanism Compatible?" 6:15-6:30 p.m.

October 18. Open Session of Conference 6: "The Boundaries of Humanistic Studies." Marjorie Nicolson and James B. Conant. McCarter Theatre, 8:30 p.m.

October 19. Visit of Representatives of Foreign Academies.

October 19. Charter Day Convocation. University Chapel, 10:30 a.m.

October 19. Re-enactment of Princeton-Rutgers Football Game, 1869. Palmer Stadium. Broadcast by television, NBC.

October 20. Bicentennial Sermon: The Rt. Rev. Donald B. Aldrich. University Chapel, 11:00 a.m.

October 20. Broadcast, CBS: "What Are the Boundaries of Human Studies?" 12:00-12:30 p.m.

October 20. Dedication of the Princeton Battlefield. Sponsored by the State Department of Conservation. 2:00 p.m.

October 20. Bicentennial Student Christian Forum, under auspices of the Student Christian Association: "The Sacraments." The Rt. Rev. Donald B. Aldrich. Murray-Dodge Hall, 7:00 p.m.

October 20. Concert by the Pro Arte Quartet. McCarter Theatre, 8:30 p.m.

October 22-24. Annual Meeting of the Association of American Universities.

October 27-December 29. Exhibition: "Princeton University through Two Centuries." New Jersey State Museum, Trenton, New Jersey.

October 28-November 30. Exhibition: "Princeton and the American Revolution." Treasure Room, University Library.

November 1. Annual Meeting of the Institute of Mathematical Statistics. Fine Hall, 10:00 a.m.

November 2. Annual Meeting of the American Mathematical Society. Palmer Laboratory, 10:00 a.m.

November 3. Bicentennial Sermon: Emil Brunner, D.D., Professor of Theology, University of Zürich. University Chapel, 11:00 a.m.

November 3. Bicentennial Student Christian Forum. "Revelation—1946": Dr. Emil Brunner. Murray-Dodge Hall, 7:30 p.m.

November 12. Broadcast, MBS: Debate, "Is the British Government Career Service Better than the American?" 9:30-10:30 p.m.

November 13-14. Conference 1, Series II (No. 7): "University Education and the Public Service." Princeton Inn.

November 13. Broadcast, WPEN: Round Table, "University Education and the Public Service." 6:45-7:00 p.m.

November 14. Broadcast, NBC: Address by James Forrestal, Secretary of the Navy, in connection with Conference 7. 6:15-6:45 p.m.

December 1. Bicentennial Sermon: Reinhold Niebuhr, D.D., Professor of Applied Christianity, Union Theological Seminary. University Chapel, 11:00 a.m.

December 1. Bicentennial Student Christian Forum: "Justification by Faith": Dr. Reinhold Niebuhr. Room 50, McCosh Hall, 7:30 p.m.

December 16. Vanuxem Lecture: "Hypothesis and Practical Judgment." G. C. Evans. Frick Auditorium, 5:00 p.m.

December 17-19. Conference 2, Series II (No. 8): "Problems of Mathematics." Princeton Inn.

December 20. Broadcast, WPEN: "The Problems of Mathematics." H. Cramer, Paul Smith, John Tukey, J. H. C. Whitehead.

December 28-30. Annual Meeting of the American Musicological Society. Clio Hall.

December 28. Organ recital of Bach and others, under auspices of the American Musicological Society: Carl Weinrich. University Chapel, 8:30 p.m.

December 27-30. Exhibition in connection with the meeting of the American Musicological Society: "Eighteenth Century Theatrical Design." Antioch Court, McCormick Hall.

1947

January 2-4. Conference 3, Series II (No. 9): "Genetics, Paleontology, and Evolution." Princeton Inn.

January 4. Broadcast, WCBS: "Adventures in Science." 4:30 p.m.

January 8. Vanuxem Lecture: "The Problem of Plan and Purpose in Nature." George Gaylord Simpson. Frick Auditorium, 5:00 p.m.

January 15. Brackett Lecture: "Post-War Industrial Relations." Jay C. Hormel '15. Engineering Lounge, 7:30 p.m.

January 22-23. Annual Meeting of the Association of American University Presses.

January 26. Bicentennial Sermon: Dr. T. Z. Koo, Secretary of the World's Student Christian Federation. University Chapel, 11:00 a.m.

January 26. Bicentennial Student Christian Forum: "The Divinity of Christ." Dr. T. Z. Koo. Murray-Dodge Hall, 7:30 p.m.

February 9. Bicentennial Recital: John Kirkpatrick '26, pianist. Sponsored by the Friends of Music. Procter Hall, 3:30 p.m.

February 17-March 22. Exhibition: "Princeton 1746-1896," Treasure Room, University Library.

February 19-21. Conference 4, Series II (No. 10): "The University and its World Responsibilities." Princeton Inn.

February 20. Broadcast, CBS: "Is a World University Desirable?" C. Mildred Thompson, Stuart Grumman. 6:15-6:30 p.m.

February 20. Open Session of Conference 10: "One World, One History." Arnold D. Toynbee. McCosh 50, 8:30 p.m.

February 21. Open Session of Conference 10: "International Intellectual Cooperation." Alexander Hall, 8:30 p.m.

February 22. Alumni Bicentennial Convocation. University Chapel, 11:00 a.m.

February 22. National Alumni Luncheon. Address by George Catlett Marshall, Secretary of State. Baker Rink, 1:00 p.m.

February 22. Broadcast, NBC: "Can UNESCO Combat Nationalism?" Ben Cherrington, William E. Rappard, George Shuster. 6:15-6:30 p.m.

February 23. Bicentennial Sermon: Douglas Horton '12, Chairman of the American Committee of the World Council of Churches. University Chapel, 11:00 a.m.

February 23. Bicentennial Student Christian Forum: "The Ecumenical Movement." Dr. Douglas Horton. Murray-Dodge Hall, 7:30 p.m.

February 25. Broadcast, BBC: Bicentennial Greetings between Princeton and Oxford.

February 25, 26, 27. Vanuxem Lecture: "Group Contact in Contemporary Society." Professor Frederic Charles Bartlett, St. John's College, Cambridge. Frick Auditorium, 5:00 p.m.

March 5-6. Conference 5, Series II (No. 11): "Planning Man's Physical Environment." Princeton Inn.

March 6. Broadcast, NBC: "Citizen Participation in Planning Cities." Henry Churchill, William Wuerster, and Louis Justement. 6:15-6:30 p.m.

March 6. Open Session of Conference 11. Robert Moses and Frank Lloyd Wright. Procter Hall, 8:30 p.m.

March 13. Vanuxem Lecture: "Progress in the Transformation of Energy." P. C. Keith, President of Hydrocarbon Research, Inc. Frick Auditorium, 8:00 p.m.

March 16. Bicentennial Sermon: Robert D. McCracken, D.D., Rector of the Riverside Church, New York. University Chapel, 11:00 a.m.

March 16. Bicentennial Student Christian Forum: "Sin, Repentance, and Forgiveness." Dr. R. D. McCracken. Murray-Dodge Hall, 7:30 p.m.

March 23. Bicentennial Recital: George Newton, '29, baritone. Sponsored by the Friends of Music. Procter Hall, 3:30 p.m.

March 25-April 26. Exhibition: Arabic, Turkish, and Persian Manuscripts. Treasure Room, University Library.

March 25-27. Conference 6, Series II (No. 12): "Near Eastern Culture and Society." Princeton Inn.

March 26. Broadcast, NBC: "Report from the Near East." Emil Zaidan, Egypt; Charles Malik, Lebanon; Muzaffar Sherif Basoglu, Turkey. 6:15-6:45 p.m.

March 27. Broadcast, CBS: "Can East meet West?" 6:15-6:30 p.m.

March 31. Preview of Bicentennial Exhibitions of Chinese Art. Museum of Historic Art and Antioch Court.

April 1-3. Conference 7, Series 2 (No. 13): "Far Eastern Culture and Society." Princeton Inn and McCormick Hall.

April 1. Open Session of Conference 13: "The Background of Chinese Philosophy." Fung Yu-han. McCormick Hall, 8:30 p.m.

April 2. Broadcast, NBC: "What Should our Policy be in China?" 1:15-1:30 p.m.

April 2. Open Session of Conference 13: "Communication and Acculturation in Modern China." McCormick Hall, 8:30 p.m.

April 3. Spring Convocation. Nassau Hall, 4:30 p.m.

April 3. Dinner and Concluding Session of Conference 13: "The Future of Chinese Studies in America." George E. Taylor. Procter Hall, 8:00 p.m.

April 6. Broadcast, CBS: "Can China Achieve a Working Democracy?" Quincy Howe, John R. Fairbank, Harold D. Lasswell, David H. Rowe. 1:00-1:30 p.m.

April 8-27. Exhibition of Chinese Art, including the DuBois S. Morris Collection. Museum and Antioch Court, McCormick Hall.

April 9-10. Annual Meeting of the Society of Experimental Psychologists.

April 16. Brackett Lecture: "The Engineer in Business." John R. Munn '06. Engineering Lounge, 7:30 p.m.

April 20. Bicentennial Sermon: John A. Mackay, President, Princeton Theological Seminary. University Chapel, 11:00 a.m.

April 20. Bicentennial Recital: James Sykes '30, pianist. Sponsored by the Friends of Music. Procter Hall, 3:30 p.m.

April 20. Bicentennial Student Christian Forum: "Salvation." Dr. John A. Mackay. Murray-Dodge Hall, 7:30 p.m.

April 22-24. Conference 8, Series II (No. 14): "Scholarship and Research in the Arts." Princeton Inn.

April 24. Expedition to Baltimore and Washington to view Exhibitions of Byzantine Art at the Baltimore Museum and the Freer Gallery.

April 24. Recital of sixteenth century part-songs under direction of Professor Randall Thompson. Procter Hall, 8:30 p.m.

April 25-26. Conference 14 continued at Dumbarton Oaks on invitation of Harvard University.

April 25-26. Conference 9, Series II (No. 15): "The Role of the Undergraduate in University Life."

April 28. Broadcast, WPEN: "What Is Liberal College Education?" James L. Kirby, William C. Campbell, Richard Bostwick, William McKenzie.

May 4. Bicentennial Sermon: The Rt. Rev. H. St. George Tucker, former Presiding Bishop in the Protestant Episcopal Church of America. University Chapel, 11:00 a.m.

May 4. Bicentennial Student Christian Forum: "The Kingdom of God." The Rt. Rev. H. St. George Tucker. Murray-Dodge Hall, 7:30 p.m.

May 11. Bicentennial Recital: Joseph Hawthorne '30, violist. Sponsored by the Friends of Music. Procter Hall, 3:30 p.m.

May 12-14. Conference 10, Series II (No. 16): "Secondary Education in the Years Ahead." Princeton Inn.

May 12. Broadcast, CBS: "What Should High Schools Teach?" H. A. Ferguson, Frederick Kahler. 6:15-6:30 p.m.

May 14. Broadcast, NBC: "How Can Secondary School Education Be Improved?" William H. Cornog, William G. Avirett, John deQ. Briggs, Lester W. Nelson. 6:15-6:45 p.m.

May 19-20. Spencer Trask Lecture: "Samuel Johnson as Critic and Poet." T. S. Eliot. McCosh 50, 8:00 p.m.

June 13. 1927 Forum: "Planning for Princeton's Third Century."

June 13-15. Reunions of the Classes of 1882, 1897, 1898, 1900, 1902-1905, 1907, 1909-1917, 1919-1922, 1924, 1927-1948.

June 14. Dedication of the Dillon Gymnasium. 11:00 a.m.

June 14. Alumni Parade and Baseball Game with Yale. 1:30 p.m.

June 14. Historical and Musical Revue, *Going Back*. McCarter Theatre, 8:00 p.m.

June 15. Service of Remembrance. University Chapel, 11:00 a.m.

June 15. Meeting of National Alumni Association. Front Campus, 12:00 a.m.

June 15. Garden Party for Visiting Delegates. Prospect, 5:00 p.m.

June 15. Concert by the Boston Symphony Orchestra. Dillon Gymnasium, 8:00 p.m.

June 16. Service of Dedication. University Chapel, 11:00 a.m.

June 16. Laying of the Cornerstone of the Harvey S. Firestone Library. 11:30 a.m.

June 16. Luncheon for the Delegates. University Dining Halls, 12:30 p.m.

June 16. Convocation for the Official Reception of Delegates. Alexander Hall, 3:30 p.m.

June 16. Garden Party for Delegates. Wyman House, 5:00 p.m.

June 16. Formal Dinner for Delegates, Hosts, and Friends. Dillon Gymnasium, 7:30 p.m.

June 17. Final Convocation. Front Campus, 11:00 a.m.

June 17. Luncheon for Delegates, Hosts, and Friends. University Dining Halls, 1:00 p.m.

September 20. Dedication of Langlotz Memorial Tablet, the Bicentennial Gift of the Class of 1901. 160 Mercer Street, 5:45 p.m.

RADIO BROADCAST NOTES

1. In the calendar above, the following abbreviations have been used: CBS—Columbia Broadcasting System; ABC—American Broadcasting Company; NBC—National Broadcasting Company; MBS—Mutual Broadcasting System; BBC—British Broadcasting Corporation. Radio Station WPEN is located in Philadelphia, Pa.

2. In addition to the broadcasts listed in the calendar, WAAT, Newark, N.J., gave 15-minute broadcasts of Bicentennial news and general news of Princeton five and six evenings a week from September 23 to January 10; and WPAT, Paterson, N.J., gave 15-minute reports weekly from September 29 to May 25.

2

Bicentennial Committees

EXECUTIVE COMMITTEE

Honorary Chairman	HAROLD W. DODDS
Chairman	WALTER E. HOPE
Vice-Chairman	WHITNEY DARROW
Treasurer	GEORGE A. BRAKELEY
Secretary	ARTHUR E. FOX

J. DOUGLAS BROWN
EDMUND S. DELONG
HAROLD H. HELM
ALEXANDER LEITCH
SHERLEY W. MORGAN
DATUS C. SMITH, JR.
EDWARD E. WATTS, JR.

FACULTY COMMITTEE

The Advisory Council of the Faculty, consisting of the chairmen of departments of instruction, was constituted as the Faculty Committee on the Bicentennial

FACULTY ADMINISTRATIVE SUBCOMMITTEE

SHERLEY W. MORGAN, *Chairman*

JULIAN P. BOYD
J. DOUGLAS BROWN
GILBERT CHINARD
KENNETH H. CONDIT
LUTHER P. EISENHART
DATUS C. SMITH, JR.

DIRECTORS OF ACADEMIC CONFERENCES

J. DOUGLAS BROWN, *Director of First Series*
WHITNEY J. OATES, *Director of Second Series*

UNIVERSITY PARTICIPATION IN FORMAL CEREMONIES

ALEXANDER LEITCH, *Director*
CHAUNCEY BELKNAP, *Bicentennial Chief Marshal*
JOHN N. DURRIE, *Aide to Chief Marshal*

UNDERGRADUATE BICENTENNIAL COMMITTEE

William A. Chisolm '45, *Chairman*
Albridge C. Smith III '36, *ex officio*
Francis R. B. Godolphin '24, *ex officio*
David Gray '48, *Assistant Chairman*

DeWitt C. Jones, III '44
Allen F. Colley '45
Philip W. Bell '46
Judson Decker '46
Frazier D. MacIver, Jr. '47
Thomas F. Spoehr '47
Benjamin F. Houston, IV '48

ALUMNI ASSOCIATION REPRESENTATION

Director of Alumni Participation: Harold H. Helm '20
October Events: Edward E. Watts, Jr. '21
February Events: Robert M. Green '13
June Events: Clarence D. Kerr '01

OFFICERS AND MEMBERS OF THE GRADUATE COUNCIL

ALUMNI ASSOCIATION BICENTENNIAL CHAIRMEN

Alabama	Joseph F. Johnston '27
Northern California & Nevada	Robbins Milbank '25
Rocky Mountain	Farrington R. Carpenter '09
Connecticut Valley	Richard H. Valentine '11
Delaware	Jasper E. Crane '01
Washington, D.C.	Breckinridge Long '03
Southeastern Florida	James V. Johnson '03
Georgia	G. Arthur Howell, Jr. '39
Idaho	Pasco B. Carter '05
Chicago	John D. Ames '28
Indiana	Garvin Morris Brown '08
	Robert B. Failey '08
Central Kentucky	Jesse Herrmann '10
Louisiana	Wilmer J. Thomas '18
Maryland	Frank B. Ober '10
Northwest	Hugh W. Arthur '36
Kansas City	John C. Long '03
Hudson County	Alan H. Pendlebury '29

Montclair & Vicinity	F. H. Kingsbury, Jr. '29
Passaic, Paterson, & Ridgewood	George W. Warch '34
St. Louis	Donald D. Danforth '20
Northern New Jersey	John C. Kerr '96
Oranges & Maplewood	Ralph D. Osborne, Jr. '35
Trenton	James L. Martin '07
Broome County, N.Y.	Brewster W. Smith '33
New York	Montgomery B. Angell '11
Rochester & Vicinity	Percival D. Oviatt, Jr. '39
Schenectady	Martin S. McVay '22
Northern New York	Roger D. Sidford '29
Western New York	Thomas W. Mitchell '25
Central Ohio	Daniel A. Carmichael, Jr. '41
Northern Ohio	Ralph L. McGean '19
Southern Ohio	Frank Peabody '27
Youngstown	Wm. H. Yeckley '32
Oregon	Edmund Hayes '18
Central Pennsylvania	Edgar Z. Wallower '05 John McI. Smith '15
Erie	Spencer A. Sisson '12
Northeastern Pennsylvania	Bruce Payne '11
Philadelphia	John Bishop, vi '33
Western Pennsylvania	William H. Rea '34
Nashville & Middle Tennessee	R. Walter Hale, Jr. '27
Houston	William A. Kirkland '19
West Virginia	Joseph H. Gaines '86
Princeton Engineering Association	A. Donald Hay '39

HOUSING

B. Franklin Bunn, *Chairman*

Mrs. George C. Wintringer
Mrs. James Barnes
Mrs. Charles Browne
Luther P. Eisenhart
Howard Menand, Jr.

PHYSICAL ARRANGEMENTS AND DECORATION

Stephen F. Voorhees, *Chairman*

Sherley W. Morgan
George R. Meyers
E. A. MacMillan
John F. Bliss
Norvell B. Samuels

BICENTENNIAL COMMITTEES

RELIGIOUS ACTIVITIES

HENRY P. VAN DUSEN, *Chairman*

JOHN A. MACKAY
GEORGE F. THOMAS
ROBERT R. WICKS
E. HARRIS HARBISON

EXHIBITIONS

E. BALDWIN SMITH, *Chairman*

JULIAN P. BOYD
GLENN L. JEPSEN
DONALD D. EGBERT
EDMUND S. DELONG

MUSIC

ROY D. WELCH, *Chairman*
RANDALL THOMPSON
OLIVER STRUNK
RUSSELL A. COOK

PUBLIC RELATIONS

EDMUND S. DELONG, *Director*
JOHN C. WILLIAMS, *Chairman*
CALEB COFFIN, *Vice-Chairman*

FRANKLYN S. ADAMS
T. HART ANDERSON
LINCOLN K. BARNETT
EDWARD W. BARRETT
ROY S. DURSTINE
WILBUR FORREST
ALDEN D. GROFF
PAUL HOLLISTER
RUSSELL W. HOLMAN
ANDREW C. IMBRIE
JAMES KERNEY, JR.
EDWARD JOHN NOBLE
STERLING NOEL
WILLIAM S. PALEY
MORGAN S. A. REICHNER
NORVELL B. SAMUELS

PUBLICATIONS

DATUS C. SMITH, JR., *Chairman*

JULIAN P. BOYD
J. DOUGLAS BROWN
E. HARRIS HARBISON
DENVER LINDLEY

Bicentennial Executive Staff

ARTHUR E. FOX, *Director*

Executive Assistants

H. Nevin Gehman, Howard Menand, Norvell B. Samuels, Dorothy Hunt Smith

Staff

Bernice R. Baldini, Anna H. Clement, Elizabeth D. Connelly, A. Gloria Davison, Margaret W. Frantz, Evelyne M. Harper, Madge P. Harper, Katie L. Horn, Carolyn B. Munro, Mary E. Wall

Former Staff Members

Edna C. Carreck, Ann Honore, Florence V. Horner, Dorothy D. Storey, Mildred Van Overen, C. K. Wallace, Catherine C. Welch

3

Government Participation

UNITED STATES COMMISSION

THE PRESIDENT OF THE UNITED STATES, *Honorary Chairman*

JAMES FORRESTAL
ERNEST J. KING
BRECKINRIDGE LONG
GEORGE C. MARSHALL

UNITED STATES SENATE

ARTHUR H. VANDENBERG, *ex officio*
ALBEN W. BARKLEY
ALBERT W. HAWKES
WILLIS ROBERTSON
H. ALEXANDER SMITH, *Commission Chairman*

HOUSE OF REPRESENTATIVES

JOSEPH W. MARTIN, JR., *ex officio*
W. GRESHAM ANDREWS
MICHAEL E. FEIGHAN
RALPH A. GAMBLE, *Commission Secretary*
FRANK A. MATHEWS, JR.

NEW JERSEY COMMISSION

ALFRED E. DRISCOLL, *Honorary Chairman*
JOHN H. BOSSHART
CLARENCE E. CASE

SENATE

CHARLES K. BARTON, *ex officio*
C. WESLEY ARMSTRONG
H. RIVINGTON PYNE

ASSEMBLY

LEON LEONARD, *ex officio*
DUANE E. MINARD
BERNARD W. VOGEL

PRINCETON COMMISSION

MINOT C. MORGAN JR., *ex officio*
IRVING W. MERSHON, *Chairman*

B. FRANKLIN BUNN
B. WOODHULL DAVIS
HAROLD M. HINKSON
JAMES PACE
JOSEPH J. REDDING

[Public Law 367—79th Congress]
[Chapter 233—2d Session]
[H. J. Res. 331]

JOINT RESOLUTION

To authorize suitable participation by the United States in the observance of the two-hundredth anniversary of the founding of Princeton University.

Whereas there are to be held at Princeton, New Jersey, and at other places, during the academic year beginning September 22, 1946, and ending June 17, 1947, ceremonies, convocations, and conferences commemorating the two-hundredth anniversary of the founding of Princeton University; and

Whereas such ceremonies, convocations, and conferences will be devoted to applying, in consultation with scholars throughout the world, our common skills, knowledge, and wisdom to the reconsideration of the fundamental obligations of higher learning to human society, with a view to contributing to the advancement of the comity of all nations and to the building of a free and peaceful world; and

Whereas Nassau Hall, for two centuries the traditional center of the university, is intimately associated with the earliest days of the Republic, having been alternately occupied by British and American troops and seriously damaged, and having then become temporarily the seat of the National Government in 1783 upon the removal of the Congress from Philadelphia to Princeton, and having been the site of the reception by Congress of the first properly accredited minister from abroad to the United States of America; and

Whereas graduates of Princeton were signers of the Declaration of Independence; and

Whereas alumni of Princeton played a distinctive part in the drafting and adoption of the Constitution of the United States; James Madison having taken the lead in the calling of the Constitutional Convention and in shaping and procuring the ratification of the document, and more alumni of Princeton than of any other college having been members of the Convention; and

Whereas many Princeton men have served with distinction in the executive, judicial, and legislative branches of the Government of the United States; and

Whereas Princeton has given to the United States of America two great Presidents and to the world two great contributors to the cause of human freedom, namely James Madison and Woodrow Wilson; and

Whereas since its founding Princeton has dedicated itself to the ideals of freedom in thought and in spirit; and

Whereas at the end of its second century and the beginning of its third it has, through its president, trustees, and faculty rededicated itself to such ideals: Therefore be it

Resolved by the Senate and House of Representatives of the United States of America in Congress assembled, That the Government and the people of the United States unite with Princeton University in a fitting and appropriate observance of the two-hundredth anniversary of its founding.

Sec. 2. There is hereby established a commission to be known as the United States Princeton University Bicentennial Commission (hereinafter referred to as the "Commission") to be composed of fifteen Commissioners, as follows: The President of the United States and four persons to be appointed by him, the President of the Senate and four Members of the Senate to be appointed by the President of the Senate, and the Speaker of the House of Representatives and four Members of the House to be appointed by the Speaker. Any vacancies occurring in the membership of the Commission shall be filled in the same manner in which original appointments to such Commission are made.

Sec. 3. The Commission, on behalf of the United States, shall cooperate with the representatives of Princeton University, the State of New Jersey, and the Borough of Princeton, New Jersey, in the appropriate observance of such anniversary, and shall extend appropriate courtesies to the delegates of foreign universities and other foreign learned bodies, or individuals, attending the celebrations as guests of Princeton University. The Commission is authorized in performing its functions under this section to utilize the services and facilities of the various agencies and instrumentalities of the United States, with the consent of such agencies and instrumentalities.

Sec. 4. The members of the Commission shall serve without compensation. They shall select a chairman and a secretary from among their number, but the President of the United States shall be designated as the honorary chairman of the Commission.

Approved April 26, 1946.

J.R. #2 P.L. 1946
State of New Jersey

A Joint Resolution relating to the bicentennial of Princeton University, and providing for a State commission with certain duties and powers in connection therewith.

Whereas, Princeton University, the first college to be founded in the Middle Colonies and originally known as the College of New Jersey, received its first charter on October twenty-second, one thousand seven hundred and forty-six, and is preparing to observe the bicentennial thereof; and

Whereas, The said charter, to which on the day and year aforesaid the Great Seal of the Province of New Jersey was affixed by John Hamilton, then serving as Governor of the Province, antedates by nearly a third of a century the establishment of independent government in New Jersey; and

Whereas, Princeton University, during its two centuries of service as an institution of learning, has enriched the intellectual life of people not only in New Jersey but throughout the world, and because of its renown in the field of higher education has brought appreciable distinction to this State; and

Whereas, The Princeton University bicentenary celebration will extend through the academic year beginning September, one thousand nine hundred and forty-six, and ending June, one thousand nine hundred and forty-seven, and, in a manner appropriate to the times as well as to the occasion, will feature the assembling at Princeton of the world's great scholars in a series of conferences treating with the advancement of learning and the welfare of society throughout the world; and

Whereas, It is the sense of this Legislature that there should be accorded to Princeton University the sovereign recognition it merits for its salutary influence upon the history of this State and upon the life of the people, and also for its outstanding contributions to education generally; and that the State should co-operate in every desirable manner towards the complete observance of the bicentennial of said University; now, therefore,

BE IT RESOLVED *by the Senate and General Assembly of the State of New Jersey:*

1. A commission is hereby created, which shall be known as the New Jersey State Commission for the Princeton University Bicentennial and which shall consist of nine members. The Governor, the President of the Senate, and the Speaker of the General Assembly shall be members ex officio of the commission and shall each, within ten days after this joint resolution takes effect, appoint two persons to be members thereof for the time the commission shall remain in existence. The six persons so appointed may, but need not, be members of the Legislature. Members of the commission shall serve without compensation. Any vacancy occurring from any cause shall be filled by appointment by the Governor, and members so appointed shall serve for the balance of the time the commission shall remain in existence.

2. The Commission shall organize by the selection of a chairman and a secretary from among its members, but the Governor shall be designated honorary chairman.

3. It shall be the duty of the commission formally to convey to the President and Trustees of Princeton University, at such time during the bicentennial celebration period as shall be deemed opportune for the purpose, the greetings and felicitations of the State of New Jersey. It shall also be the duty of the commission to extend appropriate greetings and courtesies to scholars, delegates of universities and colleges, and others who, at the invitation of Princeton University, may participate in or attend the bicentennial ceremonies throughout the celebration period. It shall further be the duty of the commission to co-operate with the representatives of said University and of the borough of Princeton so that the celebration activities of the commission may be properly co-ordinated with those of the University and the borough.

4. The commission shall have authority otherwise to unite, on behalf of the State, with Princeton University and others in the observance of said bicentennial; and to request of the head of any department of the State Government co-operation in any manner the commission may deem necessary or feasible to effectuate the purposes of this joint resolution, and all heads of departments shall have the duty of complying with all such requests.

5. This joint resolution shall take effect immediately.

Approved April 8, 1946.

Proclamation by the Governor of New Jersey of the Observance of the Bicentennial Year

I WALTER E. EDGE, Governor of the State of New Jersey, do hereby make public proclamation of this great event in New Jersey history, and

I HEREBY enjoin and urge all agencies and departments of the State Government and our municipal and county governments, our educational institutions, churches and civic organizations to take just pride in the accomplishments of Princeton's distinguished past and its part in the development of this great state and nation, and

FURTHER, I suggest that all citizens show their interest and cooperation in this bicentennial program and the significance of this great academic convocation of the post-war era as representing the real road to a just and lasting peace.

GIVEN, under my hand and the Great Seal of the State of New Jersey this nineteenth day of October in the year of Our Lord nineteen hundred and forty-six and in the Independence of the United States the one hundred and seventy-first,

WALTER E. EDGE
Governor

SECRETARY OF STATE
LLOYD B. MARSH

4

List of Delegates
from Colleges, Universities, Academies and Other Educational Institutions

Processional No.	*Date of Founding*	
310	1889	Agnes Scott College, Dean S. G. Stukes
262	1871	University of Akron, Dean Donfred H. Gardner
265	1872	University of Alabama, Dean Marten ten Hoor
135	1836	Alfred University, Mr. Asa F. Randolph
60	1780	American Academy of Arts and Sciences, Dr. Howard M. Jones
328	1894	American Academy in Rome, Mr. Randall Thompson
378	1917	American College of Surgeons, Dr. Allen O. Whipple
380	1918	American Council on Education, Dr. George F. Zook
383	1919	American Council of Learned Societies, Dr. Richard H. Shryock
249	1869	American Museum of Natural History, Dr. Albert E. Parr
48	1743	American Philosophical Society, Dr. Thomas S. Gates
323	1893	American University, Chancellor Paul F. Douglass
101	1821	Amherst College, Dean C. Scott Porter
85	1808	Andover Newton Theological School, The Reverend Professor Austin P. Guiles
189	1853	Antioch College, Dr. Austin M. Patterson
373	1915	Association of American Colleges, Dr. Guy E. Snaveley
220	1864	Bates College, President Charles F. Phillips
164	1846	Beloit College, President Carey Croneis
403	1932	Bennington College, Dr. Peter F. Drucker
199	1855	Berea College, President Francis S. Hutchins

Processional No.	*Date of Founding*	
348	1904	Berkeley Baptist Divinity School, The Reverend President Sandford Fleming
152	1840	Bethany College, President Wilbur H. Cramblet
243	1868	Bloomfield College and Seminary, The Reverend President Frederick Schweitzer
263	1871	Bonebrake Theological Seminary, The Reverend President Walter N. Roberts
217	1863	Boston College, The Very Reverend William L. Keleher, S.J.
149	1839	Boston University, Dr. John Philip Mason
73	1794	Bowdoin College, President Kenneth C. M. Sills
401	1930	Brooklyn College, Dr. Harris F. MacNeish
51	1764	Brown University, Dean Samuel T. Arnold
293	1885	Bryn Mawr College, President Katharine E. McBride
165	1846	Bucknell University, President Herbert L. Spencer
166	1846	University of Buffalo, Chancellor Samuel P. Capen
316	1891	California Institute of Technology, Dr. Theodore von Karman
244	1868	University of California, President Robert G. Sproul
179	1850	Capital University, The Reverend President Harold L. Yochum
233	1866	Carleton College, Dr. Arthur Mizener
360	1911	Carnegie Corporation of New York, Dr. Howard J. Savage
349	1905	Carnegie Foundation for the Advancement of Teaching, Dr. Howard J. Savage
338	1900	Carnegie Institute of Technology, Dr. Robert F. Mehl
344	1902	Carnegie Institution of Washington, Dr. Vannevar Bush
167	1846	Carroll College, President Nelson V. Russell
253	1870	Carthage College, Dr. James Sterenberg
284	1880	Case School of Applied Science, President William E. Wickenden
303	1887	Catholic University of America, Dean Martin Rawson Patrick McGuire
54	1770	College of Charleston, President George D. Grice

Processional No.	*Date of Founding*	
298	1886	University of Chattanooga, President David A. Lockmiller
317	1891	University of Chicago, President Ernest C. Colwell
200	1855	Chicago Theological Seminary, The Reverend President Arthur C. McGiffert, Jr.
304	1887	Clark University, President Howard B. Jefferson
95	1819	University of Cincinnati, President Raymond Walters
333	1898	Clemson Agricultural College, President Robert F. Poole
370	1913	Cleveland Museum of Art, Dr. William M. Milliken
90	1813	Colby College, The Reverend President Julius S. Bixler
96	1819	Colgate University, President Everett N. Case
270	1874	Colorado College, President Thurston Davies
276	1876	University of Colorado, Dr. E. F. D'Arms
50	1754	Columbia University, Acting President Frank D. Fackenthal
361	1911	Connecticut College for Women, President Rosemary Park
285	1881	University of Connecticut, Dr. John B. Lucke
212	1859	Cooper Union, Dr. Garrett Mattingly
225	1865	Cornell University, President Edmund E. Day
281	1878	Creighton University, The Reverend President William H. McCabe, S.J.
245	1868	Crozer Theological Seminary, The Reverend President Edwin E. Aubrey
53	1769	Dartmouth College, President John S. Dickey
140	1837	Davidson College, President John R. Cunningham
127	1833	University of Delaware, Dean Francis H. Squire
120	1831	Denison University, President Kenneth I. Brown
221	1864	University of Denver, Dr. Donald H. Menzel
141	1837	DePauw University, Mr. Bernard Kilgore
279	1877	University of Detroit, The Reverend Dr. Samuel K. Wilson, S.J.
56	1773	Dickinson College, The Reverend President William W. Edel
379	1917	Cleveland H. Dodge Foundation, Inc., Dr. Cleveland E. Dodge

Processional No.	Date of Founding	
237	1867	Drew University, The Reverend President Arlo A. Brown
318	1891	Drexel Institute of Technology, President James Creese
147	1838	Duke University, Professor Malcolm McDermott
282	1878	Duquesne University, The Reverend President Francis P. Smith, C.S.Sp.
201	1855	Elmira College, President William S. A. Pott
136	1836	Emory University, President Goodrich C. White
226	1865	Fisk University, President Charles S. Johnson
206	1857	Florida State University, President Doak S. Campbell
191	1853	University of Florida, Dr. Robert F. Davidson
156	1841	Fordham University, The Reverend Demetrius B. Zema, S.J.
68	1787	Franklin and Marshall College, President Theodore A. Distler
111	1826	Furman University, President John L. Plyler
345	1902	General Education Board, Dr. Raymond B. Fosdick
174	1848	Geneva College, Dr. Georgiana Wylie
103	1821	George Washington University, Dean Henry Grattan Doyle
69	1789	Georgetown University, The Very Reverend President Lawrence C. Gorman, S.J.
227	1865	Georgia School of Technology, President Emeritus Marion L. Brittain
66	1785	University of Georgia, Dean G. H. Boyd
352	1908	Georgian Court College, The Reverend President M. Mary John Considine
124	1832	Gettysburg College, President Henry W. A. Hanson
294	1885	Goucher College, President David A. Robertson
277	1876	Grove City College, President Weir C. Ketler
88	1812	Hamilton College, The Reverend Dr. Robert R. Wicks
57	1776	Hampden-Sydney College, Dean David C. Wilson
130	1834	Hartford Seminary Foundation, The Reverend President Russell H. Stafford
34	1636	Harvard University, President James B. Conant, Provost Paul H. Buck, Dean A. Chester Hanford

Processional No.	Date of Founding	
128	1833	Haverford College, President Gilbert F. White
325	1893	Headmasters Association, The Reverend Dr. Walden Pell, II
180	1850	Hiram College, President Paul H. Fall
157	1843	College of the Holy Cross, The Reverend Dr. William J. Healy, S.J.
238	1867	Howard University, President Mordecai W. Johnson
254	1870	Hunter College, President George N. Shuster
319	1891	College of Idaho, President William W. Hall, Jr.
118	1829	Illinois College, Dr. Edward M. Collins
321	1892	Illinois Institute of Technology, Dean John D. Larkin
239	1867	University of Illinois, Dr. Ernest L. Bogart
100	1820	Indiana University, Dr. Norman T. Pratt
402	1930	Institute for Advanced Study, Dr. Frank Aydelotte
384	1919	Institute of International Education, Dr. Edgar J. Fisher
170	1847	State University of Iowa, President Virgil M. Hancher
240	1867	Johns Hopkins University, Vice President Lowell J. Reed
228	1865	University of Kansas, Dr. Clara W. Nigg
229	1865	University of Kentucky, President Herman L. Donovan
106	1824	Kenyon College, President Gordon K. Chalmers
143	1837	Knox College, Mr. Victor Elting
112	1826	Lafayette College, The Reverend President Ralph C. Hutchinson
208	1857	Lake Forest College, President Ernest A. Johnson
230	1865	Lehigh University, President Martin D. Whitaker
79	1800	Library of Congress, Dr. Luther H. Evans
197	1854	Lincoln University, President Horace M. Bond
192	1853	Louisville Presbyterian Seminary, The Reverend President Frank H. Caldwell
113	1826	Lutheran Theological Seminary, Gettysburg, Pennsylvania, The Reverend Dr. Harry F. Baughman
222	1864	Lutheran Theological Seminary, Mt. Airy, Philadelphia, Pa., The Reverend President Paul J. Hoh
295	1885	Macalester College, President Charles J. Turck

Processional No.	Date of Founding	
231	1865	University of Maine, President Arthur A. Hauck
193	1853	Manhattan College, The Reverend President B. Thomas
134	1835	Marietta College, The Honorable George White, President William A. Shimer
84	1807	University of Maryland, Dean H. F. Cotterman
97	1819	Maryville College, President Ralph W. Lloyd
71	1791	Massachusetts Historical Society, Dr. Charles H. McIlwain
215	1861	Massachusetts Institute of Technology, Professor John E. Burchard
241	1867	University of Massachusetts, Dr. Charles F. Fraker
255	1870	Metropolitan Museum of Art, Dr. Francis H. Taylor
299	1886	Michigan College of Mining and Technology, President Grover C. Dillman
202	1855	Michigan State College, President John A. Hannah
93	1817	University of Michigan, Vice President Marvin L. Niehuss
80	1800	Middlebury College, President Samuel S. Stratton
350	1905	Milbank Memorial Fund, Dr. Clyde V. Kiser
183	1851	University of Minnesota, Vice-President Malcolm M. Willey
114	1826	Mississippi College, President Dotson M. Nelson
150	1839	University of Missouri, Vice President Thomas A. Brady
326	1893	University of Montana, Chancellor Ernest O. Melby
47	1742	Moravian College for Women, Dean Edith J. Stauffer
144	1837	Mount Holyoke College, President Roswell G. Ham
168	1846	Mount Union College, President Charles B. Ketcham
175	1848	Muhlenberg College, President Levering Tyson
256	1870	Museum of Fine Arts, Boston, Dr. Edward J. Holmes
145	1837	Muskingum College, The Reverend Robert P. Montgomery
218	1863	National Academy of Sciences, Dean Luther P. Eisenhart

Processional No.	*Date of Founding*	
405	1934	National Archives, Dr. Solon J. Buck
407	1937	National Gallery of Art, Dr. David E. Finley
65	1784	New Brunswick Theological Seminary, The Reverend President Joseph R. Sizoo
235	1866	University of New Hampshire, President Harold W. Stoke
203	1855	New Jersey State Teacher Colleges, President Harry A. Sprague
171	1847	College of the City of New York, Dr. Nelson P. Mead
121	1831	New York University, Chancellor Harry W. Chase
286	1881	Newark College of Engineering, President Allan R. Cullimore
70	1789	University of North Carolina, President Frank P. Graham
314	1890	North Dakota Agricultural College, Dr. W. C. Hunter
312	1889	University of North Dakota, Mr. William S. Holmes
334	1898	Northeastern University, President Carl S. Ell
185	1851	Northwestern University, Vice President Fred D. Fagg, Jr.
158	1842	University of Notre Dame, The Reverend Charles J. Mahony C.S.C.
129	1833	Oberlin College, President William E. Stevenson
258	1870	Ohio State University, Dr. Henry R. Spencer
83	1804	Ohio University, President John C. Baker
410	1941	Oklahoma Agricultural and Mechanical College, President Henry G. Bennett
315	1890	University of Oklahoma, Dr. Joseph A. Brandt
246	1868	Oregon State College, Dr. Walther H. Ott
267	1872	University of Oregon, Dr. Allen H. Eaton
172	1847	Otterbein College, The Reverend President J. Gordon Howard
274	1875	Park College, President George I. Rohrbough
204	1855	Pennsylvania State College, President Ralph D. Hetzel
46	1740	University of Pennsylvania, President George W. McClelland

Processional No.	*Date of Founding*	
58	1776	Phi Beta Kappa, Dr. Christian Gauss
74	1794	Pittsburgh-Xenia Theological Seminary, The Reverend Dr. H. Ray Shear
195	1854	Polytechnic Institute of Brooklyn, President Harry S. Rogers
306	1887	Pomona College, Dr. Frank W. Pitman
307	1887	Pratt Institute, President Charles Pratt
89	1812	Princeton Theological Seminary, The Reverend President John A. Mackay
347	1903	University of Puerto Rico, Dr. José Padin
308	1888	College of Puget Sound, The Reverend Everett F. Hallock
250	1869	Purdue University, Dean W. L. Ayres
210	1857	Queens College, Charlotte, North Carolina, President Hunter B. Blakely
408	1937	Queens College, Flushing, New York, President Paul Klapper
119	1830	Randolph-Macon College, President J. Earl Moreland
327	1893	Randolph-Macon Woman's College, President Theodore H. Jack
411	1941	Radio Corporation of America Laboratories, Mr. Elmer W. Engstrom
355	1909	University of Redlands, Dr. J. Russell Andrus
364	1911	Reed College, Dr. Blair Stewart
107	1824	Rensselaer Polytechnic Institute, President Livingston W. Houston
322	1892	Rhode Island State College, President Carl R. Woodward
367	1912	Rice Institute, President William V. Houston
125	1832	University of Richmond, President George M. Modlin
232	1865	Rider College, President Franklin F. Moore
186	1851	Ripon College, President Clark G. Kuebler
371	1913	Rockefeller Foundation, Dr. Raymond B. Fosdick
341	1901	Rockefeller Institute for Medical Research (New York), Dr. Warfield T. Longcope
342	1901	Rockefeller Institute for Medical Research (Princeton), Dr. Carl TenBroeck

Processional No.	*Date of Founding*	
173	1847	Rockford College, President Mary A. Cheek
296	1885	Rollins College, Dean Wendell C. Stone
376	1916	Russell Sage College, Dr. Bernice Smith
377	1916	Russell Sage Foundation, Dr. Shelby M. Harrison
52	1766	Rutgers University, President Robert C. Clothier
104	1822	Colleges of the Seneca, Dean James W. Bunting
205	1856	Seton Hall College, The Right Reverend President James F. Kelley
287a	1881	Society of Sigma Xi, Dr. Harlow Shapley
337	1899	Simmons College, Vice President J. Garton Needham
363	1911	Skidmore College, President Henry T. Moore
264	1871	Smith College, President Herbert J. Davis
169	1846	Smithsonian Institution, Dr. Alexander Wetmore
211	1857	University of the South, Dean George M. Baker
176	1848	Southwestern University, President Charles E. Diehl
81	1801	University of South Carolina, Dean Wilford H. Calcott
365	1911	Southern Methodist University, Dr. John W. Bowyer
336	1899	College of St. Elizabeth, Dr. Frank W. Naggi
40	1696	St. John's College, Acting President John S. Kieffer
269	1872	St. Peter's College, The Reverend President Vincent J. Hart, S.J.
297	1885	Stanford University, The Honorable Herbert Hoover
259	1870	Stevens Institute of Technology, President Harvey N. Davis
224	1864	Swarthmore College, Vice President James A. Perkins
343	1901	Sweet Briar College, President Martha B. Lucas
260	1870	Syracuse University, Chancellor William P. Tolley
291	1884	Temple University, President Robert L. Johnson
392	1923	Texas Technological College, President William M. Whyburn
412	1942	Textile Research Institute, Dr. John H. Dillon
110	1825	Theological Seminary of the Evangelical and Reformed Church, The Reverend Dr. Allen S. Meck

Processional No.	*Date of Founding*	
61	1780	Transylvania College, The Reverend President Raymond F. McLain
105	1823	Trinity College, President Keith Funston
188	1852	Tufts College, President Leonard Carmichael
132	1834	Tulane University, Dr. Joseph C. Morris
75	1794	Tusculum College, President George K. Davies
287	1881	Tuskegee Institute, Dr. Clarence T. Mason
78	1795	Union College, President Carter Davidson
137	1836	Union Theological Seminary, The Reverend President Henry P. Van Dusen
278	1876	United States Coast Guard Academy, Rear Admiral James Pine, USCG
82	1802	United States Military Academy, Colonel Boyd W. Bartlett, U.S.A.
162	1845	United States Naval Academy, Rear Admiral James L. Holloway, Jr., USN
251	1869	Ursinus College, President Norman E. McClure
309	1888	Utah State Agricultural College, President Franklin S. Harris
181	1850	University of Utah, President Albert R. Olpin
213	1859	Valparaiso University, The Reverend President Otto P. Kretzmann
216	1861	Vassar College, President Sarah G. Blanding
159	1842	Villanova College, The Reverend President Francis X. N. McGuire
151	1839	Virginia Military Institute, Brigadier General Stewart W. Anderson
98	1819	University of Virginia, Dr. Thomas J. Wertenbaker
126	1832	Wabash College, Dr. Lee McCanliss
404	1933	Walters Art Gallery, Mr. Edward S. King
63	1782	Washington College, President Gilbert W. Mead
62	1780	Washington and Jefferson College, President James H. Case, Jr.
49	1749	Washington and Lee University, Dean Lucius J. Desha
315a	1890	Washington State College, Dr. Lyle G. Gilbertson
194	1853	Washington University, Chancellor Arthur H. Compton
247	1868	Wayne University, Dean Arthur Neef

Processional No.	*Date of Founding*	
261	1870	Wellesley College, President Mildred M. Horton
248	1868	Wells College, Dean Evelyn C. Rusk
122	1831	Wesleyan University, Dr. John C. Blankenagel
292	1844	Western Theological Seminary, The Reverend President John R. Mulder
396	1925	Westminster Choir College, The Reverend Vice President W. Edward Jordan
290	1882	Westminster Theological Seminary, The Reverend President Lester A. Welliver
214	1860	Wheaton College, The Reverend Mr. M. Allen Kimble
177a	1849	William Jewell College, Mr. Judson W. Jones
39	1693	College of William and Mary, President John E. Pomfret
72	1793	Williams College, Dr. Freman Foote
252	1869	Wilson College, President Paul S. Havens
177	1848	University of Wisconsin, Dr. George H. Brown
163	1845	Wittenberg College, The Reverend Dr. Roy S. Bowers
198	1854	Wofford College, Dr. William B. Hunter, Jr.
42	1701	Yale University, President Charles Seymour, Provost Edgar S. Furniss, Dean William C. DeVane

Delegates from Foreign Universities and Academies

ARGENTINA

27	1613	Universidad Nacional de Córdoba, His Excellency, the Ambassador from Argentina, Oscar Ivanissevich

AUSTRALIA

190	1853	University of Melbourne, The Envoy Extraordinary and Minister Plenipotentiary from Australia, the Honorable Alfred Stirling
356	1910	University of Queensland, Dr. Douglas Harry Kedgwin Lee

Processional No.	*Date of Founding*	
178	1850	University of Sydney, Vice-Chancellor Archibald K. McIntyre
		BELGIUM
55	1772	Académie Royale des Sciences des Lettres et des Beaux-Arts de Belgique, Dr. Harlow Shapley, Dr. Edwin G. Conklin
123	1832	Université Libre de Bruxelles, Dr. George Boas
92	1816	Université de Liège, Dr. J. D. H. Donnay
10	1425	Université Catholique de Louvain, Dr. Edgar G. Gillon
139	1837	Faculté Polytechnique de Mons, Professor Richard Vincotte
99	1820	Rijksuniversiteit te Gent, Dr. N. Goormaghtigh
		BRAZIL
375	1916	Academia Brasileira de Ciencias, Dr. Alvaro Alberto da Motta
115	1827	Universidade de São Paolo, Professor Paulo Sawaya, Professor Ernesto de Moraes Leme, Professor Paul Hugon
		BURMA
387	1920	University of Rangoon, Dr. G. E. Gates
		CANADA
146	1838	Acadia University, Dr. Frederick S. Goucher
359	1911	University of Alberta, Mr. G. Allen Mail
372	1914	University of British Columbia, Dr. Otis J. Todd
94	1818	Dalhousie University, Dr. Roy D. McNutt
187	1852	Université Laval, The Right Reverend Alphonse-Marie Parent, Dean Paul E. Gagnon
102	1821	McGill University, Dr. Walter W. Colpitts
302	1887	McMaster University, Dean Charles E. Burke
275	1876	Université de Montréal, The Right Reverend Rector Olivier Maurault
154	1841	Queen's University, Dr. W. E. McNeill
288	1882	Royal Society of Canada, Dr. David A. Keys
116	1827	University of Toronto, Principal W. R. Taylor

Processional No.	Date of Founding	
		CHINA
400	1928	Academia Sinica, Dr. Y. R. Chao
374	1915	Ginling College, Dr. Ruth M. Chester
369	1913	Hua Chung University, The Reverend Dr. Arthur M. Sherman
324	1893	Lingnan University, Lt. Col. Harold B. Hoskins
332	1898	National Nankai University, Dr. Chih Meng
335	1898	National Peking University, Professor Ch'ang-p'ei Lo
366	1912	National Tsing Hua University, Dr. Fung Yu-lan
399	1926	National WuHan University, Professor Yung-ching Yeh
283	1879	St. John's University, Professor Ellis N. Tucker
357	1910	West China Union University, Chancellor Joseph Beech
311	1889	Yenching University, Dr. T. C. Chao
		COLOMBIA
236	1867	Universidad Nacional de Colombia, Dr. Eduardo Guzmán-Esponda, Dr. Rubén García
		COSTA RICA
409	1940	Universidad de Costa Rica, Rector Fernando Baudrit
		CZECHOSLOVAKIA
6	1348	Karlova Universita, Rector Dr. Bohumil Bydžovský
65a	1784	Česká Akademie věd a Urnění, Rector Dr. Bohumil Bydžovský
		DENMARK
117	1829	Polytekniske Laereanstalt, Dr. Harald Trap Friis
41	1700	Kongelige Danske Videnskabernes Selskab, Dr. Heinz Holter
		DOMINICAN REPUBLIC
20	1538	Universidad de Santo Domingo, His Excellency, the Ambassador from the Dominican Republic, Julio Ortega Frier

Processional No.	Date of Founding	
		ECUADOR
29	1622	Universidad Central, Dr. Neptalí Ponce
		EGYPT
351	1908	Farouk I University, Vice-Rector, Dr. Mahmoud Sami Guenena Bey
		EIRE
358	1910	National University of Ireland, Dr. Vincent Hurley
67	1785	Royal Irish Academy, Professor John L. Synge
160	1845	University College, Cork, Dr. Michael V. Hurley
24	1593	Trinity College, Dublin, Mr. Francis C. Coulter
354	1909	University College, Dublin, Dr. F. D. Murnaghan
		EL SALVADOR
155	1841	Universidad Autonoma de El Salvador, Dr. Luis E. Chaparro
		FINLAND
351a	1908	Suomalainen Tiedeakatemia, The Honorable K. I. Jutila, The Minister from Finland
		FRANCE
30a	1635	Académie Française, Mr. François Charles-Roux
37	1663	Académie des Inscriptions et Belles Lettres, Dr. Jeremiah D. M. Ford
38	1666	Académie des Sciences, President M. L. Blaringhem
76	1795	Académie des Sciences Morales et Politiques, Professor Gilbert Chinard, Dr. Jacques Rueff, Professor Paul Bastid
16	1530	Collège de France, Dr. André Grabar
33	1636	École Nationale des Beaux-Arts, Mr. Julian Clarence Levi
77	1795	École Normale Supérieure, Dr. Pierre Samuel
271	1875	Université d'Alger, Dr. Paul Queney
272	1875	Université Catholique de L'Ouest d'Angers, Professor Catta
11	1447	Université de Bordeaux, Dr. Jean Dufrenoy
17	1530	Université de Lille, Professor Jean Simon

Processional No.	*Date of Founding*	
280	1877	Université Catholique de Lille, Dr. Léon Legrain
86	1808	Université de Lyon, Dr. Clinton J. Davisson
196	1854	Université de Nancy, Dean Jean Delsarte
2	XIII CENT.	Université de Paris, Professor Henri Seyrig, Professor Georges Daux
5	XIII CENT.	Université de Toulouse, Dr. Orville W. Mosher
31	1635	Muséum National d'Histoire Naturelle, Dr. Achille Urbain

GREECE

397	1926	Academy of Athens, Dr. John Kalitsounakis
142	1837	University of Athens, Dr. John Kalitsounakis
398	1926	University of Salonica, Mr. John D. Kallerghis, Greek General Consul

HUNGARY

19	1538	Magyar Királyi Tisza István Tudományegyetem Debrecen (Royal Hungarian "Stephen Tisza" University of Debrecen), Dr. Béla Vasady
33	1635	Magyar Királyi Pázmány Péter Tudományegyetem (Royal Hungarian "Péter Pázmány" University of Sciences), Dr. Paul H. Schiller
44	1726	Magyar Királyi Jozsef Nádor Müegyetem (Royal Hungarian Palatine-Joseph University of Technical and Economic Sciences), Professor Géza Zemplén
266	1872	Magyar Királyi Ferenca Jozsef Tudományegyetem Szeged (Royal Hungarian "Francis Joseph" University), Dr. John von Neumann

ICELAND

362	1911	Háskoli Íslands, Dr. Niels Dungal

INDIA

305	1887	University of Allahabad, Professor P. E. Dustoor
394	1925	Andhra University, Dr. Subharamish Minakshisundaram
207	1857	University of Calcutta, Vice Chancellor Banerjee

Processional No.	Date of Founding	
389	1922	University of Delhi, His Excellency, the Ambassador from India, Dr. Asaf Ali
289	1882	University of the Panjab, Dr. F. Mowbray Velte
182	1851	University of Madras, Professor M. S. Sundaram
		IRAQ
385	1919	University of Baghdad, President R. W. LaShaum
		ITALY
26	1605	Accademia Nazionale dei Lincei, Professor Giorgio Levi della Vida, His Excellency Dr. Giovanni Giorgi
7	1361	Universitá di Pavia, Professor Carlo Alberti
5a	1303	Universitá di Roma, Professor Giorgio Levi della Vida
5b	1321	Universitá di Firenze, Professor Renzo Rava
		JUGOSLAVIA
25	1596	Univerza v Ljubljana, Dean Božidar Lavrič
		LEBANON
234	1866	American University at Beirut, Dean Harold W. Close
273	1875	Université Saint Joseph, The Reverend Henri Charles
		NETHERLANDS
184	1851	Koninklijke Nederlandsche Akademie van Wetenschappen, Dr. H. A. Kramers
30	1632	Universiteit van Amsterdam, Professor S. van Creveld, Professor A. M. J. F. Michels
157a	1842	Technische Hoogeschool te Delft, Dr. H. A. Kramers
28	1615	Rijksuniversiteit te Groningen, Dr. H. A. Kramers
22	1575	Rijksuniversiteit te Leiden, Dr. H. A. Kramers
390	1923	Roomsch-Katholieke Universiteit te Nijmegen, The Reverend Peter Mommersteeg
35	1636	Rijks-Universiteit te Utrecht, Professor H. M. H. A. van der Valk

Processional No.	*Date of Founding*	
		NEW ZEALAND
242	1867	Royal Society of New Zealand, Mr. James A. D. Nash
257	1870	University of New Zealand, The Minister from New Zealand, the Honorable Sir Carl Berendsen
330	1897	Victoria University College, Sir Carl Berendsen
		NICARAGUA
90a	1815	Universidad de Léon, Dr. Jose H. Montalváee
		NORWAY
108	1825	Bergens Museum, Dr. Bjørn Trumpy
209	1857	Norske Videnskaps-Akademi i Oslo, Dr. Olaf Devik
393	1924	Instituttet for Sammenlignende Kulturforskning Dr. Gutorm Gjessing
87	1811	Kongelige Frederiks Universitet (Oslo), Dean Torleif Dale
339	1900	Norges Tekniske Høgskole (Trondheim), Dr. Ole Singstad
		PALESTINE
395	1925	Hebrew University, Professor L. Farkas
		PANAMA
406	1936	Universidad de Panamá, Dr. Diógenes A. Arosemena
		PHILIPPINES
353	1908	University of the Philippines, His Excellency Dr. Carlos P. Romulo
15	1525	University of Santo Tomás, Dr. Edmundo A. Reyes
		POLAND
268	1872	Polska Akademia Umiejetności, Dr. Oswald Veblen
381	1918	Katolicki Uniwersytet Lubelski Polonii, Dr. Adolf Tymczak
8	1364	Uniwersytetu Jagiellonskiego w Krakowie, Dr. Waclaw Lednicki

Processional No.	*Date of Founding*	
22a	1579	Uniwersytet Mikolaja Kopernika w Toruniu, Dr. Manfred Kridl
		Uniwersytet i Politechnika, Wroclaw, Dr. Hugo Steinhaus
		PORTUGAL
4a	1290	Universidade de Coimbra, Dr. Manuel Neto Murta
59	1779	Academia das Ciências de Lisboa, Dr. Amorim Ferreira
		RUMANIA
300	1886	Academia Romana, The Honorable Dr. Mihail Ralea
223	1864	Universitatea din Bucuresti, Rector Al. Rosetti
		SOUTH AFRICA
329	1896	University of the Witwatersrand, Dr. C. W. de Kiewiet
		SPAIN
43	1714	Real Academia Española, Dr. Miguel Romera-Navarro
1	XII CENT.	Universidad de Salamanca, Professor Jesús Cosin
		SWEDEN
320	1891	Göteborgs Högskola, Dr. Axel I. Romdahl
109	1825	Kungliga Tekniska Högskolan, Dr. Erik Hallén
45	1739	Kungliga Svenska Vetenskapsakademien, Dr. Göran Liljestrand
		SWITZERLAND
91	1815	Société Helvétique des Sciences Naturelles, Dr. Jean J. Weigle
131	1834	Universität Bern, Professor Beno Eckmann
313	1889	Universität Freiburg, Professor Beno Eckmann
21	1565	Université de Genève, Dr. Jean J. Weigle, Monsieur Augustin Lombard
18	1537	Université de Lausanne, Dr. Beno Eckmann
148	1838	Université de Neuchâtel, Dr. Beno Eckmann

Processional No.	*Date of Founding*	
		SYRIA
388	1921	Arab Academy, Damascus, Dr. Philip K. Hitti
386	1919	Syrian State University, His Excellency, the President of the Syrian Parliament, Faris el-Khouri
		TURKEY
219	1863	Robert College, Dr. Walter L. Wright, Jr.
13	1471	University of Istanbul, Professor Siddik Sami Onar
		UNITED KINGDOM
14	1505	University of Aberdeen, Dr. Alan H. Cruickshank
340	1900	University of Birmingham, Dean Sir Leonard Parsons
346	1902	British Academy, Professor Campbell Bonner
4	XIII CENT.	University of Cambridge, Dr. John C. Burkill
64	1783	Royal Society of Edinburgh, Dr. Alan W. C. Menzies, Dr. Henry Norris Russell
23	1582	University of Edinburgh, Dr. Alan W. C. Menzies
12	1451	University of Glasgow, Dr. William Thomson
368	1912	University of Leeds, Dr. Alexander Gillies
301	1886	University of Liverpool, Professor R. Flenley
138	1836	University of London, Sir Owen Richardson
3	XIII CENT.	University of Oxford, Dr. Herbert J. Davis
161	1845	Queen's University, Belfast, Dr. Foster Kennedy
133	1834	Royal Institute of British Architects, Dr. Stephen F. Voorhees
36	1660	The Royal Society, Dr. C. J. Mackenzie
331	1897	University of Sheffield, Dr. George B. Waterhouse
9	1411	University of St. Andrews, Principal Sir James Irvine, Dr. William Darrach
382	1918	University College of Swansea, Mr. J. C. Jones
		URUGUAY
153	1840	Universidad de Montevideo, The Honorable José A. Mora, Mr. Juan Felipe Yriart

Delegates Who Were Unable to be Present in June but Who Participated in Earlier Phases of the Bicentennial Program

Processional No.	*Date of Founding*	
		CHINA
	1909	National Tsing Hua University, Professor Ta Chen
		SWITZERLAND
	1559	Université de Genève, Professor William E. Rappard
	1833	Universität Zürich, Professor Emil Brunner
		URUGUAY
153	1840	Universidad de Montevideo, Dr. Felipe Gil

5

Recipients of Honorary Degrees

Conferred During the Bicentennial Year Together with the Citations which accompanied the conferring of the degrees

Inauguration of Bicentennial Year September 22, 1946

The Most Reverend and Right Honorable GEOFFREY FRANCIS FISHER, Lord Archbishop of Canterbury, Primate of all England, *Doctor of Divinity*.

"After a brilliant career as a student at Oxford and a three-year apprenticeship as assistant master in his old school, Marlborough, he was appointed, at the age of 27, Headmaster of Repton School. Here for eighteen years he administered high standards of scholarship and endeared himself to successive generations of schoolboys by his wise counsel and warm human understanding.

"In 1932 he was consecrated Bishop of Chester and continued to develop his strong administrative talents and to evidence his growing stature as an ecclesiastical statesman. Seven years later, in the fateful year of 1939, he was appointed Bishop of London, and almost immediately became enveloped in London's ordeal by fire. Daily by his example he gave eloquent proof of the words of the Psalmist:

" 'Thou shalt not be afraid for the terror by night;
Nor for the arrow that flieth by day;

Nor for the pestilence that walketh in darkness;
Nor for the destruction that wasteth at noonday.'

"Tirelessly he ministered to the congregations committed to his charge, helping to hold firm the faith and courage of England's capital and to plan wisely for its rebuilding. Early in 1945 he was elevated to the exalted office he now holds, as chief pastor of the Established Church of England, succeeding in this office one of Princeton's adopted sons, the late William Temple. In this ultimate achievement, he is bringing to effective service the fruits of long years of preparation and training, his native qualities of courage, energy, and wisdom, his strong belief in the need for greater cooperation among the churches, and his sympathetic understanding of the needs of his people, to the end that religious statesmanship may do its full part in the progress of his country in these troubled times.

"Princeton is particularly happy to honor at this, the opening of its Bicentennial Celebration, a devoted and distinguished servant of man's highest ideals, who in the dedication of his life to education and religion, exemplifies the purposes and hope upon which this University was founded."

Charter Day Convocation
October 19, 1946

NIELS BOHR, *Doctor of Science*. "World famous scientist, who, through his own work and that of his students, has stimulated and guided theoretical physics for more than thirty years; his steadfast loyalty to the ideals of science and humanity have made him honored and loved in many lands."

EMIL BRUNNER, *Doctor of Divinity*. "Distinguished and influential leader in the theological revival which prepared European Protestantism for its epic resistance to tyranny; teacher in Swiss and American schools of divinity, he serves as a bridge for the traffic of theological thought between Europe and America."

YUEN REN CHAO, *Doctor of Letters*. "A founder of the Science Society of China and distinguished contributor to the work of the Chinese National Academy; scholar and historian of his native language, explorer and recorder of his country's many dialects, by his researches he has eased the path of Westerners who seek to learn, in the Chinese language, the thoughts and ideals of the Chinese people."

SIR HENRY HALLETT DALE, *Doctor of Science*. "Past president of the Royal Society, scientific adviser to his country's War Cabinet in perilous times, wise organizer of medical research in which he himself has excelled."

FRANK PORTER GRAHAM, *Doctor of Laws*. "President of the University of North Carolina and valiant supporter of liberal education in the South; by his qualities of mind and character he has brought new distinction to a great university in whose founding a Princeton graduate was privileged to play a leading part."

SIR HAROLD HARTLEY, *Doctor of Science*. "An authority on transportation on the earth and in the air, a pure scientist and resourceful engineer with unique ability to integrate scientific and engineering thought and action."

SIR HECTOR JAMES WRIGHT HETHERINGTON, *Doctor of Laws*. "Principal and vice-chancellor of the University of Glasgow, a philosopher who has put his learning to practical use in international affairs and in labor relations, whose social purpose has worked steadfastly to improve the conditions of man's daily life."

FRANK HYNEMAN KNIGHT, *Doctor of Letters*. "A devoted and learned student of political economy, to whom the ever accumulating facts of human experience are the ore from which to refine the better social theory."

TRYGVE LIE, *Doctor of Laws*. "A statesman distinguished in the service of his own country who has now been entrusted with a major role in the great undertaking of world cooperation; with respect to which 'humanity with all its fears, with all the hopes of future years, is hanging breathless on its fate.' "

LORD LINDSAY OF BIRKER, *Doctor of Laws*. "Master of Balliol and former vice-chancellor of the University of Oxford, a philosopher of international influence, who has thought deeply about the enduring values in democracy, in education, and in religious truths; a writer who has given new validity to our belief in the dignity of the individual."

CYRIL NORMAN HUGH LONG, *Doctor of Science*. "A versatile investigator of the physiology and chemistry of the glands of internal secretion; his research has illumined new pathways to an understanding of the correlative nature of endocrine activity."

SALVADOR DE MADARIAGA Y ROJO, *Doctor of Letters*. "A native of Spain but a citizen of the world; ambassador and sympathetic interpreter between nations, his keen and searching observations find beneath the diversity of cultures the common unity of man."

JACQUES MARITAIN, *Doctor of Letters*. "A philosopher whose brilliant theological and humane thought achieves breadth with no sacrifice of depth, combines penetration with clarity, and builds, on the firm rock of times past, the structure of times present."

CHARLES HOWARD MCILWAIN '94, *Doctor of Letters*. "A graduate of Princeton; a great teacher; a scholar whose far-ranging studies of the institutions and political theories of the past have taught us with what pain and toil our concept of liberty under law has been developed and maintained."

CHARLES EDWARD MERRIAM, *Doctor of Laws*. "An educator, whose character, strength, and understanding have attracted succeeding generations of ardent students; a laboratory worker in the political life of his community who has given new direction to the study of modern government."

MARJORIE HOPE NICOLSON, *Doctor of Letters*. "An authority on English literature of high distinction, whose sound scholarship and stimulating teaching are adorned by her native wit and her lively human interest."

REINHOLD NIEBUHR, *Doctor of Divinity*. "Interpreter of the ultimate mysteries of man's nature and destiny, merciless diagnostician of the ills of an ailing civilization, recognized both here and abroad as a thinker of penetration and power."

SIR JOHN BOYD ORR, *Doctor of Laws*. "Foremost authority on nutrition and health, champion of the hungry of all lands in their struggles for a better life."

LINUS CARL PAULING, *Doctor of Science*. "A master of the geometry of single molecules and crystal structures, he now essays the hard task of defining the molecular architecture of growth and life."

MICHAEL POLANYI, *Doctor of Science*. "A physical chemist who has devised new tools to determine how fast atoms react; a veteran campaigner against those who would take from science the freedom she requires for the pursuit of truth."

CORNELIS BERNARDUS VAN NIEL, *Doctor of Science*. "An inspiring leader of young scholars and a brilliant investigator whose researches have established fundamental principles concerning the metabolism of microorganisms."

ERNEST LLEWELLYN WOODWARD, *Doctor of Letters*. "British historian, wise interpreter of the economic and political development of his own country, and painstaking investigator of the relations between the Great Powers in troubled ages, past and present."

HENRY MERRITT WRISTON, *Doctor of Laws*. "President of Brown University, in whose founding Princeton takes a justifiable pride; a vigorous contender for the values of a liberal arts education; a consistent champion of the preservation of American ideals and institutions."

Alumni Day Convocation
February 22, 1947

BENJAMIN FRANKLIN BUNN '07, *Master of Arts.* "For forty years faithful steward of the many trusts committed to him by the community of Princeton; loyal supporter of the University Administration and Faculty under three Presidents; adviser and friend of succeeding generations of undergraduates and wise counsellor in many of their activities; his tireless and selfless labors have won the grateful and affectionate regard of Princeton men."

JOSÉ VINCENTE FERRER '33, *Master of Arts.* "A distinguished actor, who learned the rudiments of his art as an undergraduate at Princeton; he has revivified for our time the masterpieces of great dramatists of the past; his devotion to the highest standards of his profession holds much promise for the future of the theatre."

FREDERICK A. KAHLER, JR. '12, *Master of Arts.* "Dean of Boys in a great public school, his sympathetic and intelligent guidance has inspired among his students the same loyalty and devotion to high ideals which he himself has evidenced as teacher and administrator during thirty-five years of service to American youth."

JAMES MAITLAND STEWART '32, *Master of Arts.* "A graduate of Princeton who, whether in his chosen profession or in the grave business of war, has demonstrated ability, modesty, leadership, and above all integrity, in a way which has warmed our hearts and stirred our pride in his achievements."

ALVAR AALTO, *Doctor of Fine Arts.* "An architect whose creative power ranges from the planning of cities and great buildings to the smallest detail of their furniture, a son of Finland internationally recognized as a leader of the modern movement in many arts."

JAMES W. ALEXANDER '10, *Doctor of Science.* "A brilliant member of a distinguished Princeton family; a profound mathematician of great originality, and one of the creators of modern topology."

NORMAN ARMOUR '09, *Doctor of Laws.* "A career diplomat of the first rank who for thirty years has represented the United States with rare distinction in important and difficult posts on four continents and under six Presidents; charged with heavy responsibilities, at times in situations of great delicacy, he has served his country with intelligence and skill and in the best American tradition."

PHILIP BARD '23, *Doctor of Science*. "One of the distinguished physiologists of our time, a versatile investigator of the complexities of the brain, his research has led to a clearer understanding of the nervous control of emotional behavior."

RALPH AUSTIN BARD '06, *Doctor of Laws*. "An able business man who as a public servant gave of himself unreservedly during World War II; his business experience, industry, wisdom, loyalty, and conscientious devotion to duty contributed greatly to building the United States Navy into the most potent sea-air power in the world."

CHESTER IRVING BARNARD, *Doctor of Laws*. "A leader of American industry in whom is combined rare talent in corporate and public administration, a scholar's zeal in the search for truth, and a pervading sense of responsibility in the solution of the social and economic problems facing our State and our Nation."

FREDERIC CHARLES BARTLETT, *Doctor of Science*. "Foremost British psychologist, a leader in the scientific study of human behavior and of the social forces which shape the culture of peoples."

DETLEV WULF BRONK, *Doctor of Science*. "A brilliant investigator, long recognized as a leader in the field of biophysics, he rendered distinguished service during the War in aviation physiology; now, as Chairman of the National Research Council, he has assumed new responsibilities for the future development of science in this country."

CHARLES C. J. CARPENTER '21, *Doctor of Divinity*. "Bishop of the Protestant Episcopal Diocese of Alabama; to the responsibilities of high ecclesiastical office he brings the same qualities which twenty-five years ago endeared him to a generation of fellow Princetonians—warm sympathies, infectious good humor, and a rare and happy combination of virility and spirituality."

EVERETT NEEDHAM CASE '22, *Doctor of Laws*. "President of Colgate University; alive both to old values and new needs, and fortified by breadth of experience, he has both in his university and beyond its walls provided alert and vigorous leadership in reshaping the objectives of a liberal education so that they may have renewed validity in the world of today."

HARALD CRAMÉR, *Doctor of Science*. "Professor of Mathematics at the University of Stockholm; leading authority on the mathematical theory of probability and statistics, internationally known for his contributions to these subjects and for his personal influence on his co-workers."

EDWARD MEAD EARLE, *Doctor of Laws*. "An historian who has inspired his colleagues by his courage, wisdom, and breadth of vision; a scholar who has shown how scholarship can serve the nation in an hour of peril."

VIRGINIA C. GILDERSLEEVE, *Doctor of Laws*. "Dean of Barnard College, sound scholar and able administrator, life-long student of international affairs and militant advocate of world peace; as delegate to the San Francisco conference she had a share in framing the charter of the United Nations, chief bulwark of hope in our sorely troubled world."

HEINRICH WILHELM HOPF, *Doctor of Science*. "Professor of Mathematics at the Federal Polytechnicum in Zurich; one of the world's greatest geometers, distinguished by his inspiring teaching no less than by the originality and power of his scholarship."

JOSEPH LUKL HROMÁDKA, *Doctor of Divinity*. "Distinguished theologian of Czechoslovakia; exiled by Nazi persecution for dauntless championship of freedom, he has accomplished a fruitful ministry of mediation between the religious thinkers of Central Europe and America; he now returns to rebuild the faith of his Fatherland against the trials of perilous days ahead."

CLAUDE SILBERT HUDSON '01, *Doctor of Science*. "A keen and persistent investigator in the field of organic chemistry, who for forty years has engaged in masterly research into the structure and properties of sugars; to the many honors which his scientific colleagues have bestowed upon him, his Alma Mater now adds her tribute of esteem."

WARREN KENDALL LEWIS, *Doctor of Engineering*. "Pioneer in developing and teaching the theory, principles, and techniques of chemical engineering; authority on the technology of amorphous materials and the processing of petroleum; important collaborator in the development of the engineering aspects of nuclear fission."

FRANCIS OTTO MATTHIESSEN, *Doctor of Letters*. "Teacher, scholar, and critic, whose teaching has not only given his students knowledge, but has kindled enthusiasm and a devotion to high standards, whose writings have given Americans a richer understanding of their own literature."

ROBERT MCLEAN '13, *Doctor of Laws*. "Publisher of a great metropolitan daily, noted for its editorial independence; head of the world's foremost newsgathering organization, with the heavy responsibility of collecting and distributing the news of the world with accuracy, impartiality, and truth; a leader in the continuing struggle for a free press."

BENJAMIN DEAN MERITT '23, *Doctor of Letters.* "Foremost American epigraphist, his brilliant and untiring researches in ancient records have widened immeasurably our knowledge of Classical Athens; he and those whom he has taught and influenced have brought American epigraphical studies to a position of first rank in the world."

JOHN JAMES MOMENT '96, *Doctor of Divinity.* "Forceful and persuasive preacher, civic leader, trusted counselor in affairs of Church and community, gracious interpreter of the things of the spirit through song and sermon; now completing his twenty-eighth year of service in his present parish, he has fulfilled all the desired qualifications of a faithful and devoted pastor."

ROBERT MOSES, *Doctor of Laws.* "A public servant, trained and dedicated from his youth to the public service. His most notable characteristic has been an ability, in spite of all obstacles, to get things done. Irrespective of future accomplishments, he needs no better monument than the incredible system of parks and parkways, playgrounds, beaches, and bridges which in the past decade have arisen in and around New York as though by the touch of Aladdin's lamp. Few men could have dreamed them; very few could have brought them to reality; and future generations of children, not to mention their parents, should rise up and call him blessed."

ALFRED DAYTON OLIPHANT '10, *Doctor of Laws.* "Eleventh Chancellor of New Jersey, the eighth Princeton alumnus to occupy the State's highest judicial office since it was established a century ago; to the task of maintaining the highest standards in the conduct of the Court of Chancery, he brings ability, experience, resourcefulness, and, above all, courage."

CARLTON S. PROCTOR '15, *Doctor of Engineering.* "An authority on structural foundations, whose work has received recognition not only at home but in foreign lands; Army engineer officer in two wars; member of the engineers' committee that planned the control of German and Japanese industry, with a view to the prevention of future wars."

ISIDOR ISAAC RABI, *Doctor of Science.* "Distinguished investigator in the field of nuclear physics and radio frequency; scientific adviser of broad knowledge and wise counselor in war and peace."

WILLIAM EMANUEL RAPPARD, *Doctor of Laws.* "Scholar, educator, statesman; interpreter to the world from Geneva of the strength and weakness of the League of Nations; faithful guardian of the interests of the Mandated Colonies and consistent defender of democracy."

GEORGE GAYLORD SIMPSON, *Doctor of Science*. "An authority upon studies of the earth and its pre-human inhabitants, an inspiring interpreter of life science, a pioneer in the synthesis of geology and biology toward a new understanding of evolution."

WILLIAM WATSON SMITH '92, *Doctor of Laws*. "Distinguished lawyer, whose life-long devotion to the highest ideals of his profession has won that priceless reward, the respect and esteem of his fellow members of the Bar; whose effective participation in many good causes has led to his recognition as one of the leading citizens of his community."

ARNOLD JOSEPH TOYNBEE, *Doctor of Laws*. "Eminent British historian, whose exact scholarship in the field of international relations has been a model for his colleagues, and whose far-ranging studies of the history of civilization have given them the hope that even in this broad and complex field of inquiry historians may be numbered among those happy ones who know the cause of things."

THEODORE VON KARMAN, *Doctor of Engineering*. "Consultant extraordinary to the aeronautical industry; an outstanding contributor to applied mechanics, who has demonstrated remarkable ability to isolate essential physical principles in complex phenomena and to interpret their consequences in engineering applications; an inspiring leader who has stimulated others to creative achievement in the engineering sciences."

GEORGE CATLETT MARSHALL, *Doctor of Laws*. "Chief architect of allied military victory, and now charged with the planning of world peace, a dual role breath-taking in its magnitude and one rarely attained by a single individual. It would be easy to recite a catalogue of his offices and achievements, for which we owe him a never to be forgotten debt; but at this time it is of greater moment to record that as he embarks upon his new and critical undertaking, he possesses in full measure the faith and confidence of the American people—a faith and confidence based upon long observation of his simplicity, integrity, forceful ability, courage, and selfless love of country. The country feels that its interests are in safe and honest hands, and its fervent hopes go with him."

Spring Convocation
April 3, 1947

ABDULHAK ADNAN ADIVAR, *Doctor of Letters.* "Turkish physician whose interests have broadened to include the history of science, philosophy, and religion; interpreter to his people of the best in the intellectual heritage of the European world, he has fused the finest scholarly traditions of both East and West; twice called to high public office in times of national crisis, he has unceasingly striven to lay firm foundations of reason, justice, and democracy for the young republic of which he is a most distinguished citizen."

JOHN TAYLOR ARMS '09, *Master of Fine Arts.* "An artist who in the years since he was an undergraduate at Princeton has acquired such a mastery of his art that today he is a dean of American etchers, President of the Society of American Etchers and of the National Committee of Engraving, and, above all, a distinguished craftsman whose fine prints will continue to enrich the homes and collections of this and other countries.

GIFFORD REYNOLDS BEAL '00, *Master of Fine Arts.* "Graduate of Princeton, and an artist whose paintings have gained him high honors and wide recognition, because his brush has had the breadth and strength to express simply and sincerely his own deep enjoyment of the American environment and the men who live by the sea."

JOHN HENRY BOSSHART, *Doctor of Laws.* "A veteran schoolman who is completing his forty-fifth year of service to American youth, as teacher, as principal, as supervising principal, and since 1943 as Commissioner of Education of the State of New Jersey; his administration, touching the lives of all the children of this State and thereby profoundly affecting its future welfare, has been marked by sound judgment, by sympathetic understanding, and by unfailing good will."

JOHN DE QUEDVILLE BRIGGS, *Doctor of Letters.* "A graduate of Harvard, coming of a family long distinguished as scholars and teachers, for more than thirty years Headmaster of St. Paul Academy in St. Paul, Minnesota; his alert, sympathetic, and versatile mind has led his students toward high achievement, and has realized in action one great type of American education: the good country day school supplementing the influence of the home."

KEPPEL A. C. CRESWELL, *Doctor of Letters.* "Professor of Moslem art and archaeology at the Fouad I University, Cairo,

Egypt, inspiring teacher, distinguished scholar, productive author, who has applied on an unprecedented scale Western methods of scientific research to vast and hitherto unorganized historical and literary materials in Arabic relating to mosques, citadels, schools, and other architectural monuments, and who has written the standard works on those important phases of Moslem culture."

WILLIAM BELL DINSMOOR, *Doctor of Letters*. "Excavator, writer, and teacher who has dug into the earth and from every stone uncovered in the ruins of an ancient past has extracted a fuller understanding of Greek architecture and the civilization which created it. By sheer coincidence the secret of his successful career as a Classical archaeologist is epitomized in the quotation carved in stone directly beneath his office window at Columbia University, which reads: 'Speak to the Earth and it Shall Teach Thee.' "

JAN JULIUS L. DUYVENDAK, *Doctor of Letters*. "Diplomat, teacher, and philologist, he is distinguished for maintaining the highest standards in Chinese studies, and for improving that understanding between cultures which eventually may make of two hemispheres one world."

ALFRED EINSTEIN, *Doctor of Letters*. "Historian of the Italian madrigal, biographer of Mozart and cataloguer of his works, for fifteen years the editor of Germany's leading journal for musical science, a scholar whose audience includes not only scholars but also composers, performers, and amateurs, a sympathetic and discerning critic, he has made himself loved and respected, here and abroad, by his personal generosity and political integrity."

HAROLD ALLEN FERGUSON, *Doctor of Letters*. "A graduate of Clark University, deeply interested in social science and the responsibility of the School to the State. Now Principal of the Montclair High School of Montclair, New Jersey, he has served as President of the New Jersey Council of Education, the New Jersey High School Teachers Association, and the New Jersey High School Principals Association, bringing to the complex problems of public education the benefit of his wide experience enlightened by his own calm and balanced judgment."

YU-LAN FUNG, *Doctor of Letters*. "A philosopher whose grasp of western scholarship has enabled him to illuminate the history of Chinese philosophy; an original thinker whose familiarity with diverse cultures and systems of thought has led his own speculations toward the creation of a new philosophy."

FRANKLIN F. HOPPER '00, *Doctor of Letters.* "A graduate of Princeton, whose responsibility for the guidance of one of the world's great libraries could not efface his genial smile, though his achievements in a fruitful career of librarianship show how close at heart he held the belief that 'oblivion would hide the wonders of the universe had not God provided for mortals the remedies of books.' "

OTTO KINKELDEY, *Doctor of Letters.* "Dean of American musicologists, a pioneer in winning for his subject a respected place in the curriculum of the American university, he is an exact scientist for whom music, past and present, is always and above all a living aesthetic experience, and whose genial personality and encyclopaedic command of his own and other fields have brought him the affection and regard of his colleagues, of his pupils, and of all who know him."

KENNETH SCOTT LATOURETTE, *Doctor of Letters.* "Historian and religious leader, whose life and works have helped to bridge the great gulf between West and East, whose monumental study of the expansion of Christianity has thrown new light on many phases of the world's history."

LIANG SSŬ-CH'ÊNG, *Doctor of Letters.* "A creative architect who has also been a teacher of architectural history, a pioneer in historical research and exploration in Chinese architecture, and a leader in the restoration and preservation of the priceless monuments of his country."

DAVID NICHOL SMITH, *Doctor of Letters.* "With half a century of distinguished, accurate, continuous productive study of English letters as part of his harvest, this scholar passes the bounds of his native Scotland, and of his adopted Oxford, and of his spiritual home in the eighteenth century; great teacher and counselor as well as literary historian, his influence on the higher studies of English literature in America may well surpass that of any scholar in the British Isles."

ERWIN PANOFSKY, *Doctor of Letters.* "An historian of Art who lives easily in all ages, his profound scholarship, comprehensive curiosity, sympathetic wit, and elasticity of spirit have made him an admired and delightful interpreter of those other humanists, the artists of the Renaissance, who also discovered pleasure, beauty, and enlightenment in the creations of the past."

GEORGE VAN SANTVOORD, *Doctor of Letters.* "A graduate of Yale, a Rhodes Scholar and later a soldier in World War I, a recipient of the Croix de Guerre, for more than a score of years he has been Headmaster of the Hotchkiss School at Lakeville, Connecticut; skilled both in university and secondary school education, he delights most of all to teach and to instill in youth that love of truth and devotion to duty which have so singularly marked his own career."

Concluding Convocation
June 17, 1947

BEN MOREELL, *Doctor of Engineering*. "A brilliant engineer both ashore and afloat, whose scholarly and energetic application of the engineering approach has produced significant technological advances of a high order. Organizer and first in command of the Seabees, whose fabulous exploits and achievements played so substantial a part in the victory of the Pacific."

WALTER SYDNEY ADAMS, *Doctor of Science*. "A life-long student of the spectra of the sun and stars, his original and precisely detailed studies of the light given off by thousands of stars in hundreds of different wave-lengths have revealed their distance from the earth and their composition. For more than twenty years the distinguished director of the world's foremost observatory."

WALTER HERMAN BUCHER, *Doctor of Science*. "An inspiring teacher and outstanding authority on the structure of the earth's crust; his analyses and deductions in theoretical geology have stimulated and enlightened geologists throughout the world."

EDWARD DELOS CHURCHILL, *Doctor of Science*. "Brilliant surgeon, sympathetic teacher, and outstanding investigator. His work in the surgery of the chest and in the functions of the parathyroid gland, and his fundamental clarification of the problems of wound healing in the war, establish his place as one of the great figures of present-day surgery."

JOHN VON NEUMANN, *Doctor of Science*. "Mathematician and physicist, whose wide-ranging genius is equally at home with the abstract principles of quantum mechanics and the practical effects of shock waves from high explosives. In the devotion of his versatile talents to the grave problems of war, he rendered outstanding service."

WALTER WALKER PALMER, *Doctor of Science*. "An outstanding man of medicine, whose early researches in the field of biochemistry contributed to the present-day application of the techniques of the fundamental sciences to the solution of the problems of clinical medicine. His capacity for leadership and for helpful human relationships have been especially effective in developing and inspiring his younger associates and have helped to make his medical clinic one of the great teaching and research organizations of the country."

WENDELL MEREDITH STANLEY, *Doctor of Science.* "Nobel Laureate in Chemistry; his studies in the virus diseases of plant and animal life have revealed new crystalline units, giant chemical molecules which extend the range of scientific observation to the very threshold of living organisms."

ALFRED HENRY STURTEVANT, *Doctor of Science.* "Eminent theorist, biologist, and field naturalist; by his researches on genes and chromosomes he has laid the foundation upon which much of the modern science of genetics is built."

SELMAN ABRAHAM WAKSMAN, *Doctor of Science.* "A pioneer in the investigation of antibiotic substances, the discoverer of streptomycin; his brilliant studies of the endless conflict between microorganisms has enabled medical science to enlist armies of microbes in the service of mankind."

PAUL HERMAN BUCK, *Doctor of Letters.* "Provost of Harvard, an historian whose penetrating insight into the political and social forces which influence a free society has made him a recognized leader in the development of a pattern of education adapted to the needs of a great democracy."

THOMAS STEARNS ELIOT, *Doctor of Letters.* "Critic and poet of distinction, whose work has affected the course of literature and exerted a strong influence upon all contemporary writing. As a critic, he has made possible by his perceptions a new and more coordinated view of the whole of literature. As a poet, he has widened the scope of the art to include the everyday life of the average man. Keenly aware of the trends of the time, he has become the literary conscience of an era."

DOUGLAS SOUTHALL FREEMAN, *Doctor of Letters.* "Distinguished editor and scholar, trusted adviser of our great educational foundations, biographer of Lee and his lieutenants, master of the spoken and written word with a discriminating sense of values, a man of warm human sympathies and wide-ranging interests, he has enhanced our knowledge and enriched its enjoyment."

EDGAR STEPHENSON FURNISS, *Doctor of Letters.* "Provost of Yale and Dean of its Graduate School. A teacher and scholar whose interest has ever centered upon the advancement of man's estate; whose deep understanding of the ways of teachers and scholars enables him to discharge with rare insight the responsibilities of our sister institution for standards of scholarship and research."

ANDRÉ GRABAR, *Doctor of Letters*. "Professor of the Collège de France, eminent historian of the Art of the Eastern Roman Empire, worthy successor to the great tradition of Russian Byzantine scholarship. His penetrating and subtle studies of the development of Imperial Iconography and of the origins of Christian Architecture have opened a new understanding of the knowledge of the religious bases of our civilization."

MILDRED MCAFEE HORTON, *Doctor of Letters*. "President of Wellesley College. First woman to be commissioned in the United States Navy and first to become a captain. Her brilliant success in that unique capacity has been attributed, in part, to what has been termed her 'unerring sense of *how* to rule the Waves and *when* to waive the rules.' Of more substantial importance, however, is her outstanding ability as an educator and administrator, her keen and active mind, her warm human qualities, and a God-given sense of humor."

SERGE KOUSSEVITZKY, *Doctor of Letters*. "Distinguished representative of the great musical tradition of Russia, wise and imaginative educator, generous friend and mentor of young conductors, performers, and composers; uncompromising champion of contemporary music, inspired conductor of the Boston Symphony Orchestra, through whose knowledge and understanding his players and listeners are led together to the heart of music."

ROBERT MORRISON MACIVER, *Doctor of Letters*. "A scholar whose penetrating analysis of human institutions and social change has brought new depth and discipline to American sociology and political philosophy. A son of Scotland, whose work is in the best tradition of that stronghold of tough-fibered thinking to which scholarship in general and Princeton in particular owe so much."

TSU-CH'EN CHAO, *Doctor of Divinity*. "Dean of the School of Religion of Yenching University; foremost interpreter of Christian Faith to Oriental minds; scholar, inspiring teacher, distinguished poet, gentle mystic; representative of a great university of the East with which Princeton has long maintained close and friendly ties."

HENRY KNOX SHERRILL, *Doctor of Divinity*. "The accepted leader of the Protestant Episcopal Church, recently chosen in recognition of his enlightened and forceful service in its spiritual and temporal advancement. A fearless advocate of the Church's commitment to its world-wide obligations in the fields of unity and Christian helpfulness, he has by his breadth and his integrity already given the Church a new vision of its mission and its opportunities in a changing world."

LUTHER ALLAN WEIGLE, *Doctor of Divinity*. "Dean of the Yale University Divinity School and Sterling Professor of Religious Education; indefatigable leader in unnumbered Christian causes—theological education, foreign missions, the revision of the Bible, church cooperation and unity; humble and fruitful servant of the Church of Christ."

WARREN ROBINSON AUSTIN, *Doctor of Laws*. "Born and reared in the Vermont tradition, he has served his State and the Nation in posts of steadily mounting importance. For fifteen years a member of the United States Senate, from which he resigned to become, by appointment of the President, Chief Representative of the United States in the United Nations. As such, he serves as representative upon the General Assembly, the Atomic Energy Commission, the Commission for Conventional Armaments, and in other important capacities. A man of sound judgment and training, of steady thinking and action, with a New Englander's ability to adhere to a position with firmness and assurance, when once he is convinced he is in the right, he brings a well-rounded equipment to a task of unprecedented difficulty and of critical importance to ourselves and the world."

BERNARD MANNES BARUCH, *Doctor of Laws*. "For over thirty years he has devoted himself without stint to public service, first as the friend and adviser of President Woodrow Wilson and thereafter through successive administrations, serving with distinction both here and abroad in many and diverse fields and an amazing variety of undertakings. He has brought to these important undertakings a keen and well-trained mind, a wide knowledge of men and affairs, a passion for facts as the only sound basis for decisions, and the courage to make and uphold those decisions. In brief, a wise counselor and patriotic American citizen who has given expression to his love of country by continued and devoted labors in the nation's service."

VANNEVAR BUSH, *Doctor of Laws*. "President of the Carnegie Institution of Washington. A man of science, whose distinguished career as an electrical engineer, inventor, and administrator found fitting fruition in his selection as Director of the Office of Scientific Research and Development in Washington, where during the war years he mobilized with striking effectiveness the country's scientific personnel and resources, and became their brilliant commander in chief."

EDMUND EZRA DAY, *Doctor of Laws.* "President of Cornell University, distinguished scholar, stimulating teacher, and able administrator. During his earlier years, as a teacher of economics, he kindled the interest and zeal of his students, who have reason to recall him with gratitude. Thereafter he engaged in broader fields of business and social activities and gave convincing demonstration of his ability for effective application of abstract theories in the world of practical affairs. Thus he has brought to the presidency of Cornell a broad experience and equipment, which with his fine personal qualities and abilities have steadily advanced the interests and prestige of that great university."

DWIGHT DAVID EISENHOWER, *Doctor of Laws.* "Supreme Allied Commander in the war and unofficial ambassador of good will, of whom it has been aptly said 'His character and skill made of a coalition a triumphant army of democracy.' Bringing to his task the intensive preparation of a lifetime, he revealed qualities of simplicity, self-effacing efficiency, unerring good judgment, and dynamic but friendly personality, which quickly brought about an acceptance of his leadership with remarkable unanimity not unmixed with real affection. In his daily decisions he was just and fair and wise, and held the respect and warm admiration of his officers and men. In his post-war missions to other countries, his tact, humor, and refreshing frankness left a lasting and happy impression. For his service to his country, we owe him a debt never to be forgotten."

FRANK DIEHL FACKENTHAL, *Doctor of Laws.* "Acting President of Columbia University. Educator and skilled administrator, who has dedicated his life, with singleness of purpose and rare devotion to the welfare of his famous alma mater. Becoming Provost in 1937, he served as the trusted and able lieutenant of his illustrious predecessor, and with self-effacing efficiency conducted the day-to-day operations of that far-flung organization with smoothness and ease of execution. Upon the retirement of Dr. Butler, he became Acting President, without disruption or dissent, without commotion or loss of motion, and with the complete confidence and friendly support of trustees, faculty and undergraduates. Such a result could only have been achieved through qualities of fairness, modesty, thoughtful consideration, courage, and the best type of constructive leadership. In his own quiet way he has made an outstanding contribution, not only to Columbia but to American education."

LEARNED HAND, *Doctor of Laws.* "A United States Judge, who in thirty-eight years of active service has builded steadily the respect and esteem for his Court, not merely in his own jurisdiction but throughout the land. He has maintained with vigor the reign of law, without fear of its adjustment to meet changing conditions, dignity without sacrifice of approachability, a profound and ever-growing knowledge without claim of infallibility, courage to state things as he sees them regardless of consequences; and above all else, a native and shining integrity which no man has ever thought to question."

CHARLES FRANKLIN KETTERING, *Doctor of Laws.* "Engineer, inventive genius extraordinary, possessed of a restless curiosity combined with a driving persistency which never admits the possibility of defeat; he, with the aid of his associates, has provided an incredible succession of creative achievements which have contributed to the comfort and well-being of millions and heightened the joy of their living. His active mind, with its passion for productive research tempered by canny common sense, penetrates widely varied fields of human interest and leaves each the richer for its presence."

ALFRED PRITCHARD SLOAN JR., *Doctor of Laws.* "His career reads like an epic of American success. Starting from modest beginnings, by virtue of hard work and native abilities, he rose step by step to the headship of a great industry. Modest, retiring, always insistent upon teamwork with his associates, he provided the driving force essential to outstanding achievement. More recently, with the lightening of business responsibilities, he has turned his attention increasingly to interests of public welfare, and with his life-long associates, has organized and made munificent provision for the Sloan-Kettering Institute for Cancer Research. It is understandable that this approach might appear unorthodox to certain members of the medical profession, but the public, mindful of past achievements on the part of this incomparable team, will be content to wait patiently but hopefully for progress in the solution of the world's most baffling medical problem."

CHESTER WILLIAM NIMITZ, *Doctor of Laws.* "An Admiral in the best tradition of the United States Navy. Called to the command of the Pacific Fleet in its darkest hour, after the disaster at Pearl Harbor, this son of Texas took up his difficult task with quiet and assured determination. Reconstructing his shattered command with amazing results, he turned at the first possible moment from defensive to offensive warfare and by daring leadership and brilliant strategy achieved a succession of victories which culminated in one of the greatest triumphs in naval history. In this accomplishment his personal qualities played an important part. Modest, resolute, and wise, firm but human, his faith in his officers and men was reflected in their confidence and enthusiastic loyalty to him. His decisions were dictated by unerring judgment and a sturdy common sense which won whole-hearted support and were executed with skill and vigor. Today, in well-merited recognition of his achievements, he is commanding our Navy in its adjustments to new responsibilities in a troubled world."

ROBERT GORDON SPROUL, *Doctor of Laws*. "President of the University of California. Since his election in 1930, he has by his leadership and able administration advanced the distinction of that great institution on San Francisco Bay, not only in his own state but throughout the nation. With all his responsibilities in the field of education, he has found time to take an active part in the intellectual and civic activities of his community and has brought to its people the resources of his great university, reinforced by his own vigorous personality."

EUGÈNE CARDINAL TISSERANT, *Doctor of Laws*. "Distinguished scholar and eminent churchman, interpreter of early Christian documents, expert in the liturgical arts of the Eastern rites, world authority on the Oriental languages, master of manuscripts. Knowing full well the ancient needs of scholars and the modern means for their greater satisfaction, he has helped to make the Biblioteca Apostolica Vaticana the most cooperative of all institutions of learning and by his ever-friendly response has earned the gratitude of scholars in many lands."

"Mr. President, I have the honor to present for the degree of Doctor of Laws, *honoris causa*:

"THE CHIEF JUSTICE OF THE UNITED STATES (Frederick M. Vinson).

"THE GOVERNOR OF THE STATE OF NEW JERSEY, whose early predecessor granted our charter 200 years ago (Alfred E. Driscoll).

"HIS EXCELLENCY, THE GOVERNOR-GENERAL OF CANADA (Field Marshal Viscount Alexander of Tunis).

"THE PRESIDENT OF THE UNITED STATES."

6

Conferences

First Series

J. Douglas Brown, *Director*

1. The Future of Nuclear Science

September 23-25

Eugene P. Wigner, *Director*

Advisory Committee

Luther P. Eisenhart
Henry Eyring
N. Howell Furman
R. Ladenburg
H. P. Robertson
Henry N. Russell
H. D. Smyth
J. Q. Stewart
Hugh S. Taylor
John A. Wheeler

Staff

Paul Busse
Karl K. Darrow
Robert H. Dicke
Donald R. Hamilton
George T. Reynolds

Radio Broadcasts: Eugene P. Wigner, Harlow Shapley, Karl T. Compton, J. R. Oppenheimer, P. M. S. Blackett, Farrington Daniels, Glenn Seaborg, J. T. Tate, M. S. Vallarta, H. N. Russell, H. A. Kramers.

PROGRAM

Cooperation of Universities with other Institutions in Science
- Scholarship in the Secondary School
- The relation of research in universities to government and commercial laboratories
- The place of the large laboratory in nuclear research
- On problems of scientific cooperation: the uses and hopes of scientific societies

Nuclear Physics
- Elementary particles
- Proton scattering

CONFERENCES

Application of artificial radioactive tracers to chemistry and medicine

Experimental methods of nuclear physics

Physical Science and Human Values

The physical sciences and their bearing on philosophy and human values

Foundation of freedom in science

New vistas for intelligence

PUBLIC SESSIONS

1. The Observation Problem in Atomic Physics—Niels Bohr
2. The Scientist's Role in International Relations—M. S. Vallarta H. N. Russell, H. A. Kramers

GUESTS OF THE UNIVERSITY WHO PARTICIPATED

J. W. Alexander, Institute for Advanced Study, Princeton
Samuel K. Allison, University of Chicago
Edoardo Amaldi, University of Rome, Italy
Ernest F. Barker, University of Michigan
H. J. Bhabha, Tata Institute of Fundamental Research, Bombay, India
P. M. S. Blackett, University of Manchester, England
Niels Bohr, University of Copenhagen, Denmark
John H. Bosshart, Commissioner of Education, New Jersey
Gregory Breit, University of Wisconsin
P. W. Bridgman, Harvard University
C. Vernon Cannon, Clinton Laboratories
S. Chandrasekhar, Yerkes Observatory, University of Chicago
Arthur H. Compton, Washington University
Karl T. Compton, Massachusetts Institute of Technology
James B. Conant, Harvard University
Edward U. Condon, National Bureau of Standards
Charles D. Coryell, Massachusetts Institute of Technology
Paul C. Cross, Brown University
Farrington Daniels, University of Wisconsin
Karl K. Darrow, Bell Telephone Laboratories
C. J. Davisson, Bell Telephone Laboratories
G. H. Dieke, The Johns Hopkins University
P. A. M. Dirac, Cambridge University, England
Lee A. DuBridge, California Institute of Technology

FRANK G. DUNNINGTON, Rutgers University
W. J. ECKERT, International Business Machines Corporation
E. FERMI, University of Chicago
R. P. FEYNMAN, Cornell University
EVERETT J. FORD, Boston English High School, Boston
GAYLORD P. HARNWELL, University of Pennsylvania
DAVID HAWKINS, George Washington University
JOHN C. HOGG, Phillips Exeter Academy, New Hampshire
ALBERT W. HULL, General Electric Company
Research Laboratories
J. C. JACOBSEN, University of Copenhagen, Denmark
ZAY JEFFRIES, General Electric Company
FREDERIC JOLIOT, Collège de France
IRENE CURIE-JOLIOT, Faculté des Sciences, Paris
D. W. KERST, University of Illinois
JOHN G. KIRKWOOD, Cornell University
GEORGE B. KISTIAKOWSKY, Harvard University
L. KOWARSKI, Collège de France
H. A. KRAMERS, University of Leyden, Holland
ERNEST O. LAWRENCE, University of California
O. MAASS, McGill University, Canada
EDWARD MACK, Ohio State University
HENRY MARGENAU, Yale University
JOSEPH E. MAYER, University of Chicago
DEAN B. MCLAUGHLIN, University of Michigan
C. E. K. MEES, Eastman Kodak Company
M. G. MESCHERJAKOV, Leningrad Radium Institute, Russia
PHILIP MORRISON, Cornell University
F. S. C. NORTHROP, Yale University
J. R. OPPENHEIMER, University of California
M. POLANYI, University of Manchester, England
I. I. RABI, Columbia University
MARCEL SCHEIN, University of Chicago
GLENN T. SEABORG, University of California
HARLOW SHAPLEY, Harvard College Observatory
MANNE SIEGBAHN, Royal Academy of Science, Sweden
FRANCIS T. SPAULDING, Commissioner of Education,
New York State
C. G. SUITS, General Electric Company
JOHN T. TATE, University of Minnesota
WENDELL H. TAYLOR, The Lawrenceville School, New Jersey

Charles A. Thomas, Monsanto Chemical Company
Richard C. Tolman, California Institute of Technology
Louis A. Turner, University of Iowa
Harold C. Urey, University of Chicago
M. Sandoval Vallarta, Comision Impulsora y Coordinaria de la Investigacion Cientifica, Mexico
J. H. Van Vleck, Harvard University
Victor S. Vavilov, Leningrad University, Russia
Oswald Veblen, Institute for Advanced Study, Princeton
Victor F. Weisskopf, Massachusetts Institute of Technology
Hermann Weyl, Institute for Advanced Study, Princeton
Rupert Wildt, Yale University
E. Bright Wilson, Harvard University
Robert R. Wilson, Harvard University
V. K. Zworykin, Radio Corporation of America

2. The Chemistry and Physiology of Growth

September 27-30

Arthur K. Parpart, *Director*

Advisory Committee	*General Committee*
Elmer G. Butler	Aurin M. Chase
Gregg Dougherty	Kenneth W. Cooper
Henry Eyring	Gerhard Fankhauser
E. Newton Harvey	Frank H. Johnson
Wilbur Swingle	Eugene Pacsu
Hugh S. Taylor	Charles E. Wilde, Jr.
Everett S. Wallis	

Radio Broadcasts: Arthur K. Parpart, Linus Pauling, Francis Schmitt, C. C. Little, Herbert M. Evans, J. S. Fruton, M. Delbruck, John H. Northrop, Cyril N. H. Long, Baldwin Lucke, C. P. R. Rhoads, Paul A. Weiss.

PROGRAM

Proteins and Growth, and Growth Promoting Compounds
Synthesis of proteins
Molecular morphology and growth

Plant growth hormones
Unidentified vitamins and growth factors
Kinetics of Growth and Problems of Morphogenesis
Kinetics of growth of micro-organisms
Cellular enzymatic reactions and growth
Differential growth
Problems of organization
Hormonal Control of Growth and Abnormal Growth
The growth hormone of the anterior pituitary
Abnormal growth

PUBLIC SESSION

"Quel est l'usage des glandes surrénales?" Académie des Sciences, Bordeaux, 1716—C. N. H. Long

GUESTS OF THE UNIVERSITY WHO PARTICIPATED

A. Elizabeth Adams, Mount Holyoke College
H. G. Albaum, Brooklyn College
M. L. Anson, Continental Foods, Hoboken, New Jersey
George Avery, Brooklyn Botanic Gardens
Eric G. Ball, Harvard University
E. S. Guzman Barron, University of Chicago
Lester G. Barth, Columbia University
Stanhope Bayne-Jones, Yale University
Edgar J. Boell, Yale University
Detlev W. Bronk, University of Pennsylvania
Henry B. Bull, Northwestern University
R. Keith Cannan, New York University
George F. Cartland, The Upjohn Company, Kalamazoo, Michigan
Erwin Chargaff, Columbia University
Bacon F. Chow, Institute for Medical Research New Brunswick, New Jersey
Albert Claude, Rockefeller Institute for Medical Research, New York
E. G. Conklin, Princeton University
Ruth Snyder Cooper, Princeton University
Donald P. Costello, University of North Carolina
Ray F. Dawson, Columbia University
M. Delbruck, Vanderbilt University

John T. Edsall, Harvard University
Herbert M. Evans, University of California
I. Fankuchen, Brooklyn Polytechnic Institute
Karl Folkers, Merck and Company, Inc., Rahway, New Jersey
J. S. Fruton, Yale University
William U. Gardner, Yale University
I. Gersh, The Johns Hopkins University
Harry S. N. Greene, Yale University
Paul Gyorgy, University of Pennsylvania
Viktor Hamburger, Washington University
James B. Hamilton, Long Island College of Medicine
Ross G. Harrison, Yale University
Ethel Browne Harvey, Princeton University
Roger M. Herriott, Rockefeller Institute for Medical Research, Princeton, New Jersey
Frederick L. Hisaw, Harvard University
Albert G. Hogan, University of Missouri
J. Holtfreter, University of Rochester
Thomas H. Jukes, Lederle Laboratories, Pearl River, New York
John C. Keresztesy, Mount Sinai Hospital, New York
M. Kunitz, Rockefeller Institute for Medical Research, Princeton, New Jersey
J. H. Leathem, Rutgers University
Howard B. Lewis, University of Michigan
Warren H. Lewis, Wistar Institute, Philadelphia, Pennsylvania
Fritz Lipmann, Biochemistry Research Laboratory, Massachusetts General Hospital
C. C. Little, Roscoe B. Jackson Memorial Laboratory, Bar Harbor, Maine
C. N. H. Long, Yale University
Balduin Lucke, University of Pennsylvania
E. Lundsgaard, Institute of Physiology, Copenhagen, Denmark
C. F. W. McClure, Princeton University
Morton McCutcheon, University of Pennsylvania
Stuart Mudd, University of Pennsylvania
Warren O. Nelson, University of Iowa
John S. Nicholas, Yale University
H. C. Nicholson, National Research Council
J. H. Northrop, Rockefeller Institute for Medical Research, Princeton, New Jersey
Severo Ochoa, New York University

Ernest Oppenheimer, CIBA Pharmaceutical Products, Inc., Summit, New Jersey
Jane M. Oppenheimer, Bryn Mawr College
Philip S. Owen, National Research Council
Linus Pauling, California Institute of Technology
N. W. Pirie, Rothamsted Experimental Station, Harpenden, Herts, England
Mary E. Rawles, The Johns Hopkins University
Cornelius P. Rhoads, Memorial Hospital, New York
W. J. Robbins, New York Botanical Garden
Dorothea Rudnick, Albertus Magnus College
F. J. Ryan, Columbia University
Francis O. Schmitt, Massachusetts Institute of Technology
Oscar Schotte, Amherst College
Mildred W. S. Schram, Cancer Research Division, Donner Foundation, Philadelphia, Pennsylvania
M. G. Sevag, University of Pennsylvania
Aura E. Severinghaus, Columbia University
Richard E. Shope, Rockefeller Institute for Medical Research, Princeton, New Jersey
Folke H. Skoog, Washington University
Carl C. Speidel, University of Virginia
O. S. Sponsler, University of California
Wendell M. Stanley, Rockefeller Institute for Medical Research, Princeton, New Jersey
Kurt G. Stern, Brooklyn Polytechnic Institute
E. L. Tatum, Yale University
Kenneth V. Thimann, Harvard University
H. B. van Dyke, Columbia University
C. B. van Niel, Stanford University
J. van Overbeek, Institute of Tropical Agriculture, Mayaguez, Puerto Rico
Shields Warren, Harvard University
David F. Waugh, Massachusetts Institute of Technology
Paul A. Weiss, University of Chicago
F. W. Went, California Institute of Technology
Abraham White, Yale University
Benjamin H. Willier, The Johns Hopkins University
Emil Witschi, University of Iowa

Dillworth W. Woolley, Rockefeller Institute for Medical Research, New York
Dorothy Wrinch, Smith College

3. Engineering and Human Affairs

October 3-5

Richard H. Wilhelm, *Director*

Advisory Committee

Kenneth H. Condit
Joseph C. Elgin
Arthur M. Greene, Jr.
Frank A. Heacock
Walter C. Johnson
Philip Kissam
Lewis F. Moody
Louis F. Rahm
Daniel C. Sayre
W. Taylor Thom
Elmer K. Timby
Richard K. Toner
Clodius H. Willis

Radio Broadcasts: Richard H. Wilhelm, Hugh H. Bennett, Ralph E. Flanders, Karl T. Compton, L. Welch Pogue, Thomas H. MacDonald, Francisco Gomez-Perez, Te-Pang Hou.

PROGRAM

Engineering and the Material Aspects of Society
- Natural resource development
- The efficient utilization of materials
- Manufacturing methods and productivity
- Progress in the transformation of energy
- Improved methods of transportation and their import
- Modern communication and its import

Technology, Engineering, and the Individual
- The individual worker
- The individual engineer

Toward the Future Development of Engineering
- Engineering education
- The engineering profession
- Research in engineering

PUBLIC SESSION

Greetings from Foreign Engineers—Sir Harold Hartley, F. Gomez-Perez, Te-Pang Hou
Engineering and Human Affairs—R. E. Flanders

GUESTS OF THE UNIVERSITY WHO PARTICIPATED

John L. Alden, Western Electric Company
Earl B. Babcock, Firestone Tire and Rubber Company
Laurence W. Bass, Air Reduction Company, Incorporated.
United States Industrial Chemicals, Incorporated
Hugh H. Bennett, United States Department of Agriculture
George G. Brown, University of Michigan
Francis J. Chesterman, Bell Telephone Company of Pennsylvania
Thomas H. Chilton, E. I. DuPont de Nemours and Company
Alexander G. Christie, The Johns Hopkins University
Wallace Clark, Wallace Clark and Company
Stewart P. Coleman, Standard Oil Company of New Jersey
Karl T. Compton, Massachusetts Institute of Technology
Allen R. Cullimore, Newark College of Engineering
Clarence E. Davies, American Society of Mechanical Engineers
Harvey N. Davis, Stevens Institute of Technology
Everette L. DeGolyer, DeGolyer and McNaughton, Consulting Geologists
James C. Donnell, ii, The Ohio Oil Company
Charles R. Downs, Consulting Chemical Engineer
Elmer W. Engstrom, Radio Corporation of America
James K. Finch, Columbia University
Ralph E. Flanders, Jones and Lamson Machine Company
John A. Goff, University of Pennsylvania
Francisco Gomez-Perez, Mexican Association of Engineers and Architects
Harry P. Hammond, Pennsylvania State College
William Harrigan, Texas Oil Company and Society of Automotive Engineers
Sir Harold Hartley, British European Airways, London
Arthur W. Hixson, Columbia University
Eugene Holman, Standard Oil Company of New Jersey
Te-Pang Hou, Yungli Chemical Industries, Ltd.
Ernest E. Howard, Howard, Needles, Tammen, and Bergendorf
Jerome C. Hunsaker, Massachusetts Institute of Technology
James E. Jagges, American Society of Civil Engineers
Zay Jeffries, General Electric Company
Frank B. Jewitt, National Academy of Sciences

S. Paul Johnston, Institute of Aeronautical Sciences
H. Frazer Johnstone, University of Illinois
Paul C. Keith, Jr., Hydrocarbon Research, Incorporated
W. Julian King, Cornell University
Sidney D. Kirkpatrick, Chemical and Metallurgical Engineering
John C. Leslie, Pan American Airways System
Thomas H. MacDonald, Federal Works Agency, Public Roads Administration
Charles E. MacQuigg, Ohio State University
Joseph R. Mares, Monsanto Chemical Company
Donald H. McLaughlin, Homestake Mining Company
John C. McPherson, International Business Machines Corporation
Robert K. Merton, Columbia University
Ben Moreell, Office of the Assistant Secretary of Navy
John R. Munn, Elastic Stop Nut Corporation of America
Malcolm Pirnie, Malcolm Pirnie Engineers
Joseph E. Pogue, Chase National Bank
L. Welsh Pogue, Civil Aeronautics Board
Andrey A. Potter, Purdue University
David C. Prince, General Electric Company
Carlton S. Proctor, Moran, Proctor, Freeman, and Mueser
Harvey C. Rentschler, Westinghouse Electric Corporation
Alfred Rheinstein, Rheinstein Construction Company
Louis Ruthenburg, Servel Incorporated
David Sarnoff, Radio Corporation of America
George K. Scribner, Boonton Molding Company
Norman A. Shepard, American Cyanamid Company
Lewis K. Sillcox, New York Air Brake Company
Chester F. Smith, Standard Oil Company of New Jersey
Elliot D. Smith, Carnegie Institute of Technology
Charles M. A. Stine, E. I. DuPont de Nemours and Company
George W. Taylor, University of Pennsylvania
Frederick E. Terman, Stanford University
Stephen L. Tyler, American Institute of Chemical Engineers
James G. Vail, Philadelphia Quartz Company
Roland Voorhees, Carbide and Carbon Chemicals Corporation
Thomas N. Whitehead, Radcliffe College. Harvard Graduate School of Business Administration

Walter G. Whitman, Massachusetts Institute of Technology
Robert E. Wilson, Standard Oil Company of Indiana
D. Robert Yarnall, Yarnall-Waring Company
Earl P. Yerkes, Bell Telephone Company of Pennsylvania. American Institute of Electrical Engineers
Rufus E. Zimmerman, United States Steel Corporation

4. The Evolution of Social Institutions in America

October 7-9

John F. Sly, *Director*

Conference Committee

William S. Carpenter
Kingsley Davis
Stanley E. Howard
Paul M. Douglas
John A. Mackay
Joseph R. Strayer
George F. Thomas
Joseph E. McLean
William Miller

Conference Staff

Jeremy Blanchet
Robert C. Fisher
Herbert W. Fraser
Gabriel Gabrelian
Will E. Mason
Simeon F. Moss
Jack W. Peltason
Ray L. Strong

Radio Broadcasts: John F. Sly, William E. Hocking, Charles E. Merriam, Howard F. Lowry, Edward S. Corwin.

PROGRAM

The State
- Political theory for an industrial age
- American federalism—past, present, and future
- The social and political influences of American urbanization
- American democracy in transition

The Economy
- The changing concept of free enterprise
- Trade unions in a free society
- The social and economic determinants in the distrbution of income in the United States
- The place of the United States in the world economy

The Church
- The American religious pattern

CONFERENCES

The Church and the American community
Racial and religious minorities in the United States
The Church and American culture
The Church and the political order

PUBLIC SESSION

The Ecumenical Movement in its National and International Significance—Henry P. Van Dusen
Summary of Conference—Charles H. McIlwain, Chester I. Barnard

GUESTS OF THE UNIVERSITY WHO PARTICIPATED

E. E. Agger, Rutgers University
Chester I. Barnard, New Jersey Bell Telephone Company
Carl Bridenbaugh, Institute of Early American History, Williamsburg, Virginia
Dennis W. Brogan, Cambridge University
Emil Brunner, University of Zurich
Arthur F. Burns, National Bureau of Economic Research
Emile Cailliet, Wesleyan University
Thomas C. Cochran, New York University
Henry S. Commager, Columbia University
Morris A. Copeland, National Bureau of Economic Research
Philip Davidson, Vanderbilt University
Maurice R. Davie, Yale University
William H. Davis, N.Y. City Board of Transportation
Peter F. Drucker, Bennington College
Corwin D. Edwards, Northwestern University
William Y. Elliott, Harvard University
G. H. Evans, Jr., The Johns Hopkins University
Louis Finkelstein, Jewish Theological Seminary
E. Franklin Frazier, Howard University
E. A. Goldenweiser, Director, Division of Research and Statistics, Federal Reserve Board
Robert A. Gordon, University of California
Stuart Grummon, Redding, Connecticut

LUTHER H. GULICK, Institute of Public Administration, New York
WALTON H. HAMILTON, Yale University
PHILIP M. HAUSER, Department of Commerce, Washington, D.C.
WILLIAM E. HOCKING, Harvard University
ARTHUR N. HOLCOMBE, Harvard University
V. O. KEY, The Johns Hopkins University
FRANK H. KNIGHT, University of Chicago
HOWARD F. LOWRY, College of Wooster
CHARLES H. MCILWAIN, Harvard University
JOHN T. MCNEILL, Union Theological Seminary
ARTHUR W. MACMAHON, Columbia University
CHARLES E. MERRIAM, University of Chicago
PERRY MILLER, Harvard University
ALLAN NEVINS, Columbia University
EDWIN G. NOURSE, Brookings Institution
JOHN E. POMFRET, College of William and Mary
ROBERT S. RANKIN, Duke University
CHARLES B. ROBSON, University of North Carolina
CHARLES C. ROHLFING, University of Pennsylvania
RICHARD H. SHRYOCK, University of Pennsylvania
SUMNER H. SLICHTER, Harvard University
THEO SURANYI-UNGER, Syracuse University
RUPERT B. VANCE, University of North Carolina
ARTHUR T. VANDERBILT, New York University
HENRY P. VAN DUSEN, Union Theological Seminary
LUTHER A. WEIGLE, Yale University
AMOS N. WILDER, Chicago Theological Seminary
DONALD R. YOUNG, Social Science Research Council
KIMBALL YOUNG, Queens College
ALEXANDER C. ZABRISKIE, Virginia Theological Seminary

5. The Development of International Society

October 11-14

HAROLD H. SPROUT, *Director*

Advisory Committee

EDWARD M. EARLE
FRANK D. GRAHAM
E. HARRIS HARBISON
DANA G. MUNRO
FRANK W. NOTESTEIN
JOSEPH R. STRAYER
JACOB VINER

Conference Staff

JOHN L. CHASE
THOMAS L. CRYSTAL, JR.
REUBEN H. GROSS, JR.
WILLIAM W. LOCKWOOD
RICHARD C. SNYDER

Radio Broadcasts: Harold H. Sprout, Theodore Schultz, Eugene Staley, Brooks Emeny, Gerhart Niemeyer, Sir John Boyd Orr, Quincy Wright, Owen Lattimore, Denna F. Fleming.

PROGRAM

International Society—Objectives, Essential Conditions, and Prospects
- The prospects for international society: general view
- Bearing of living standards upon the prospects for international society
- Bearing of loyalties and ideologies on the prospects for international society

Fundamental Problems in the Development of International Society
- Problems arising from the existence of empires and dependent peoples
- Problems arising from the unequal distribution of power among nations
- Problems arising from the inter-relations and policies of the great powers

Approaches to the Problem of Developing International Society
- Approaches through human motives, beliefs, and loyalties

PUBLIC SESSION

Is an International Society Possible?—Isaiah Bowman

Next Steps in the Development of International Society—E. L. Woodward

GUESTS OF THE UNIVERSITY WHO PARTICIPATED

HAMILTON FISH ARMSTRONG, *Foreign Affairs*
HERMAN BEUKEMA, United States Military Academy
PERCY W. BIDWELL, Council on Foreign Relations
FRANK G. BOUDREAU, Milbank Memorial Fund
ISAIAH BOWMAN, The Johns Hopkins University
JOHN B. BREBNER, Columbia University
CRANE BRINTON, Harvard University
EDWARD C. CARTER, American Council, Institute of Pacific Relations
ROYDEN J. DANGERFIELD, University of Oklahoma
CORNELIS DE KIEWIET, Cornell University
TYLER DENNETT, Formerly Department of State
ALLEN W. DULLES, Council on Foreign Relations
FREDERICK S. DUNN, Yale University
E. R. DURGIN, US Navy
EDWARD M. EARLE, Institute for Advanced Study
HOWARD S. ELLIS, University of California
BROOKS EMENY, Cleveland Council on World Affairs
SYDNEY B. FAY, Harvard University
DENNA F. FLEMING, Vanderbilt University
W. T. R. FOX, Yale University
CARL J. FRIEDRICH, Harvard University
SIDNEY F. GIFFIN, US Army General Staff, War Department
CARTER GOODRICH, Columbia University
KENT R. GREENFIELD, War Department General Staff
ALFRED M. GRUENTHER, National War College
DIMITRIE GUSTI, The Rumanian Academy
GOTTFRIED HABERLER, Harvard University
RICHARD HARTSHORNE, University of Wisconsin
CHARLES W. HENDEL, Yale University
MELVILLE J. HERSKOVITS, Northwestern University
ROSS J. S. HOFFMAN, Fordham University
HAJO HOLBORN, Yale University
WILLIAM L. HOLLAND, Institute of Pacific Relations
PHILIP C. JESSUP, Columbia University
JOSEPH E. JOHNSON, Department of State
RAYMOND KENNEDY, Yale University
GRAYSON L. KIRK, Columbia University
FRANK H. KNIGHT, University of Chicago

HANS KOHN, Smith College
HAROLD J. LASKI, University of London
OWEN LATTIMORE, The Johns Hopkins University
ABBA P. LERNER, The New School for Social Research
WALTER LIPPMANN, *The New York Herald Tribune*
BRECKINRIDGE LONG, Laurel, Maryland
JOHN W. MASLAND, Dartmouth College
KIRTLEY F. MATHER, Harvard University
CHARLES H. MCILWAIN, Harvard University
DONALD C. MCKAY, Harvard University
RICHARD P. MCKEON, University of Chicago
C. WRIGHT MILLS, Columbia University
PHILIP E. MOSELEY, Columbia University
GERHART NIEMEYER, Oglethorpe University
SIR JOHN BOYD ORR, Food and Agriculture Organization of the United Nations
FREDERICK H. OSBORN, Social Science Research Council
TALCOTT PARSONS, Harvard University
DEWITT C. POOLE, Harvard University
PITMAN B. POTTER, *American Journal of International Law*
J. HERMAN RANDALL, Columbia University
CARL REMER, University of Michigan
WINFIELD W. RIEFLER, Institute for Advanced Study
BERNADOTTE SCHMITT, Department of State
THEODORE SCHULTZ, University of Chicago
H. ALEXANDER SMITH, United States Senator from New Jersey
RAYMOND J. SONTAG, University of California
EUGENE STALEY, Institute of Pacific Relations
WALTER W. STEWART, Institute for Advanced Study
FRANK TANNENBAUM, Columbia University
WARREN THOMPSON, Scripps Foundation for Research in Population Problems
RALPH E. TURNER, Yale University
ARTHUR P. WHITAKER, University of Pennsylvania
C. R. WHITTLESEY, University of Pennsylvania
ARNOLD WOLFERS, Yale University
ERNEST LLEWELLYN WOODWARD, Oxford University
ROBERT G. WOOLBERT, University of Denver
QUINCY WRIGHT, University of Chicago
DONALD YOUNG, Social Science Research Council
FLORIAN ZNANIECKI, University of Illinois

6. The Humanistic Tradition in the Century Ahead

October 16-18

DONALD A. STAUFFER, *Director*

Policy Committee
WHITNEY J. OATES
ROBERT R. PALMER
IRA O. WADE
LEDGER WOOD

Executive Committee
ROBERT H. CHAPMAN
WALLACE IRWIN, JR.
MAURICE W. KELLEY
JAMES THORPE
ALBA H. WARREN, JR.
WILLIAM H. ZIEGLER

Radio Broadcasts: Donald A. Stauffer, Irwin Edman, Christian Gauss, Ernest J. Simmons, Baron Lindsay of Birker, Lynn T. White, W. H. Auden, Robert M. MacIver.

PROGRAM

Approaches to the Humanistic Tradition
- Approaches to humanism
- The historic approach in humanistic inquiry
- The aesthetic approach to the humanistic tradition
- Permanent elements in the humanistic tradition

Contemporary Impact of Humanism
- The possibilities of adult education
- The powers of practising artists, the popular arts, and the press in developing humanistic culture
- The responsibilities of institutions toward the humanistic tradition
- The effect of democratic and totalitarian thought upon the humanistic tradition

Humanism in an Expanding World
- Social studies in the humanistic tradition
- Science in the humanistic tradition
- The humanistic tradition in "one world"

PUBLIC SESSION

The Boundaries of Humanistic Studies—Marjorie Nicolson, James B. Conant

GUESTS OF THE UNIVERSITY WHO PARTICIPATED

JAMES R. ANGELL, National Broadcasting Company, New York
W. H. AUDEN, 7 Cornelia Street, New York
FRANK AYDELOTTE, Institute for Advanced Study
JACQUES BARZUN, Columbia University
GEORGE BOAS, The Johns Hopkins University
LYMAN BRYSON, Columbia Broadcasting System, New York
JAMES B. CONANT, Harvard University
EDWARD F. D'ARMS, War Department, Washington, D.C.
HERBERT DAVIS, Smith College
JOHN W. DODDS, Stanford University
IRWIN EDMAN, Columbia University
CHRISTIAN GAUSS, Princeton University
MARGARET GILMAN, Bryn Mawr College
LOUIS GOTTSCHALK, University of Chicago
THEODORE M. GREENE, Yale University
GLEN HAYDON, University of North Carolina
CHARLES W. HENDEL, Yale University
SIR HECTOR HETHERINGTON, University of Glasgow, Scotland
HAJO HOLBORN, Yale University
ROBERT M. HUTCHINS, University of Chicago
WERNER W. JAEGER, Harvard University
HOWARD MUMFORD JONES, Harvard University
MICHAEL KARPOVICH, Harvard University
WOLFGANG KÖHLER, Swarthmore College
STURGIS E. LEAVITT, University of North Carolina
RENSSELAER W. LEE, Smith College and Institute for Advanced Study
BARON LINDSAY OF BIRKER, Balliol College, Oxford, England
ARTHUR O. LOVEJOY, The Johns Hopkins University
ROBERT M. MACIVER, Barnard College, Columbia University
ARCHIBALD MACLEISH, 34 East 70th Street, New York
SALVADOR DE MADARIAGA, 3 Church Street, Old Headington, Oxford, England
JACQUES MARITAIN, The Vatican, Rome, Italy
JOHN MARSHALL, The Rockefeller Foundation, New York
F. O. MATTHIESSEN, Harvard University
RICHARD P. MCKEON, University of Chicago
BORIS MIRKINE-GUETZEVITCH, École Libre des Hautes Études, New York

Henry Allen Moe, The Guggenheim Memorial Foundation, New York
Theodor E. Mommsen, Princeton University
David Nichol Smith, Merton College, Oxford, England
Marjorie Nicolson, Columbia University
Reinhold Niebuhr, Union Theological Seminary, New York
William A. Nitze, Pacific Coast Committee for the Humanities, Los Angeles, California
Edmundo O'Gorman, Universidad Nacional de Mexico, Mexico, D.F.
Stephen C. Pepper, University of California
Ralph Barton Perry, Harvard University
Antony E. Raubitschek, Yale University
I. A. Richards, Harvard University
George H. Sabine, Cornell University
Artur Schnabel, 2 West 86th Street, New York
Harlow Shapley, Harvard College Observatory
Richard H. Shryock, University of Pennsylvania
Ernest J. Simmons, Columbia University
Leo Spitzer, The Johns Hopkins University
Harold Spivacke, The Library of Congress
Wolfgang Stechow, Oberlin College
Walter W. Stewart, Institute for Advanced Study
Francis Henry Taylor, Metropolitan Museum of Art
Lily Ross Taylor, Bryn Mawr College
Homer A. Thompson, University of Toronto, Toronto, Canada
Chi-Chen Wang, Columbia University
Lynn T. White, Mills College, Oakland, California
Ernest H. Wilkins, Oberlin College
James Southall Wilson, University of Virginia

Second Series

WHITNEY J. OATES, *Director*

1. University Education and the Public Service

November 13-14

JAMES FORRESTAL, *Director*
JOSEPH E. MCLEAN, *Assistant Director*

Conference Committee	*Conference Staff*
WILLIAM S. CARPENTER	ISOBEL MUIRHEAD
GEORGE A. GRAHAM	GEORGE A. GRAHAM
DANA G. MUNRO	WILLIAM MILLER
JOHN F. SLY	PAUL M. DOUGLAS
HAROLD H. SPROUT	

Radio Broadcasts: Joseph E. McLean, Arthur Flemming, Sir James Grigg, Herman Finer, H. Struve Hensel, Donald C. Stone, Merle Fainsod, George A. Graham, A. R. M. Lower, Leonard D. White, H. Nevin Gehman, Harold W. Dodds, James Forrestal.

PROGRAM

The Personnel Experiences of Federal Agencies
A Top Management View of the Federal Service
Personnel Needs in the International Field
The British Experience
The Role of the University in Education for the Public Service

PUBLIC SESSION

Managing the Public's Business—James V. Forrestal, Arthur Krock

GUESTS OF THE UNIVERSITY WHO PARTICIPATED

ARTHUR J. ALTMEYER, Commissioner for Social Security
WILLIAM ANDERSON, University of Minnesota

Paul Appleby, Syracuse University
Norman Armour, Formerly Ambassador to Argentina, Chile, and Madrid
Charles S. Ascher, American Society for Public Administration
Louis Brownlow, Public Administration Clearing House. Formerly, President's Committee on Administrative Management
Selden Chapin, Office of the Foreign Service, Department of State
E. P. Chase, Lafayette College
John T. Connor, Navy Department
Wayne Coy, *The Washington Post.* Formerly, Office of Emergency Management
Herman Crystal, Department of Taxation and Finance, State of New Jersey
Robert E. Cushman, Cornell University
Frederick S. Dunn, Yale University
Edward M. Earle, Institute for Advanced Study
Ferdinand Eberstadt, New York City
Rowland Egger, University of Virginia
Herbert Emmerich, Public Administration Clearing House
Merle Fainsod, Harvard University
Herman Finer, University of Chicago
Arthur S. Flemming, U.S. Civil Service Commissioner
Patterson H. French, U.S. Bureau of the Budget
John Gaus, University of Wisconsin
Philip L. Graham, *The Washington Post*
Sir James Grigg, International Bank for Reconstruction and Development
Joseph P. Harris, University of California
H. Struve Hensel, Carter, Ledyard, and Milburn
Carl Herbert, Governmental Research Association
Henry F. Hubbard, Council of Personnel Administration
Philip C. Jessup, Columbia University
William A. Jump, U.S. Department of Agriculture
H. Eliot Kaplan, National Civil Service League
George F. Kennan, National War College
Arthur Krock, *The New York Times*
Robert A. Lovett, Brown Brothers Harriman & Company
A. R. M. Lower, University of Manitoba
William P. Maddox, Division of Foreign Service Studies, Department of State

WILFRED J. MCNEIL, Navy Department
LEWIS MERIAM, The Brookings Institution
CHARLES P. MESSICK, New Jersey Civil Service Commission
FRANK C. NASH, Georgetown University
SAMUEL H. ORDWAY, JR., New York City
HENRY REINING, JR., The Port of New York Authority
WILLIAM C. ROGERS, Public Administration Clearing House
WILLIAM J. RONAN, New York University
THE HONORABLE LEVERETT SALTONSTALL, United States Senate
THE HONORABLE H. ALEXANDER SMITH, United States Senate
THE HONORABLE HAROLD E. STASSEN, South St. Paul, Minnesota
JOHN A. STEVENSON, The Penn Mutual Life Insurance Company
DONALD C. STONE, U.S. Bureau of the Budget
M. H. TRYTTEN, National Research Council
ARTHUR T. VANDERBILT, New York University
DONALD H. WALLACE, Council of Economic Advisers
SCHUYLER WALLACE, Columbia University
KENNETH O. WARNER, U.S. Office of Education
E. L. WOODWARD, Oxford University
DONALD R. YOUNG, Social Science Research Council

2. Problems of Mathematics

December 17-19

S. LEFSCHETZ, *Director*

Conference Committee
The Department of Mathematics

Conference Staff
JOHN W. TUKEY
ALBERT W. TUCKER
RALPH H. FOX
HOWARD P. ROBERTSON
DOUGLAS R. CROSBY

Radio Broadcasts: Samuel S. Wilks, Saunders MacLane, Harald Cramér, Paul Smith, J. W. Tukey, J. H. C. Whitehead.

PROGRAM

Algebra
Algebraic Geometry
Differential Geometry
Mathematical Logic
Topology
New Fields
Mathematical Probability
Analysis
Analysis in the Large

GUESTS OF THE UNIVERSITY WHO PARTICIPATED

L. V. Ahlfors, Harvard University
A. A. Albert, University of Chicago
J. W. Alexander, Institute for Advanced Study
C. B. Allendoerfer, Haverford College
G. Ancochea, University of Salamanca, Spain
E. G. Begle, Yale University
G. Birkhoff, Harvard University
R. P. Boas, *Mathematical Reviews*, Brown University
H. F. Bohnenblust, California Institute of Technology
K. Borsuk, University of Warsaw, Poland
R. Brauer, University of Toronto, Canada
S. S. Cairns, Syracuse University
L. F. Chiang, Academia Sinica, Shanghai, China
I. S. Cohen, University of Pennsylvania
R. Courant, New York University
H. Cramér, University of Stockholm, Sweden
P. A. M. Dirac, Cambridge University
J. L. Doob, University of Illinois
N. Dunford, Yale University
S. Eilenberg, Indiana University
A. Einstein, Institute for Advanced Study
L. P. Eisenhart, Princeton University
G. C. Evans, University of California
W. Feller, Cornell University
K. Gödel, Institute for Advanced Study
O. G. Harrold, Princeton University
G. A. Hedlund, University of Virginia
T. H. Hildebrandt, University of Michigan
E. Hille, Yale University
V. Hlavaty, Charles University of Prague, Czechoslovakia
G. P. Hochschild, Harvard University
W. V. D. Hodge, Cambridge University

H. Hotelling, University of North Carolina
H. Hopf, Federal Institute for Technology, Zurich, Switzerland
L. K. Hua, National Tsing Hua University, Peiping, China
W. Hurewicz, Massachusetts Institute of Technology
N. Jacobson, The Johns Hopkins University
M. Kac, Cornell University
S. C. Kleene, University of Wisconsin
J. R. Kline, University of Pennsylvania
N. Levinson, Massachusetts Institute of Technology
S. MacLane, Harvard University
W. Mayer, Institute for Advanced Study
J. C. C. McKinsey, Oklahoma Agricultural and Mechanical College
E. J. McShane, University of Virginia
D. Montgomery, Yale University
M. Morse, Institute for Advanced Study
F. D. Murnaghan, The Johns Hopkins University
J. von Neumann, Institute for Advanced Study
M. H. A. Newman, Victoria University of Manchester, England
J. Neyman, University of California
W. V. Quine, Harvard University
H. Rademacher, University of Pennsylvania
T. Radó, Ohio State University
M. Riesz, University of Lund, Sweden
R. M. Robinson, University of California
J. B. Rosser, Cornell University
R. Salem, Massachusetts Institute of Technology
I. J. Schoenberg, University of Pennsylvania
M. Shiffman, New York University
P. A. Smith, Columbia University
D. C. Spencer, Stanford University
N. E. Steenrod, University of Michigan
M. H. Stone, University of Chicago
J. L. Synge, Carnegie Institute of Technology
A. Tarski, University of California
T. Y. Thomas, Indiana University
O. Veblen, Institute for Advanced Study
A. Wald, Columbia University
R. J. Walker, Cornell University
J. L. Walsh, Harvard University
J. H. M. Wedderburn, Princeton University

H. Weyl, Institute for Advanced Study
J. H. C. Whitehead, Oxford University
H. Whitney, Harvard University
G. T. Whyburn, University of Virginia
D. V. Widder, Harvard University
N. Wiener, Massachusetts Institute of Technology
R. L. Wilder, University of Michigan
J. W. T. Youngs, Indiana University
O. Zariski, University of Illinois
A. Zygmund, University of Pennsylvania

3. Genetics, Paleontology, and Evolution

January 2-4

Glenn L. Jepsen, *Director*

Conference Advisory Committee

Kenneth W. Cooper
Theodosius Dobzhansky
Ernst Mayr
G. G. Simpson
G. Ledyard Stebbins

Conference Staff

Arthur F. Buddington
Elmer G. Butler
Kenneth W. Cooper
Erling Dorf
Gerhard Fankhauser
Steven K. Fox
B. F. Howell
G. H. Shull
F. van Houten
C. E. Wilde, Jr.

Radio Broadcasts: Curt Stern, J. B. S. Haldane, Alfred S. Romer, Theodosius Dobzhansky, G. H. R. von Koenigswald.

PROGRAM

Time in Earth History
Gene and Character
Gene and Mutation
Time Series, Trends, in Animals
Time Series, Trends, in Plants
Rates of Evolution in Animals
Rates of Evolution in Plants
Speciation and Systematics
Adaptation and Selection
Summation

PUBLIC SESSION

Man's Evolution, Past and Future—J. B. S. Haldane

GUESTS OF THE UNIVERSITY WHO PARTICIPATED

E. Anderson, Missouri Botanical Garden
Henry N. Andrews, Jr., Missouri Botanical Garden
G. W. Beadle, California Institute of Technology
Arthur Bevan, National Research Council
Harold F. Blum, National Cancer Institute, Bethesda, Maryland. (Princeton University)
Walter H. Bucher, Columbia University
Charles L. Camp, University of California
Ralph W. Chaney, University of California
Edwin H. Colbert, American Museum of Natural History
G. Arthur Cooper, U.S. National Museum
D. Dwight Davis, Chicago Natural History Museum
M. Demerec, Carnegie Institution of Washington, Cold Spring Harbor
Lee R. Dice, University of Michigan
Th. Dobzhansky, Columbia University
Carl O. Dunbar, Yale University
Emmett Reid Dunn, Haverford College
Maxim K. Elias, Nebraska Geological Survey
Carl Epling, University of California at Los Angeles
E. B. Ford, University Museum, Oxford, England
Bentley Glass, Goucher College. (The Johns Hopkins University)
Myron Gordon, New York Zoological Society
Joseph T. Gregory, Yale University
J. B. S. Haldane, University College, London, England
William Hovanitz, University of Michigan
Carl L. Hubbs, Scripps Institution of Oceanography, University of California
Patrick M. Hurley, Massachusetts Institute of Technology
Theo. Just, Chicago Natural History Museum
J. Brookes Knight, U.S. National Museum
Adolph Knopf, Yale University
Gustav Heinrich Ralph von Koenigswald, The Geological Survey of the N.E.I., Java. (University of Utrecht, Holland)
David Lack, Edward Grey Institute, Oxford, England
S. E. Luria, Indiana University
Paul O. McGrew, University of Wyoming
Klaus Mampell, University of Pennsylvania

Herbert L. Mason, University of California
Ernst Mayr, American Museum of Natural History
Charles D. Michener, American Museum of Natural History
A. K. Miller, State University of Iowa
John A. Moore, Barnard College
H. J. Muller, Indiana University
Norman D. Newell, American Museum of Natural History
E. Novitski, University of Rochester. (University of Missouri)
Marion Ownbey, State College of Washington
Bryan Patterson, Chicago Natural History Museum
C. S. Pittendrigh, Columbia University. (Princeton University)
Alfred S. Romer, Harvard University
Bobb Schaeffer, American Museum of Natural History
Karl P. Schmidt, Chicago Natural History Museum
G. G. Simpson, American Museum of Natural History
T. M. Sonneborn, Indiana University
Warren P. Spencer, College of Wooster
Lewis J. Stadler, University of Missouri
Harrison D. Stalker, Washington University Missouri
G. Ledyard Stebbins, Jr., University of California
Curt Stern, University of Rochester. (University of California)
R. A. Stirton, University of California
A. H. Sturtevant, California Institute of Technology
D. M. S. Watson, University College, London, England
T. Stanley Westoll, Marischal College, Scotland
Horace E. Wood, 2nd, The Newark Colleges of Rutgers University
Sewall Wright, University of Chicago

4. The University and Its World Responsibilities

February 19-21

Gordon A. Craig and Cyril E. Black, *Directors*

Conference Committee

W. O. Aydelotte
Carlos H. Baker
Elmer A. Beller
E. Harris Harbison
Theodor E. Mommsen
Svein Rosseland
George F. Thomas
Roy D. Welch

CONFERENCES

Conference Staff

THOMAS L. CRYSTAL
RALPH GREENLAW
REUBEN H. GROSS, JR.
E. L. KATZENBACH

Radio Broadcasts: G. A. Borgese, Garrett Mattingly, David Daiches, Arnold J. Toynbee, C. Mildred Thompson, Stuart E. Grummon, Ben Cherrington, William E. Rappard, George Shuster.

PROGRAM

The Problem of the University Today
The University, its mission and its problems
University Education and Intercultural Cooperation
Education for intercultural understanding
A sample discipline: the teaching of history
Toward a new *jus gentium*
Toward a Federative Policy in Higher Education
Should there be a world federation of universities?
UNESCO: New Demands on Universities
The universities' relation to UNESCO

PUBLIC SESSION

International Intellectual Cooperation—His Excellency Henri Bonnet,* Archibald MacLeish

GUESTS OF THE UNIVERSITY WHO PARTICIPATED

EUGENE N. ANDERSON, Department of State
FRANK AYDELOTTE, Institute for Advanced Study, Princeton
EDWARD W. BARRETT, *Newsweek*
JACQUES BARZUN, Columbia University
SARAH GIBSON BLANDING, Vassar College
G. A. BORGESE, University of Chicago
GRAY C. BOYCE, Northwestern University
LYMAN BRYSON, Columbia Broadcasting System
SCOTT BUCHANAN, St. John's College
EVERETT CASE, Colgate University
BEN M. CHERRINGTON, University of Denver
GEORGE P. CUTTINO, Swarthmore College
DAVID DAICHES, Cornell University

*Unable to be present. Speech read by Armand Berand

Edmund E. Day, Cornell University
C. W. de Kiewiet, Cornell University
Edward Mead Earle, Institute for Advanced Study, Princeton
Louis Finkelstein, Jewish Theological Seminary of America
Ralph H. Gabriel, Yale University
Leo Gershoy, New York University
Felix Gilbert, Bryn Mawr College
Stuart E. Grummon, Redding, Connecticut
Oscar Halecki, Fordham University
John N. Hazard, Columbia University
Hajo Holborn, Yale University
Sidney Hook, New York University
Bryn J. Hovde, New School for Social Research, New York
Erich Kahler, Princeton, New Jersey
Horace M. Kallen, New School for Social Research, New York
Fred J. Kelly, Palo Alto, California
Cornelius Krusé, Wesleyan University
Waldo G. Leland, American Council of Learned Societies, Washington
Archibald MacLeish, UNESCO
Katharine E. McBride, Bryn Mawr College
Anne O'Hare McCormick, *The New York Times*
Charles H. McIlwain, Harvard University
John A. Mackay, Princeton Theological Seminary
John Marshall, Rockefeller Foundation
Garrett Mattingly, The Cooper Union
Alexander Meiklejohn, St. John's College
Boris Mirkine-Guetzvitch, École Libre des Hautes Études, New York
David Mitrany, Institute for Advanced Study, Princeton
Arnold S. Nash, McCormick Theological Seminary
Emery Neff, Columbia University
Sigmund Neumann, Wesleyan University
F. S. C. Northrop, Yale University
Anton Charles Pegis, Pontifical Institute of Medieval Studies, Toronto, Canada
Pittman B. Potter, *American Journal of International Law*
Roscoe Pound, Harvard University
William E. Rappard, Institut Universitaire des Hautes Études Internationales, Geneva, Switzerland

George L. Ridgeway, International Business Machines Corporation
Robert Kilburn Root, Princeton University
George N. Shuster, Hunter College
Henry E. Sigerist, The Johns Hopkins University
David H. Stevens, Rockefeller Foundation
Walter W. Stewart, Institute for Advanced Study, Princeton
C. Mildred Thompson, Vassar College
Charles A. Thomson, U.S. National Commission for UNESCO, Department of State
Arnold J. Toynbee, Royal Institute of International Affairs, Chatham House, London, England
Ralph Turner, Yale University
Robert Ulich, Harvard University
Joseph H. Willits, Rockefeller Foundation
Howard E. Wilson, Carnegie Endowment for International Peace
Silvio Zavala, Long Island, New York
George F. Zook, American Council on Education, Washington

5. Planning Man's Physical Environment

March 5-6

Arthur C. Holden, *Director*

Conference Committee

Henry A. Jandl
Kenneth S. Kassler
Jean Labatut
Sherley W. Morgan
Robert B. O'Connor

Conference Staff

John K. Shear
Henry A. Jandl
William F. Shellman
Francis A. Comstock

Radio Broadcasts: Thomas Creighton, Louis Justement, Henry Churchill, George Howe.

Exhibits: Examples of the work of Frank Lloyd Wright, Robert Moses, Tony Garnier, and Alvar Aalto. Demonstrations of the psychology of vision from the Dartmouth Eye Institute. Architectural exhibit in McCormick Hall.

PROGRAM

The Visual and Social Basis of Design
Physical Possibilities and Limitations of Design
Philosophy of Form and the Psychological Effect of Form
Review of Social, Physical, and Intellectual Attributes of Design
Extensive Environment
The Building as the Limiting Element of Space
The Design of Individual Objects and their Place in Environment

GUESTS OF THE UNIVERSITY WHO PARTICIPATED

Alvar Aalto, Massachusetts Institute of Technology
Frederick J. Adams, Massachusetts Institute of Technology
Adelbert Ames, Jr., Dartmouth Eye Institute
Leopold Arnaud, Columbia University
Walter Baermann, Industrial Designer, New York City
Catherine Bauer, Harvard University
Richard M. Bennett, Architect, Chicago
Wells I. Bennett, University of Michigan
T. L. Blakeman, Department of New Jersey Economic Development
John E. Burchard, Massachusetts Institute of Technology
Hadley Cantril, Princeton University
Serge Chermayeff, Institute of Design, Chicago
Henry S. Churchill, Architect, New York City
Carlos Contreras, Architect, Mexico City
Thomas H. Creighton, *Progressive Architecture*
Aymar Embury, II, Architect, New York City
Hugh Ferriss, Architect, New York City
A. M. Friend, Jr., Princeton University
Sigfried Giedion, Zurich, Switzerland
William Roger Greeley, Architect, Boston
Theodore M. Greene, Yale University
Walter Gropius, Harvard University
Talbot F. Hamlin, Columbia University
George Howe, Architect, Philadelphia
Joseph Hudnut, Harvard University
Philip C. Johnson, Museum of Modern Art, New York City
B. Kenneth Johnstone, Carnegie Institute of Technology
Roy Childs Jones, University of Minnesota

Louis Justement, Architect, Washington, D.C.
Henry L. Kamphoefner, University of Oklahoma
George Fred Keck, Architect, Chicago
Gyorgy Kepes, Massachusetts Institute of Technology
Morris Ketchum, Jr., Architect, New York City
A. Lawrence Kocher, College of William and Mary
Ernest J. Kump, Architect, San Francisco
Liang Ssŭ-Ch'êng, Academia Sinica, Nanking, China
A. Gordon Lorimer, Architect, Douglaston, Long Island
Theodore T. McCrosky, Greater Boston Development Committee, Inc., Boston
Robert W. McLaughlin, Architect, New York City
C. L. V. Meeks, Yale University
Arthur E. Morgan, Community Service, Inc., Yellow Springs, Ohio
Robert Moses, New York City
Richard J. Neutra, Architect, Los Angeles
Marcelo Roberto, Architect, Rio de Janeiro, Brazil
Walter T. Rolfe, Architect, Houston
Jose Luis Sert, City Planning Consultant, New York City
Fred N. Severud, Engineer, New York City
G. E. Kidder Smith, Architect, New York City
Walter A. Taylor, American Institute of Architects
Mies van der Rohe, Illinois Institute of Technology
Howard P. Vermilya, American Houses Inc., New York City
Konrad Wachsmann, Engineer, New York City
Ralph Walker, Architect, New York City
J. Kendall Wallis, M.D., Princeton University
Roland A. Wank, Architect, New York City
George Grey Wornum, R.I.B.A., London, England
Frank Lloyd Wright, Architect, Spring Green, Wisconsin
William W. Wurster, Massachusetts Institute of Technology

6. Near Eastern Culture and Society

March 25-27

Philip K. Hitti, *Director*

Conference Committee

Dana C. Munro, Edward J. Jurji, George Rowley

Conference Staff

WALTER L. WRIGHT, JR.	WILLARD BELING
R. BAYLY WINDER	ERNEST DAWN
JIBRA'IL JABBUR	HARRY HAZARD
IZZ-AL-DIN AL YASIN	WILFRED SMITH

Radio Broadcasts: John A. Wilson, Walter L. Wright, Jr., Emile Zaidan, Charles Malik, Matta Akrawi, Ananda Coomaraswamy, Jibra'il Jabbur, Edward J. Jurji, Costi K. Zurayk, Philip K. Hitti.

Exhibit: Arabic, Turkish, and Persian manuscripts from the Garrett Collection, Treasure Room, University Library.

PROGRAM

Art and Archaeology
- Islamic Art: new approaches in research
- Islamic Archaeology: new approaches in research

Literature and Religion
- Arabic Scientific Literature: new approaches in research
- Arabic Religious Literature: new approaches in research
- Arabic Language and Literature: new approaches in research

Cultural and Political Problems
- Interaction of Islamic and Western thought in retrospect and prospect
  - Turkey—Iran—the Arab World

Religious, Social, and Political Problems
- The Arab peoples in their national and international relationship
- The Arab World in its relation to the United States of America

GUESTS OF THE UNIVERSITY WHO PARTICIPATED

BARCLAY ACHESON, International Editions of the *Reader's Digest*

ABDULHAK ADNAN ADIVAR, *Turkish Encyclopedia of Islām*, Istanbul

MEHMET AGA-OGLU, New York City

MATTA AKRAWI, Government of Iraq

E. P. ARBEZ, Catholic University of America

GEORGE M. BARAKAT, Advisory Council, Princeton University Department of Oriental Languages

ERIC F. F. BISHOP, Kennedy School of Missions; Newman School of Missions, Jerusalem

AMIR BOKTOR, American University at Cairo; University of Illinois
W. NORMAN BROWN, University of Pennsylvania
EDWIN E. CALVERLEY, The Hartford Seminary Foundation; *The Moslem World*
HAROLD W. CLOSE, American University of Beirut
ANANDA K. COOMARASWAMY, Museum of Fine Arts, Boston
K. A. C. CRESWELL, King Fouad I University
FLORENCE E. DAY, Dumbarton Oaks, Washington, D.C.
G. LEVI DELLA VIDA, University of Pennsylvania
MAURICE S. DIMAND, Metropolitan Museum of Art
BASILE D'OUAKIL, Fordham University
JAMES T. DUCE, Arabian American Oil Company
RICHARD ETTINGHAUSEN, Freer Gallery of Art; *Ars Islamica*
CHARLES B. FAHS, Rockefeller Foundation
JOHN W. GARDNER, Carnegie Corporation of New York
MOORE GATES, Advisory Council, Princeton University Department of Oriental Languages
H. A. R. GIBB, Oxford University
SIDNEY S. GLAZER, Library of Congress
CYRUS GORDON, Dropsie College
MORTIMER GRAVES, American Council of Learned Societies
GUSTAVE E. VON GRUNEBAUM, University of Chicago
WILLIAM S. HAAS, School of Asiatic Studies
MOSTAFA M. HAFEZ, Princeton Graduate College; King Fouad I University
HARVEY P. HALL, *The Middle East Journal*
M. HESSABY, University of Teheran
WILLIAM ERNEST HOCKING, Harvard University
HALFORD L. HOSKINS, Middle East Institute and School of Advanced International Study
HAROLD HOSKINS, Advisory Council, Princeton University Department of Oriental Languages
HABIB A. KURANI, Office of International Information and Cultural Relations, Department of State; American University of Beirut
ILSE LICHTENSTADTER, School of Asiatic Studies
ALBERT H. LYBYER, University of Illinois
HANNAH E. MCALLISTER, Metropolitan Museum of Art
CHARLES MALIK, American University of Beirut

George C. Miles, American Numismatic Society
Walter S. Rogers, Institute of Current World Affairs
Franz Rosenthal, Hebrew Union College
George Sarton, Carnegie Institution; Harvard University; *Isis, Osiris*
G. Howland Shaw, Former Assistant Secretary of State, Washington, D.C.
M. Sherif Basoglu, University of Ankara
Solomon L. Skoss, Dropsie College
Myron B. Smith, University of Chicago
Harry R. Snyder, Near East Colleges Association
Robert R. Solenberger, Upper Darby, Pennsylvania
Afif I. Tannous, Department of Agriculture
William Thomson, Harvard University
Allen O. Whipple, Memorial Hospital, New York
Wilbur W. White, Western Reserve University
Donald N. Wilber, School of Asiatic Studies
Charles K. Wilkinson, Metropolitan Museum of Art
John A. Wilson, University of Chicago
J. Christy Wilson, Princeton Theological Seminary
T. Cuyler Young, University of Toronto
Emile Zaidan, *al-Hilal*, Cairo
Costi K. Zurayk, American University of Beirut

7. Far Eastern Culture and Society

April 1-3

George Rowley, *Director*
David N. Rowe, *Associate Director*

Conference Staff

Chinese Art and Archaeology

James D. Breckenridge
Ernest T. DeWald
Ransom R. Patrick
George B. Tatum
David R. Coffin

Chinese Society

William W. Lockwood
Reuben H. Gross, Jr.
H. D. Barnett
William W. Marvel
Sandy M. Pringle
Richard F. Bortz
Anthony H. C. Hill

CONFERENCES

Exhibitions

Installations	*Catalogues*
M. Lester Cooke, Jr.	Yiu Tung
Frances F. Jones	Wang Ch'i-ch'en
P. Joseph Kelleher	Wang Chung-min
William F. Shellman, Jr.	Wu Kwang-tsing

Radio Broadcasts: George E. Taylor, Owen Lattimore, Michael Lindsay, William L. Holland, John R. Fairbank, Harold D. Lasswell, David N. Rowe.

Exhibit: Chinese Paintings and Bronzes, Museum of Historic Art.

PROGRAM

Chinese Art and Archaeology
- Historical development, figure style
- Historical development, landscape style
- Special problems, bronze vessels
- Special problems: garden design and iconography
- Recent discoveries and future investigations
- The stone reliefs in Shoshoin
- T'ang and Sung sculpture
- Architectural discoveries

Chinese Society
- China's social heritage
  - Geographical influence
  - Political and social philosophy
  - Economic and political elements
- Social transition in modern China: Demographic elements
- China's potentialities as a modern state: industrialization, political

PUBLIC SESSION

The Background of Chinese Philosophy—Fung Yu-lan

Communication and Acculturation in Modern China—David N. Rowe

The Future of Chinese Studies in America—George E. Taylor

GUESTS OF THE UNIVERSITY WHO PARTICIPATED

William R. B. Acker, Freer Gallery of Art, Smithsonian Institution

Ludwig F. Bachhofer, University of Chicago

Knight Biggerstaff, Cornell University
Derk Bodde, University of Pennsylvania
Chen Han-seng, The Johns Hopkins University
Ch'en Meng-chia, University of Chicago
Chen Shou-chiang, Columbia University
Chen Ta, Tsing Hua University
Chu Tung-tsu, Columbia University
Herrlee G. Creel, University of Chicago
George B. Cressey, Syracuse University
J. J. L. Duyvendak, University of Leyden
Roger Evans, Rockefeller Foundation
Charles B. Fahs, Rockefeller Foundation
John K. Fairbank, Harvard University
Fung Yu-lan, Tsing Hua University
Charles S. Gardner, Cambridge, Massachusetts
L. Carrington Goodrich, Columbia University
Mortimer Graves, American Council of Learned Societies
Chauncey J. Hamlin, Chinese Art Society of America, Inc.
William L. Holland, Institute of Pacific Relations
Ernest R. Hughes, Oxford University
Arthur W. Hummel, Library of Congress
Horace H. F. Jayne, Metropolitan Museum of Art
Harold D. Lasswell, Yale University
Kenneth S. Latourette, Yale University
Owen Lattimore, The Johns Hopkins University
Liang Ssŭ-Ch'êng, Tsing Hua University
Michael Lindsay, Harvard University
Du Bois Schanck Morris, New York City
John E. Orchard, Columbia University
James M. Plumer, University of Michigan
John A. Pope, Freer Gallery of Art, Smithsonian Institution
Alan Priest, Metropolitan Museum of Art
Laurance P. Roberts, New York City
David N. Rowe, Yale University
Benjamin Rowland, Harvard University
Alfred Salmony, New York University
Laurence K. Sickman, William Rockhill Nelson Gallery of Art
Osvald Siren, National Museum, Stockholm
Alexander C. Soper, Bryn Mawr College
George E. Taylor, University of Washington
Warren S. Thompson, Miami University

Wang Kan-yu, University of Washington
Langdon Warner, Harvard University
Archibald G. Wenley, Freer Gallery of Art, Smithsonian Institution
C. Martin Wilbur, Division of Research for Far East, Department of State
Karl A. Wittfogel, Columbia University
Arthur N. Young, National Government of China

Together with a number of additional scholars and graduate students, members of the Princeton faculty were also invited to attend the conference.

8. Scholarship and Research in the Arts

April 22-24

E. Baldwin Smith, *Director*
A. M. Friend, Jr. and Oliver Strunk, *Associate Directors*

Conference Committee

Randall Thompson
Roy D. Welch
Ernest T. DeWald

Conference Staff

William L. M. Burke
Edward T. Cone
David R. Coffin
Robert A. Koch
Joseph W. Kerman
Donald D. Egbert
Richard Stillwell
J. Merrill Knapp

Exhibits: Drawings by G. H. Forsyth, Jr., of the Church of St. Martin at Angers. Exhibit of Byzantine Art, organized by Walters Art Gallery, Baltimore Museum of Art. Exhibit of Byzantine Art at the Freer Gallery, Washington, D.C.

PROGRAM

I The Architectural Historian and the Problems of Fact and Interpretation
- Fact and interpretation in the work of the architectural historian
- From concept to structure; the architectural profession in the Age of Pericles

Architectural design and contemporary thought: Gothic and Scholasticism

The Architectural historian and the Present

II Studies in Byzantine Art and the Future Need of Scholarly Cooperation Between Institutions of Learning

Les Peintures de la Synagogue de Dura et L'Art Chrétien du haut moyen-âge et du moyen-âge oriental

Saint-Sophie d'Edesse d'apres une hymne syriaque

Significance of Old Testament illustrations and the publication of the Septuagint

Research in Byzantine liturgy and music

PUBLIC SESSION

Scholarship in the Arts, Its Past and Future—Paul H. Buck, C. R. Morey

The Vatican and Byzantine Studies—Eugène Cardinal Tisserant

III Music and the Renaissance

Expression and Symbol in the Italian Madrigal

PUBLIC CONCERT

Program of sixteenth century part-songs under the direction of Randall Thompson

GUESTS OF THE UNIVERSITY WHO PARTICIPATED

Milton V. Anastos, Harvard University, Dumbarton Oaks
Myrtilla Avery, Wellesley College
Turpin C. Bannister, Alabama Polytechnic Institute
Franklin Biebel, The Frick Collection
Hon. Robert Woods Bliss, Washington, D.C.
Mrs. Robert Woods Bliss, Washington, D.C.
Herbert Bloch, Harvard University
Mark Brunswick, College of the City of New York
Paul H. Buck, Harvard University
Manfred F. Bukofzer, University of California
William L. M. Burke, Princeton University
Edward Capps, Jr., Oberlin College
Kenneth Conant, Harvard University
Walter W. S. Cook, New York University
John P. Coolidge, University of Pennsylvania
Sumner McK. Crosby, Yale University

Sirarpie Der Nersessian, Harvard University, Dumbarton Oaks
Ernest T. DeWald, Princeton University
George S. Dickinson, Vassar College
William B. Dinsmoor, Columbia University
Glanville Downey, Harvard University, Dumbarton Oaks
Donald D. Egbert, Princeton University
Alfred Einstein, Smith College
George W. Elderkin, Princeton University
Richard Ettinghausen, Freer Gallery of Art, Smithsonian Institution
James Ford, Princeton University
George H. Forsyth, Jr., University of Michigan
William H. Forsyth, Metropolitan Museum of Art
Charles W. Fox, Eastman School of Music
Paul Frankl, Institute for Advanced Study
Albert M. Friend, Jr., Princeton University
Otto Gombosi, Michigan State College
Donald Goodchild, American Council of Learned Societies
André Grabar, Collège de France and Harvard University, Dumbarton Oaks
Donald J. Grout, Cornell University
Meta Harrsen, Pierpont Morgan Library
Glen Haydon, University of North Carolina
Carl K. Hersey, University of Rochester
Erich Hertzmann, Columbia and Princeton Universities
Helen Hewitt, University of Texas
Richard S. Hill, Library of Congress
Henry Russell Hitchcock, Wesleyan University
Clark Hopkins, University of Michigan
Francis Hyslop, Pennsylvania State College
R. P. G. de Jerphanion, Institut Pontifical Oriental
Raymond Kendall, University of Michigan
Fiske Kimball, Philadelphia Museum of Art
Edward S. King, Walters Art Gallery
Otto Kinkeldey, Cornell University, Emeritus and Harvard University
Ernst Kitzinger, Harvard University, Dumbarton Oaks
Carl Kraeling, Yale and Harvard Universities; Dumbarton Oaks
Richard Krautheimer, Vassar College
George Kubler, Yale University

Stephen Kuttner, Catholic University of America
Paul H. Lang, Columbia University
Marion Lawrence, Barnard College
Rensselaer W. Lee, Smith College and Institute for Advanced Study
Karl Lehmann, New York University
Edward E. Lowinsky, Black Mountain College
John McAndrew, Wellesley College
Duncan McKensie, New Jersey College for Women
Carroll L. V. Meeks, Yale University
Arthur Mendel, New York
Benjamin D. Meritt, Institute for Advanced Study
The Very Reverend Father P. T. Michels, O.S.B., St. Paul's Priory
Ulrich Middeldorf, University of Chicago
C. Rufus Morey, Department of State
Hugh S. Morrison, Dartmouth College
Hans Nathan, Michigan State College
Erwin Panofsky, Institute for Advanced Study
Carl Parrish, Westminster Choir School
Dragan Plamenac, New York, New York
Gustave Reese, New York University
David M. Robb, University of Pennsylvania
James J. Rorimer, Metropolitan Museum of Art
Walter H. Rubsamen, University of California at Los Angeles
Curt Sachs, New York University
Paul J. Sachs, Harvard University
Leo Schrade, Yale University
Joseph C. Sloane, Jr., Bryn Mawr College
Carlton Sprague Smith, New York Public Library
E. Baldwin Smith, Princeton University
Alexander C. Soper, Bryn Mawr College
Harold Spivacke, Library of Congress
F. W. Sternfeld, Dartmouth College
Richard Stillwell, Princeton University
W. Frederick Stohlman, Princeton University
Dom Anselm Strittmatter, O.S.B., St. Anselm's Priory
Oliver Strunk, Princeton University
Emerson H. Swift, Columbia University
Hanns Swarzenski, Institute for Advanced Study

Mary H. Swindler, Bryn Mawr College
James Sykes, Longport, New Jersey
John Thacher, Harvard University, Dumbarton Oaks
His Eminence Eugene Cardinal Tisserant, The Vatican
Randall Thompson, Princeton University
Dimitris T. Tselos, New York University
Stephen Tuttle, University of Virginia
Paul A. Underwood, Harvard University, Dumbarton Oaks
Everard M. Upjohn, Columbia University
Alexander A. Vasiliev, Harvard University, Dumbarton Oaks
Frederick O. Waage, iii, Cornell University
Clarence Ward, Oberlin College
Carl Weinrich, Princeton University
Kurt Weitzmann, Princeton University and Institute for Advanced Study
Roy D. Welch, Princeton University
Egon T. Wellesz, Oxford University
Donald Wilber, School of Asiatic Studies
Harold R. Willoughby, University of Chicago
Emanuel Winternitz, Metropolitan Museum of Art
Helen Woodruff, Princeton, New Jersey
G. Wallace Woodworth, Harvard University
Stephen G. Xydis, United Nations
Frederick Yeiser, *Cincinnati Enquirer*

9. The Role of the Undergraduate in University Life

April 25-26

Frazier D. MacIver, Jr., *Director*
DeWitt C. Jones iii, *Chairman*
William A. Chisholm, *Adviser*
R. Harry Webster, *Recorder*

Conference Committee

Benjamin F. Houston   Philip W. Bell

Radio Broadcasts: James L. Kirby, William C. Campbell, Richard Bostwick, William McKenzie.

PROGRAM

The Role of Student Government
The Pattern of Social Organization on the Campus
The Four Sides of a Liberal Education

MEMBERS OF THE CONFERENCE

Richard G. Axt, Harvard University
Arnold M. Berlin, Princeton University
Allen I. Bildner, Dartmouth College
Richard C. Bostwick, University of Pennsylvania
Currie L. Brewer, Williams College
William C. Campbell, Princeton University
Randolph B. Cardozo, University of Virginia
Everett Case, Colgate University
Judson Decker, Princeton University
Francis R. Drury, Jr., Dartmouth College
John Curtis Farrar, Yale University
Peter W. Fay, Harvard University
Willard B. Fernald, Brown University
Christian Gauss, Princeton University
Frank F. Gibson, Amherst College
Edward Gold, Columbia University
David C. Huntington, Princeton University
Alexander M. Keith, Amherst College
James L. Kirby, Jr., Princeton University
Edwin L. Knetzger, Princeton University
Tremper Longman, Princeton University
William H. MacKenzie, Rutgers University
William E. McAuliffe, Brown University
Thomas Morse, Cornell University
John D. Mosser, Princeton University
Alfred A. Neuschaefer, Jr., Rutgers University
Charles R. Nielsen, Princeton University
Michael J. O'Neill, University of Pennsylvania
Richard A. Paddock, Cornell University
Norman Redlich, Williams College
Lilburn T. Talley, University of Virginia
Sherman Tibbets, Colgate University
Thomas B. Turley, Colgate University
H. Bradford Westerfield, Yale University
Bernard Wishy, Columbia University

10. The Responsibilities of Secondary Education in the Years Ahead

May 12-14

RADCLIFFE HEERMANCE, *Director*
ALBERT ELSASSER, *Associate Director*

Conference Committee
WILLIAM G. AVIRETT
HAROLD A. FERGUSON
CLAUDE M. FUESS
E. S. WELLS KERR
LEDLIE I. LAUGHLIN
JOHN F. SLY
E. LAWRENCE SPRINGER

Conference Staff
HAMILTON COTTIER
MINOT C. MORGAN, JR.
WILLIAM LIPPINCOTT
GARDNER CUNNINGHAM
MACPHERSON RAYMOND
H. NEVIN GEHMAN
FREDERICK S. OSBORNE
JOHN KAUFFMANN
CHARLES S. SHAIN
JAMES HARLE

Radio Broadcasts: Frederick Kahler, Harold Ferguson, Lester Nelson, William Avirett, John DeQ. Briggs, William H. Cornog.

PROGRAM

Exploratory
- The college looks at the schoolmaster
- The schoolmaster looks at the college
- The layman looks at both

Whom to Teach?
- Searching for talent
- Testing for talent
- Burying talent
- Developing talent
- Providing for different kinds of talent

Who Shall Teach?

What to Teach?
- Curriculum planning in America
- Secondary education in England
- Educational planning in Europe

To What End?
- Religious and spiritual factors

GUESTS OF THE UNIVERSITY WHO PARTICIPATED

Hymen Alpern, Evander Childs High School, New York City
Frank D. Ashburn, Brooks School, Andover, Mass.
William G. Avirett, *The New York Herald Tribune*, New York City
Francis L. Bacon, Evanston Township High School, Evanston, Ill.
L. S. Beattie, Ontario Department of Education, Toronto, Canada
John H. Bosshart, State Department of Education, Trenton, N.J.
Frank L. Boyden, Deerfield Academy, Deerfield, Mass.
John DeQ. Briggs, St. Paul Academy, St. Paul, Minn.
Henry H. Callard, Gilman Country School, Baltimore, Md.
William G. Carr, National Education Association, Washington, D.C.
Hollis L. Caswell, Columbia University
Henry Chauncey, College Entrance Examination Board, Princeton, N.J.
John T. Christie, Westminster School, London, England
James S. Collins, North Quincy High School, North Quincy, Mass.
William H. Cornog, Central High School, Philadelphia, Pa.
B. Woodhull Davis, Princeton Public Schools, Princeton, N.J.
John E. Dugan, Beaver College, Jenkintown, Pa.
Edward W. Eames, Governor Dummer Academy, South Byfield, Mass.
Paul E. Elicker, National Association of Secondary School Principals, Washington, D.C.
Harold A. Ferguson, Montclair High School, Montclair, N.J.
Burton P. Fowler, Germantown Friends School, Germantown, Pa.
Will French, Columbia University
Claude M. Fuess, Phillips Academy, Andover, Mass.
Christian Gauss, Princeton University
Albert J. Geiger, St. Petersburg High School, St. Petersburg, Fla.
Alonzo G. Grace, State Department of Education, Hartford, Conn.

JOHN F. GUMMERE, William Penn Charter School, Germantown, Pa.
ERDMAN HARRIS, Shady Side Academy, Pittsburgh, Pa.
GREVILLE HASLAM, Episcopal Academy, Overbrook, Pa.
ALLAN V. HEELY, Lawrenceville School, Lawrenceville, N.J.
MAX HERZBERG, Weequahic High School, Newark, N.J.
C. LAMBERT HEYNIGER, Darrow School, New Lebanon, N.Y.
WILLIAM C. HILL, Classical High School, Springfield, Mass.
ELWOOD F. IRELAND, Gould Academy, Bethel, Me.
EDGAR G. JOHNSTON, University of Michigan
GALEN JONES, United States Office of Education, Washington, D.C.
FREDERICK A. KAHLER, New Trier High School, Winnetka, Ill.
E. S. WELLS KERR, Phillips Academy, Exeter, N.H.
HUGH LYON, Rugby School, Rugby, England
BURR J. MERRIAM, School Department, Framingham, Mass.
NORMAN B. NASH, Diocesan House, Boston, Mass.
LESTER W. NELSON, Scarsdale High School, Scarsdale, N.Y.
NORMAN J. NELSON, Public Schools, District of Columbia
GEORGE R. H. NICHOLSON, Kingswood School, West Hartford, Conn.
H. DEAN PEARL, Edmunds High School, Burlington, Vt.
JOSEPH L. POWERS, Public Latin School, Boston, Mass.
MERVYN W. PRITCHARD, British Embassy, Washington, D.C.
EDWARD PULLING, Millbrook School, Millbrook, N.Y.
PAUL A. REHMUS, Board of Education, Lakewood, Ohio
ARTHUR S. ROBERTS, Natick, Mass.
HEBER H. RYAN, State Department of Education, Trenton, N.J.
WILLIAM G. SALTONSTALL, Phillips Academy, Exeter, N.H.
WILBOUR E. SAUNDERS, Peddie School, Hightstown, N.J.
HERBERT W. SMITH, Francis W. Parker School, Chicago, Ill.
PERRY D. SMITH, North Shore Country Day School, Winnetka, Ill.
WILLIAM R. SMITHEY, University of Virginia
PAUL R. SPENCER, Central High School, Trenton, N.J.
E. LAURENCE SPRINGER, Pingry School, Elizabeth, N.J.
CHARLES L. STEEL, Teaneck High School, Teaneck, N.J.
IAN M. B. STUART, Enniskillen, North Ireland
JOHN W. STUDEBAKER, United States Office of Education Washington, D.C.
ANSON S. THACHER, Thacher School, Ojai, Calif.

Charles C. Tillinghast, Horace Mann School for Boys, New York City
Charles S. Tippetts, Mercersburg Academy, Mercersburg, Pa.
Robert Ulich, Harvard University
George Van Santvoord, Hotchkiss School, Lakeville, Conn.
George A. Walton, George School, George School, Pa.
James I. Wendell, Hill School, Pottstown, Pa.
Lambert F. Whetstone, Detroit University School, Grosse Pointe Woods, Mich.
M. H. Willing, University of Michigan
O. N. Wing, Central YMCA High School, Chicago, Ill.
Sydney H. Wood, Ministry of Education, London, England
Eugene Youngert, Oak Park Township High School, Oak Park, Ill.

7

Musical Events
of the Bicentennial Year

September 29. ORGAN RECITAL, *Carl Weinrich*, Procter Hall, Graduate College. This recital was given as part of the program of the Conference on "The Chemistry and Physiology of Growth."

October 13. ORGAN RECITAL, *Carl Weinrich*, Procter Hall, Graduate College. This recital was given as part of the program of the Conference on the "Development of International Society."

October 19. BICENTENNIAL COMMEMORATIVE ANTHEM: "Let Us Now Praise Famous Men." This anthem, sung by the Chapel Choir and the University Glee Club at the Charter Day Convocation, was composed especially for the occasion by Edward T. Cone '39. The text is from Ecclesiasticus XLIV.

October 20. CHAMBER MUSIC CONCERT, *Pro Arte Quartet.* This concert, made possible by the generosity of Mrs. Elizabeth Sprague Coolidge, included the first performance of the Third Quartet by Arnold Schoenberg.

December 28. ORGAN RECITAL, *Carl Weinrich*, University Chapel. This recital was given in honor of the Twelfth Annual Meeting of The American Musicological Society.

Four Recitals by Princeton Alumni, sponsored by the Friends of Music at Princeton:

February 9. *John Kirkpatrick* '26, pianist
March 23. *George Newton* '29, baritone
April 20. *James Sykes* '30, pianist
May 11. *Joseph Hawthorne* '30, violist

April 24. MUSIC OF THE RENAISSANCE. The program of French Chansons and Italian Madrigals under the direction of Randall Thompson was presented as part of the Conference on "Scholarship and Research in the Arts."

June 15. BICENTENNIAL CONCERT, Herbert Lowell Dillon Gymnasium. Boston Symphony Orchestra, Serge Koussevitsky conducting.

PROGRAM

Thompson — Finale, "The Testament of Freedom"
Men's Chorus was provided by the combined Chapel Choir and University Glee Club.

Bach — Suite No. 3 in D major

Brahms — Academic Festival Overture, Op. 80

Beethoven — Symphony No. 3 in E-flat major, "Eroica," Op. 55

8

Bicentennial Exhibitions

Dedication and Exhibition of Joseph Henry Murals, Engineering Lounge, October 4, 1946.

Princeton Bicentennial Exhibition, International Business Machines Building, Fifth Avenue at 57th Street, New York, New York.

Two centuries of Princeton History, New Jersey State Museum, Trenton, New Jersey.

"Princeton 1746-1896," an exhibition of Princetoniana based on material used by Professor T. J. Wertenbaker in the preparation of his Bicentennial history, Treasure Room, University Library.

Three exhibitions as part of the Bicentennial Conference on "Planning Man's Physical Environment":

Examples of the work of Frank Lloyd Wright, Robert Moses, Tony Garnier, and Alvar Aalto.

Demonstrations of the psychology of vision from The Dartmouth Eye Institute.

Architectural exhibit in McCormick Hall.

Arabic, Turkish, and Persian manuscripts from the Garrett Collection were displayed in the Treasure Room of the University Library as part of the conference on "Near Eastern Culture and Society."

Chinese bronzes, paintings and rare books were exhibited in McCormick Hall as part of the Bicentennial Conference on "Far Eastern Culture and Society."

Three exhibitions as part of the conference on "Scholarship and Research in the Arts":

Early Christian and Byzantine Art

(Organized by the Walters Art Gallery and displayed at the Baltimore Museum of Art.)

Drawings by G. H. Forsyth, Jr., of the Church of St. Martin at Angers.

Byzantine Art, Freer Gallery, Washington, D.C.

9

Bicentennial Sermons

GEOFFREY FRANCIS FISHER Archbishop of Canterbury	September 22
DONALD B. ALDRICH Former Bishop-Coadjutor of the Diocese of Michigan	October 20
EMIL BRUNNER Professor of Theology, University of Zurich	November 3
REINHOLD NIEBUHR Professor of Applied Christianity, Union Theological Seminary	December 1
T. Z. KOO Secretary of the World's Student Christian Federation	January 26
DOUGLAS HORTON '12 Chairman, American Committee of the World Council of Churches	February 23
ROBERT J. MCCRACKEN Pastor, Riverside Church, New York City	March 16
JOHN A. MACKAY President, Princeton Theological Seminary	April 20
HENRY ST. GEORGE TUCKER Former Presiding Bishop, Protestant Episcopal Church of America	May 4

10

Bicentennial Publications

The Princeton University Press published during 1946-1950 the following books relating to Princeton and her history:

AUTHOR	TITLE
V. Lansing Collins	Princeton Past and Present (revised)
Thomas J. Wertenbaker	Princeton 1746-1896
Willard Thorp, ed.	The Lives of Eighteen from Princeton
William Starr Myers, ed.	Woodrow Wilson: Some Princeton Memories
Arthur S. Link	Wilson: Road to the White House
Charles G. Osgood, et al.	The Modern Princeton
Donald D. Egbert	Princeton Portraits
Wheaton J. Lane	Pictorial History of Princeton
Arthur L. Bigelow	Tower and Bells of the Princeton Graduate College
Alfred H. Bill	The Battle of Princeton
Samuel Chamberlain	Princeton in Spring

The Press published also the following books based on Bicentennial Conferences:

E. P. Wigner, ed.	Physical Science and Human Values
Glenn L. Jepsen, George G. Simpson, Ernst Mayr, eds.	Genetics, Paleontology, and Evolution
Arthur K. Parpart, ed.	Chemistry and Physiology of Growth
Joseph E. McLean, ed.	The Public Service and University Education
Thomas H. Creighton, ed.	Building for Modern Man
T. Cuyler Young, ed.	Near Eastern Culture and Society

The discussion in particular Bicentennial Conferences was related to the following books published by Princeton University Press:

George Rowley	Principles of Chinese Painting
Kurt Weitzmann	Illustrations in Roll and Codex
Alfred Einstein	The Italian Madrigal

The Bicentennial Office also issued fourteen pamphlets summarizing the various Bicentennial Conferences and listing the participants.

11

Service of Dedication

June 16, 1947

University Chapel

ORDER OF SERVICE

ORGAN PRELUDE: "Kyrie, Gott heiliger Geist" Bach
PROCESSIONAL HYMN NO. 1: "O God our Help in Ages Past"
CALL TO WORSHIP

Thus saith the Lord, let not the wise man glory in his wisdom, neither let the mighty man glory in his might; let not the rich man glory in his riches; but let him that glorieth glory in this that he hath understanding and knoweth me, that I am the Lord who executeth loving kindness, justice, and righteousness in the earth; for in these things I delight, saith the Lord.

¶ *After which the Minister and people shall read in unison the following Psalm*:

God be merciful unto us, and bless us; and cause his face to shine upon us;
That thy way may be known upon earth, thy saving health among all nations.
Let the people praise thee, O God; let all the people praise thee.
O let the nations be glad and sing for joy: for thou shalt judge the people righteously, and govern the nations upon earth.
Let the people praise thee, O God: let all the people praise thee.
Then shall the earth yield her increase; and God, even our own God, shall bless us.
God shall bless us; and all the ends of the earth shall fear him.

THE SANCTUS

¶ *Minister*: The Lord be with you
¶ *People*: And with thy spirit
¶ *Minister*: Let us pray
¶ *Here, all being seated, the Minister shall bid the prayers of the people as follows*:

AN ACT OF THANKSGIVING

Let us thank God for his over-ruling providence which shapes our ends, rough-hew them how we will, and for our faith that by his greatness round about our littleness, more can be done with human instruments than we can ask or think.

Let us give thanks that God enabled our fathers to build better than they knew, and since out of small beginnings he wrought so great a work for this nation, let us pray that now again our devotion to the cause of truth may, by his grace, outweary this time of chaos and frustration.

Let us praise God that the operations of his grace are never absent but always hidden in the course of human events; that he did attest his presence with the founders of this college by secret promptings to do the best things in the worst times, by making the darkest days the times of revelation, and by renewing the prophetic vision where it was dimmed by the narrowness of pious men; and let us pray that in all our doubts and uncertainties we may be granted a clear conscience and a readiness for new light to break forth.

Let us remember before God, with special honor, the fathers and mothers of the sons of Princeton, whose unapplauded sacrifice enabled their sons to enter upon a richer heritage, and who first taught by their lives that which is not learned from books, and without which all training here would have been in vain.

Let us also thank God for the lesson taught here that nothing can be taken in exchange for a faithful friend who is a medicine of life; and more especially let us praise him for his priceless gift of the beloved community of teachers and scholars who here added to the store of human knowledge and wrought patiently to transform the original selfishness of human nature in generations of young men that they might be of service to the nation and the world.

Let us acknowledge our gratitude for the pioneers who served God's purpose here without reward of fame, and for that company of presidents of this institution known to the world as famous men.

And finally let us yield unto God most high praise for those Princeton men who gave their lives for their country—from the early struggle for our independence unto the World Wars of these latter days, acknowledging in silence our unspeakable debt.

Thine they are, O Lord, and naught shall wrest them out of thy hand.

¶ *Choir*:

Justorum animae in manu Dei sunt, et non tanget illos tormentum malitiae: visi sunt oculis insipientium mori, illi autem sunt in pace.

¶ *Minister*:

We humbly beseech thee, O Father, mercifully to look upon our infirmities; and for the glory of thy name, turn from us all those evils that we most justly deserved; and grant, that in all our troubles we may put our whole trust and confidence in thy mercy, and evermore serve thee in holiness and pureness of living, to thy honor and glory, through Jesus Christ our Lord. Amen.

Anthem: "Veni Creator" Downes

Veni Creator Spiritus,
Mentes tuorum visita,
Imple superna gratia
Quae tu creasti pectora.

Da gaudiorum praemia,
Da gratiarum munera,
Dissolve litis vincula,
Adstringe pacis foedera.

Sit laus patri cum filio
Sancto simul paraclito,
Nobisque mitat filius
Charisma sancti spiritus. Amen.

AN ACT OF DEDICATION

¶ *Minister*: O Lord, deal not with us according to our sins.

¶ *People*: Neither reward us according to our iniquities.

¶ *Minister*: Let us pray. From all self-sufficiency that holds not thee in awe, from knowledge that stores the mind without opening the heart, from skill that gives power without wisdom and equips men to take unwitting part in man's inhumanity to man,

¶ *People*: Good Lord, deliver us.

¶ *Minister*: From the pride of race and class that would prevent our service to those who need most what we enjoy; from isolation in a world created to be one,

¶ *People*: Good Lord, deliver us.

¶ *Minister*: From the temptations of greed that draw men after one another in the fever of covetous quest and so confound the purposes of our creator; from narrow pride in outworn ways, and from blind eyes that will not see the need of change,

¶ *People*: Good Lord, deliver us.

¶ *Minister*: We who have all fallen short do beseech thee to hear us, good Lord; and that it may please thee to give Princeton a richer usefulness and higher distinction in her third century of life, as she carries on the torch of truth, which was brought here from lands older than our own, and from which her sons have lighted their torches and borne the light even to the ends of the earth,

¶ *People*: We beseech thee to hear us, good Lord.

¶ *Minister*: That it may please thee to strengthen and sustain this Princeton family of loyal men who in these troublous days labor for the fulfillment of our high calling in the years before us,

¶ *People*: We beseech thee to hear us, good Lord.

¶ *Minister*: That it may please thee to keep this institution in generous comity with other colleges and universities, here and abroad, in common defence of the wisdom that can make of one mind those whom thou hast made of one blood to dwell on all the face of the earth,

¶ *People*: We beseech thee to hear us, good Lord.

¶ *Minister*: That it may please thee to preserve and enhance our heritage of culture that outlives the temporal riches of this world, in books that hold the thoughts of our human race, and in the living minds of scholarly men who gladly teach that new minds may gain power both to know and to think, to defend opinion and to seek the truth,

¶ *People*: We beseech thee to hear us, good Lord.

¶ *Minister*: That it may please thee to confirm our devotion to the significance of the individual man responsible to his people and to thee, that all men may be makers of history and not the victims of it, and that a few may do by their excellence what numbers can not do by their strength,

¶ *People*: We beseech thee to hear us, good Lord.

¶ *Minister*: That it may please thee to prosper our efforts to unite high scholarship and spiritual discernment and bring into partnership the study of science and the study of man, lest our knowledge lead but to our doom,

¶ *People*: We beseech thee to hear us, good Lord.

¶ *Minister*: That it may please thee that in this place men may meet the thoughts which are destined to rule the future, and learn to fear no destruction that clears a way through man's obstinate desire to be undisturbed; and that it may please thee also to teach us by stern events to keep our learning close to those who do the work of the world,

¶ *People*: We beseech thee to hear us, good Lord.

¶ *Minister*: That it may please thee finally and above all to give us grace to nurture here a continuing company of men who know no lord save the Lord our God and who will be citizens first of thy Kingdom, resolved to be more thine than their country's or their own,

¶ *People*: We beseech thee to hear us, good Lord.

¶ *Minister*:

O God, who didst inspire our fathers to bring forth upon this continent a new nation, conceived in liberty and dedicated to the proposition that all men are created equal; and who didst raise up their descendants who gave their lives that this nation might live, grant that we the living be here dedicated to the unfinished work thus far so nobly carried on; that from the honored dead we may take increased devotion, that we here highly resolve that these dead shall not have died in vain, that this nation shall, under God, have a new birth of freedom, and that government of the people, by the people, and for the people shall not perish from the earth. Amen.

Anthem: "Adoramus te, Christe" Ruffo

Adoramus te, Christe, et benedicimus tibi, quia per sanctam crucem tuam et passionem tuam redemisti mundum. Domine, miserere nobis.

¶ *Then all shall stand, and repeat together* The Lord's Prayer.

Recessional Hymn No. 163: "God of our fathers, whose almighty hand"

Prayer and Benediction

Organ Postlude: Toccata and Fugue in D minor Bach

Index